World Changers

GORDON FERGUSON

World Changers

The History of the Church in the Book of Acts

World Changers —*The History of the Church in the Book of Acts*

Printed in the United States of America

PREVIOUS ISBN: 1-57782-058-4 (Revolution!)
NEW ISBN: 978-0-9839157-0-6

A note of thanks to Amy Morgan for her editorial work.
Cover and book interior design: Toney C. Mulhollan

About the Author

Gordon Ferguson is a graduate of Northwestern State University and the Harding Graduate School of Religion, earning an M.A. in New Testament Studies from the latter. With over 40 years of experience, he has served as an Evangelist, Elder, and Teacher. He trains ministers in the United States, Asia and Eurasia, with an emphasis on leadership training and teaching in his ministry. He serves as Dean and primary teacher in the Asia-Pacific Leadership Academy and the Ukrainian Institute of Ministry. Gordon has written ten books and many study guides. Gordon and his wife, Theresa, make their home in Phoenix, Arizona and have two children and five grandchildren. His website is: www.gftm.org. Contact: gordon@gftm.org.

www.ipibooks.com

Illumination Publishers International
www.ipibooks.com
6010 Pinecreek Ridge Court
Spring, Texas 77379-2513, USA

DEDICATION

The first edition of this Acts exposition was written thirteen years ago, and was dedicated to our first grandson, Bryce Gordon Ferguson, who had just been born. At that time, I recalled the words of my Dad, who once said that you haven't lived until you have grandchildren. The arrival of Bryce reminded me of those words and registered their accuracy on my heart. The Psalmist wrote, "May you live to see your children's children" (Psalm 128:6), and the writer of Proverbs added, "Children's children are a crown to the aged" (Proverbs 17:6). God has brought both of these realities to pass for Theresa and me, for which we are eternally grateful.

Since Bryce was born, we have been blessed with four more grandchildren: Aleea Hope Klinkhammer (age 11); Blayze David Ferguson (age 10); Cody Jeffry Klinkhammer (age 8) and Ronan Scott Ferguson (age 6). All five of you are a delight to our hearts, as you shower us with the kind of love that only grandchildren can give. One of our greatest desires in life as your grandparents is to pass on to you our love for God, our faith in his Son and our unswerving trust in his Word.

May what Paul said of Timothy about the spiritual influence of grandparents and parents in his life be true of each of you, our dearest grandchildren:

> I have been reminded of your sincere faith, which first lived in your grandmother Lois and in your mother Eunice and, I am persuaded, now lives in you also. (2 Timothy 1:5)

CONTENTS

CONTENTS

INTRODUCTION

The Book of Acts is history, but it is also far more than history. It is the story of how God dramatically changes the lives of those who make Jesus their Lord. It is a story waiting to be relived again and again by idealistic, faithful men and women who dare to follow the world's greatest radical Leader.

The fact is that the book of Acts may be far more radical than some of us think. Some of us have read Acts for years and have taught our favorite verses from it to others on many occasions. We think we know this book. We think we are like the people it describes. We feel comfortable in Acts. Perhaps we should not. A careful look at Acts will reinforce many of our convictions, but it will also stretch us, challenge us and even shake us up. If that is what we need, and I think it is, so be it.

Acts is really the second of a two-volume work penned by Luke, the physician. Both works are written to "Theophilus" (Luke 1:3, Acts 1:1). The man referred to may very well have been a government official—thus the term "most excellent Theophilus" in Luke 1; or since the name means "friend of God," it may have been a symbol for various people who were seeking God. If the former, the "most excellent" omission in Acts may have indicated that he became a Christian after the Gospel was written but before Luke wrote Acts.

Luke writes more of the New Testament than any other writer, including Paul—approximately one-fourth of the total New Testament, between his two books. He wrote to show how this radical movement began, far from the great seats of wisdom and power, in the womb of a Galilean teenager, and ended up shaking the great imperial city of Rome.

There is always something significant about the beginning of a great movement. Americans constantly hark back to 1776 in an effort to recover the spirit that was present at the beginning of the new democracy. As useful as that may be, there is something much more significant about the beginning of something that is from God. Jesus had said he would build his church. Acts describes its beginning. The book of Acts is important to us who want to live God's dream in our day, for it shows us the fresh and awe-inspiring way his Spirit worked in his church at the very beginning. As we study our own spiritual origins, two words Jesus spoke later to the church in Ephesus are useful to us: "remember" and "repent" (Revelation 2:5). We need to remember what God did in the beginning, what the newborn church was all about and what a change it brought to people's lives. Then, when we see our failure to be like that church, we must be ready to repent. As Peter preached in Acts, such repentance will bring times of refreshing (Acts 3:19).

Luke no doubt wrote Acts for a number of very good reasons. One was to show how the gospel spread according to Jesus' plan, to "Jerusalem, and in all Judea and Samaria, and to the ends of the earth" (Acts 1:8). Another reason was to provide the accounts of the establishment of specific congregations to whom later letters would be written. It also shows how individuals became a part of God's kingdom. The conversion process is laid out too clearly to miss, if we will but read. Combining the elements of the different accounts is an effective way to get the big picture of just what becoming saved disciples of Jesus is all about.

Yet another purpose for writing is apologetic, which means "to make an apology or defense" (not, in any sense, to apologize for anything!). Luke wants to show that the message of Jesus and his followers is "true and reasonable" (Acts 26:25). Additionally, he wants to show that Christians are not guilty, as charged by some, of being subversives. Luke presents the Roman authorities mostly in a good light compared to the Jews. However, the Jewish religion is not portrayed as the obstacle to the growth of the young church. Rather, individual Jews who will not accept the Biblical conclusion of their religion, i.e. that Jesus is the Messiah, are shown to be the source of the turmoil in various cities. In Acts, Luke shows that Paul is not in any way opposed to the Roman government but instead is a loyal Roman citizen.

Another intriguing purpose for which Luke evidently wrote

is often overlooked: He wanted to commend Paul as an apostle on equal footing with Peter, otherwise the most influential apostle. Paul's conversion and appointment came late and in a most unusual way. For these reasons some in the early church questioned his right to have the influence that he did, an influence that overshadowed to some degree that of Peter, who was given "the keys of the kingdom" by Jesus himself. Hence, Luke writes to establish clearly that Paul was "not in the least inferior to the 'super-apostles'" (2 Corinthians 12:11). Note these amazing parallels between Peter and Paul:

- Both had key sermons included in the book: Peter in Acts 2:14–40; Paul in Acts 13:16–42.
- Both healed the lame: Peter in Acts 3:1–10; Paul in Acts 14:8–10.
- Both were involved in miracles that brought judgment: Peter in Acts 5:1–11; Paul in Acts 13:6–11.
- Both were freed from prison by miraculous intervention: Peter in Acts 12:1–11; Paul in Acts 16:19–30.
- Both raised the dead: Peter in Acts 9:36–42; Paul in Acts 20:7–12.
- Both had miracles result from their persons: Peter in Acts 5:15; Paul in Acts 19:11–12.
- Both dealt with sorcerers: Peter in Acts 8:18–23; Paul in Acts 19:19.
- Both refused worship from men: Peter in Acts 10:25–26; Paul in Acts 14:11–15.
- Both saw visions from God: Peter in Acts 10:9–20; Paul in Acts 16:9–10; 18:9–10; 26:12–19.
- Both were spoken to by the Holy Spirit: Peter in Acts 10:19–20; Paul in Acts 20:22–23.

The date of the writing of Acts is normally thought to be in the 60s AD. Since Nero did not seem to be in his destructive mode yet, it could be assumed that Luke wrote earlier than 65 AD. However, an alternative idea is that he wrote in the earlier stages of Nero's persecution to show that Nero was an aberration to the normal approach of Roman officials. Whatever the date, the author (Luke, inspired by the Holy Spirit) and the purposes are well-established.

Acts is God's story of world changers which must be replicated in every generation as we volunteer to be his tools through whom he acts for the salvation of mankind. Let us drink deeply of its lessons as we begin our journey through its sacred history.

Editor's note: *In the exposition of Acts that follows, the complete text of Acts will not be included, due to its length. For each section the author has selected a few verses that will serve to introduce it.*

Questions for Further Study

1. In the Introduction, who does it say the author is, and what can you tell us about him?

2. Which individual received the letter originally, and what can you tell us about him?

3. Give the four key purposes for the writing of Acts.

4. What is the probable date of Acts being written?

5. What was the most interesting or surprising new thing you learned in the Introduction?

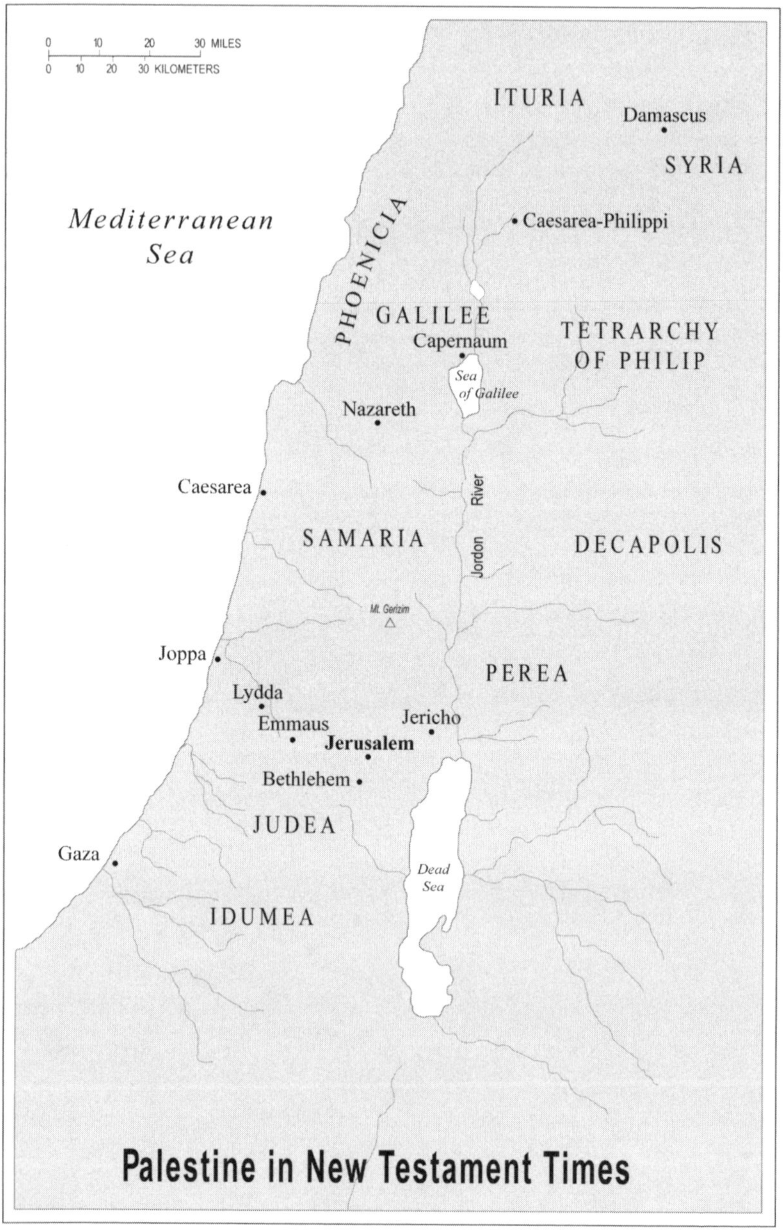

Palestine in New Testament Times

Chapter One

THE DAY IS DAWNING
ACTS 1

Having told the Jesus story in "volume one," the gospel of Luke, Luke now turns his attention to the amazing events that followed the death and resurrection of Jesus. One might say that the focus of the book of Luke is on how God's Spirit dwelled in Jesus, while the focus of the book of Acts is on how God's Spirit continued Jesus' work in the life of the church that he built.

Luke is eager to show us how the wonders of God continued. At the same time he is just as eager to show his readers that there is a sound basis for believing that these things are real and not just stories from "Never-Never Land." Throughout this work he will be both evangelist and historian. He will proclaim the Christ and describe the spiritual power that comes to those who follow him, but he will also show us that these things are true and reasonable—soundly supported by the evidence. Let's look at how he opens his book.

Knowing For Certain (Acts 1:1-3)

[1]In my former book, Theophilus, I wrote about all that Jesus began to do and to teach [2]until the day he was taken up to heaven, after giving instructions through the Holy Spirit to the apostles he had chosen. [3]After his suffering, he showed himself to these men and gave many convincing proofs that he was alive. He appeared to them over a period of forty days and spoke about the kingdom of God.

Luke begins with a series of bold assertions. He speaks of Jesus' resurrection and ascension back to heaven. He assures Theophilus that Jesus "gave many convincing proofs that he was alive" (v3). Unlike other religions that are mainly philosophical, Christianity is based on demonstrable facts, most notably that its founder lived, died and was raised from the dead—in the proximity of multitudes who could not deny those events. The enemies of Jesus paid Judas Iscariot thirty pieces of silver to betray Jesus; they no doubt would have paid many times more than this to produce the corpse of Jesus. But this was impossible because the empty tomb was a reality rather than a whimsical wish in the minds of sentimentally deluded followers.

The miracle of Jesus' resurrection was quickly preached right in the city where it happened. And the Jewish authorities, who were panic-stricken over the impact of this message, were absolutely powerless to stop it. Producing the corpse of Jesus would have sounded the death knell to gospel preaching. But no body was available, and the fact of the resurrection was unassailable. As Paul reasoned with King Agrippa, he reminded him that nothing about Christ's resurrection was unreasonable, for it did not take place "in a corner" (Acts 26:26). The apostles were proclaiming a faith built squarely on the facts, facts which could be proven beyond any reasonable doubt. No wonder they were so bold and confident!

Those not familiar with the Bible fail to see that there is a connection between faith and facts, and that this connection is not unlike what we find in worldly realms. The scientist, for example, bases his experiments on what others who preceded him have done and said; he cannot take the time to prove every principle on which his current experiment is based. He accepts the testimony of others whom he deems trustworthy. The historian cannot prove the existence of Alexander the Great, if we mean that he must produce something that we can see, taste, smell, touch or hear with our senses. We only know that he existed by accepting the testimony of others whom we trust were telling the truth as they wrote about that period of time. We trust them because of the way various independent pieces of evidence converge to make it highly unlikely that he was a mythical figure. Without question, most of what we believe in life is taken on faith—based on our acceptance of reliable and reasonable testimony.

Walking by faith in the spiritual realm does not mean that we walk without evidence or reason. Jesus' disciples had faith because they saw many convincing proofs that he was alive. For us, walking by faith means that we trust Jesus and the Bible, for which there is abundant evidence. Everything in life cannot be proven scientifically. Actually, few things can. For example, although we cannot see love, we would all agree it is nonetheless quite real. Although we cannot prove scientifically that Jesus rose from the dead, we can still be certain of it through the testimony of those who did see it. Along with Luke, let us confidently say that Christ has been proved to be true, the Bible accurate and the gospel desperately needed!

The Kingdom of God (Acts 1:4-8)

3b He appeared to them over a period of forty days and spoke about the kingdom of God....

6 So when they met together, they asked him, "Lord, are you at this time going to restore the kingdom to Israel?"

The focus and duration of Jesus' post-resurrection teaching is clearly specified by Luke in verse 3—for forty days he spoke about the kingdom of God. The kingdom was obviously central to his message and his understanding of his purpose. The statement Luke makes prompts two related questions: "What did Jesus teach about the kingdom, and why was it so important?" Few biblical subjects are addressed in more detail in the Scriptures and yet misunderstood more consistently by religious people. Many Bible believers have some erroneous views of the kingdom at worst or incomplete views at best. Admittedly it is a very broad and relatively complex subject, and for that reason, one that we cannot address in great depth here.

However, since teaching about the kingdom was the post-resurrection focus of Jesus, we will do well to examine it in at least some detail. I will also include an Appendix in the last part of the book with some observations about the kingdom that will hopefully both broaden your knowledge about the subject and whet your appetite for doing more study on your own. Anyone who reads the Appendix and does not find something new to challenge their thinking will be a rare bird indeed—and that's a promise!

Let me begin by mentioning several books for your further study. Tom Jones and Steve Brown have written *The Kingdom of God*, which is the first of a series of three. The second focuses on the teaching found in Matthew 5–7, the Sermon on the Mount. I think the authors would prefer to call this portion of Scripture the Sermon on the Kingdom. These are published by Discipleship Publications International (DPI) and are also available from Illumination Publishers International

(IPI). I would also suggest a small book by Jim McGuiggan, entitled *The Reign of God*. The Jones/Brown books are very practical regarding life application, whereas the McGuiggan book is much more doctrinal in nature, yet it provides insights that have been invaluable to me on this subject. Jim's book is available through his website (www.jimmcguiggan.com) or through the Florida College Bookstore (http://bookstore.floridacollege.edu).

Mistaken Views

Certainly many in Jesus' day held to mistaken views. The Jews expected their long-awaited Messiah to be a political king who would establish a physical kingdom. When they saw the miraculous power of Jesus, they believed the fulfillment of their dreams was imminent. "Jesus, knowing that they intended to come and make him king by force, withdrew again to a mountain by himself" (John 6:15). To the extreme disappointment of the Jews, he made it clear that his kingdom was not to be a physical one. As he stood before Pilate, he stated:

> "My kingdom is not of this world. If it were, my servants would fight to prevent my arrest by the Jews. But now my kingdom is from another place." (John 18:36)

He did not deny being a king and having a kingdom; he simply denied their views of both the nature of the King and the kingdom. Actually, his focus on a spiritual kingdom was one of the primary reasons why he was rejected and killed.

The modern incarnation of this error is found ironically in the theology of many teachers and writers in conservative Christendom. Based on a futurist interpretation of the book of Revelation, they view the kingdom of Old Testament (OT) prophecy as future, relegated to an assumed return of Christ to establish an earthly kingdom for a thousand years. However, the idea that OT prophecy was focused on a physical kingdom is biblically unfounded and flatly denied by Jesus in John 18:36.[1]

But what did the apostles mean by their question in Acts 1:6: "Lord, are you at this time going to restore the kingdom to Israel?"? Were they still quite confused at this late date, holding on to the common Jewish view that the kingdom was to be both earthly and physical? The assumption that the apostles were thus confused evidently arises from the use of the word "restore." That assumption seems highly doubtful. After all, Jesus had "opened their minds so they could understand the Scriptures" and explained in detail the gospel and its worldwide mission (Luke 24:44–49). The use of the word "restore" does not necessarily demonstrate that they held to a mistaken view. In a very real sense, Jesus was mandated by OT scripture to *restore* the Davidic kingdom.

Once the Southern nation of Judah was taken into Babylonian captivity, no king of David's line sat on his throne. The prophets were assuring those in captivity that they would return to their homeland and would once again have a king on David's throne. In Acts 15:15-18, James, quoting from Amos 9:11–12, could hardly have been clearer on the idea of restoring the Davidic kingdom:

> The words of the prophets are in agreement with this, as it is written:
> "'After this I will return
> and rebuild David's fallen tent.
> Its ruins I will rebuild,
> and I will restore it,
> that the remnant of men may seek the Lord,
> and all the Gentiles who bear my name,
> says the Lord, who does these things'
> that have been known for ages."

Based on James' comments, the kingdom was exactly that—a *restored* Davidic kingdom. Consider Hebrews 8:8–12, a quote from Jeremiah 31:31–34, which promised that a new covenant would be established "with the house of Israel and with the house of Judah." Ezekiel 37:15–28 is most graphic in showing that the then-divided nation would be gathered back together and ruled over by David the king (Jesus on David's throne) in an everlasting covenant. The Old Testament foretold that the Messiah, whom we now know is Jesus, would sit on the throne of David. (See 2 Samuel 7:13, 16; Psalm 132:11–12; Isaiah 9:6–7, and then Luke 1:32 and Acts 2:30, showing the fulfillment.) Jesus was a *Jew* who became king of the *restored* kingdom of David. Of course it was a spiritual kingdom, of which the old kingdom was but a shadow, but it clearly was the kingdom of David nonetheless. Simply stated, God did restore the spiritualized kingdom of David to the Jews and from that foundation eventually started bringing in those from other nations (the Gentiles).

Another misunderstanding of the kingdom in our day is found at the other end of the spectrum with many believing that the kingdom is only heaven and something to inherit and enjoy after this physical life ends. Perhaps that explains why many who claim to be Christians see their religion mainly as preparation for heaven, rather than seeing it as having a "heaven on earth" focus, thus making us strangers and pilgrims in this world. When Christianity is viewed primarily as "fire insurance," it is not really Christianity at all. Having said that, it is true that some passages can definitely be viewed as referring to the kingdom in heaven, and a few can be viewed *only* in this way. On the latter note, Paul spoke of our resurrection at the end of time by stating:

> I declare to you, brothers, that flesh and blood cannot inherit the kingdom of God, nor does the perishable inherit the imperishable. (1 Corinthians 15:50)

In this context, he is referring to the heavenly state of the kingdom after it has been delivered up to God at the end of time (1 Corinthians 15:24). However, most of the passages speaking about the kingdom of God (or kingdom of heaven[2]) are definitely speaking of the kingdom on earth—but not a physical entity.

An Incomplete View

Many of us understand the basics of how OT prophecies about the kingdom, such as Isaiah 2 and Daniel 2, were fulfilled in the church age. However, our view of—and appreciation for—the kingdom may yet be incomplete. We find it too easy to equate the kingdom with the church and to declare them one and the same. And, while it is correct to say that all living, saved followers of Christ are in the kingdom and therefore in the church, which is Christ's universal spiritual Body, it is quite incorrect to say that the two are exact equivalents. Jones and Brown deal with the distinctions in some detail, and although you will note in my Appendix some variations in how I would describe those distinctions, we all agree that the simple equation of *church equals kingdom* is quite flawed.

For just one simple example, those in the church are in the kingdom of God *on earth*, but the kingdom includes far, far more than the church on earth. Hebrews 12 is most important in this light. In a context describing the superiority of the New Testament (NT) kingdom to that of the Old Testament, we find this thrilling description:

> But you have come to Mount Zion, to the heavenly Jerusalem, the city of the living God. You have come to thousands upon thousands of angels in joyful assembly, to the church of the firstborn, whose names are written in heaven. You have come to God, the judge of all men, to the spirits of righteous men made perfect. (Hebrews 12:22–23)

Do you see the implications in this passage? The present kingdom includes a myriad of angels and the OT people of faith (for whom Christ also died—Romans 3:25, Hebrews 9:15), along with the church of the firstborn (that's us!). In the model prayer of Matthew 6, Jesus gave a simple yet comprehensive definition of the spiritual kingdom: "Your kingdom come, your will be done on earth as it is in heaven" (v10). Those who do the will of God are in the kingdom, whether they reside on earth or in heaven.

An Important View

Does any of this really matter? Absolutely! For one thing, it is biblically accurate. For another thing, it is extremely inspirational. When we come to a church assembly on Sunday morning, we are not coming to a small assembly, even if the visible number is small. We are entering into the presence of God and of heaven, which should cause us to tremble with awe and excitement. No wonder the writer of Hebrews ended chapter 12 with these words:

> Therefore, since we are receiving a kingdom that cannot be shaken, let us be thankful, and so worship God acceptably with reverence and awe, for our 'God is a consuming fire.' (vv28–29)

To conclude this very brief overview regarding the kingdom, in the forty-day period of teaching about it, Jesus was preparing the apostles for the revolutionary mission: the establishment and spread of his spiritual reign all over the known world in their generation! Through his message they would call men and women into a kingdom that would make a powerful impact on earth and then be ultimately fulfilled in heaven. Could there be any greater mission?

Time to Fly (Acts 1:9-12)

9 After he said this, he was taken up before their very eyes, and a cloud hid him from their sight.

Since Pentecost fell on the fiftieth day after the Sabbath of Passover week, Jesus ascended back to heaven about seven days before the Spirit descended to mark the establishment of the church of Christ. Earlier in his ministry, Jesus' mention of his going back to the Father filled the apostles with grief (John 16:5–28). Yet he promised then that they would come to understand the necessity of his leaving and would ultimately be filled with joy, the fulfillment of which we now see in Acts 1. The discipling was complete, and they were ready to embark on the greatest mission the world has ever known.

Jesus probably ascended in such a dramatic way to mark with certainty his final departure from earth (in bodily form). After the resurrection he had made at least a dozen appearances to the apostles or others. After these times he would evidently just disappear. Now he was making sure that the apostles knew that this was the culmination of their preparations and the time was at hand for the mission to be launched. They were so focused on this ascension that the presence of two angels was not immediately noticed. The angels reminded them of the finality of Jesus' departure with the promise that Jesus would one day come back in the same manner in which he departed. We understand that this return will mark the end of time as we know it and the ushering in of the great Judgment Day. No doubt filled with anticipation and perhaps a few butterflies, they returned to Jerusalem to await the great events that were soon to occur.

It was time for Jesus to "fly" back to heaven (wherever that is!), and it was also time for the apostles to leave the nest and fly on their own as the Spirit worked through them. The Great Commission in the book of Matthew was about to become a reality, as they became special witnesses to Jerusalem, Judea, Samaria and finally, to the ends of the earth (Acts 1:8). Jesus promised them in John 14:12–14 that after he left them they would do greater works than he had done, and they were only a few days away from seeing this promise fulfilled.

Given the nature of the miracles Jesus did and the impact he had, how are we to understand this promise? How did the apostles understand it? One of the most striking truths in the New Testament is in view here, which is highly sobering and highly exhilarating at the same time. And by this point, the apostles must have grasped its import fairly well. It has to do with the "greater things" of how the mission was to be carried out.

One of the reasons God became a man in the person of Jesus was to demonstrate the very nature of Deity to man (John 1:18). Until men could see God in flesh and blood, they could never really understand him. Colossians 2:9 informs us that the fullness of God lived in Jesus, meaning that the complete picture of God could be seen in him, and without that flesh and blood demonstration, men simply could not see the whole picture. Once Jesus said to one of his apostles:

> "Don't you know me, Philip, even after I have been among you such a long time? Anyone who has seen me has seen the Father. How can you say, 'Show us the Father'?" (John 14:9)

The point is clear that no one could fully understand God until they saw him in human form.

Now let's take this line of reasoning one step further. Not only was Jesus the fullness (demonstration) of God; the church is the fullness of Christ (Ephesians 1:22–23, Colossians 2:9–10). Although no individual is the fullness of Christ, if each of us is filled with God through the Holy Spirit, then the composite body of Jesus (the church) is the fullness of him (Ephesians 4:13).

God's wisdom is obvious. If he could not be really understood without being perceived in the flesh through Jesus, then Jesus also cannot be really understood without being seen in the flesh—our flesh—in every generation. God did not choose to drop leather-bound, gold-edged Bibles from heaven. He knew that the gospel had to be communicated by humans because those receiving the message would have to see it in writing and in lives. The Bible alone is sufficient to reveal the content of the truth to man, but to grasp its power we also must read it in the lives of the redeemed. This is the role of the church and the method by which the mission must be accomplished. Jesus had been limited to working in one place at a time, but soon disciples would be working all over the world at the same time. Greater things were about to begin as the apostles and early church put the principle into motion about which Paul would later write in 2 Corinthians 5:20: "We are therefore Christ's ambassadors, as though

God were making his appeal through us."

The Believers Joined Together (Acts 1:13-26)

[13]When they arrived, they went upstairs to the room where they were staying. Those present were Peter, John, James and Andrew; Philip and Thomas, Bartholomew and Matthew; James son of Alphaeus and Simon the Zealot, and Judas son of James. [14]They all joined together constantly in prayer, along with the women and Mary the mother of Jesus, and with his brothers. .

The group of believers numbered about 120 (v15). The apostles, the seventy-two of Luke 10, the family of Jesus (Matthew 13:55, Mark 6:3) and the women (including the apostles' wives) would add up to just about that amount. The mention of Jesus' family stirs the heart and the imagination. At one point, they had gone to bring him home, thinking that he had lost his mind (Mark 3:20–21, 31–35). Yet ultimately, they were converted. What won them over? Surely his refusal to compromise played a larger part than most might suspect, a point that should not be lost on us who want to see our family members come into the kingdom.

We should take special note of Acts 1:14. Here is the first of many times in Acts in which we see that the early church was a fellowship of prayer. "They all joined together constantly in prayer." Robert Coleman has said about Jesus that prayer was the air which he breathed and that the battle of the cross was fought and won on his knees. The first disciples had seen Jesus' ferocious commitment to prayer. They had heard his prayers and had longed to pray as he did. They had cried out, "Teach us to pray" (Luke 11:1). Now Doctor Luke shows us that they learned their lessons well. What they had seen in Jesus, they continued to practice. They understood that they were on the edge of something great (resurrection appearances give you that conviction!), but they were not self-confident. Like their Lord, they continued to believe that they needed God and could do nothing without him.

Prayer is mentioned in Acts nearly thirty times. It accompanied the working of miracles and the selection and appointment of leaders. As those first disciples faced persecution, they prayed so powerfully that the place where they were meeting was literally shaken (Acts 4:31). Stephen, the first Christian martyr, met his God with a prayer on his lips (Acts 7:59). The prayers of the church resulted in Peter's release from prison, although he was guarded by four squads of four soldiers each (Acts 12:1–17). Paul and Silas were beaten and locked in stocks but through prayer found the power to sing and look for the hand of God to intervene. That faith led to an earthquake and an amazing conversion story for the ages (Acts 16:16–40). Prayer for our first-century brothers and sisters was not simply what they did—it was a major part of the definition of who they were.

Are we like them? Are we known as a fellowship of prayer? Are we more known for our prayer lives or more known for our activities? Leaders, do you teach your people more about how to pray or more about how to work? The church in Acts worked. But they understood the idea of first things first. Before work must come prayer, and a lot of it. They saw prayer as a powerful use of time. "Constantly in prayer" does not sound like they always started and closed out every meeting with prayer. It sounds like it was far more important than that. In accomplishing the mission, the apostles placed prayer on equal footing with preaching the Word (Acts 6:4). Later Paul would say:

> The weapons we fight with are not the weapons of the world. On the contrary, they have divine power to demolish strongholds. (2 Corinthians 10:4)

The nearly unbelievable results we read about in Acts were produced more by prayer than by any other single element. Prayer was the chief "weapon" of the army of God. Many of us find it easier to work than to pray. We find we are more interested in planning than in praying. We rely on our skill, our knowledge and our experience far too much. We need to go back to the beginning of the church and see what these men and women who were fresh from their experiences with Jesus did. He spent forty days after the resurrection teaching them even more about the kingdom of God, and what do we see them doing next? Praying. That should tell us a great deal about the kingdom. What is most important for those wanting to evangelize their cities? Prayer. What is most important for parents wanting to raise their children to be Christians? Prayer. What is most important for those wanting to help the poor and the needy? Prayer. This is a lesson we must learn and a truth we must hold to if we are to change the world through the power of God.

Acts 1 closes with the selection of Matthias to take the place of

Judas Iscariot[3] in the apostleship (whose destiny was stated in rather blunt and bold terms[4]). When James was murdered in Acts 12, no other person was chosen to replace him. But now, the kingdom on earth was to be instituted with the full complement of twelve apostles present. As Pentecost dawned, these twelve apostles were awaiting the promised descent of the Holy Spirit to lead them into the most glorious mission the world had ever known.

Questions for Further Study

1. As stated, many references to prayer are found in Acts. Look up each of the following and list the lessons that you learn about prayer from their examples: Acts 1:14, Acts 1:24, Acts 2:42, Acts 4:24, Acts 4:31, Acts 6:4, Acts 6:6, Acts 7:59, Acts 8:15, Acts 9:11, Acts 9:40, Acts 10:2, Acts 10:4, Acts 10:9, Acts 10:30–31, Acts 11:5, Acts 12:5, Acts 12:12, Acts 13:3, Acts 14:23, Acts 16:25, Acts 20:36, Acts 21:5, Acts 22:17, Acts 26:29 and Acts 28:8.

2. Is our faith in the Bible's inspiration and accuracy based on facts or only on faith? Explain.

3. Describe right and wrong views of what Jesus taught about the "kingdom."

4. What is the main thing you read in Chapter 1 that strengthened your convictions? Explain.

Chapter Two

Stage One: A Day Like No Other

Acts 2

When does this equation work: 2 + 2 + 2 = 2? It works when Isaiah 2, Daniel 2 and Joel 2 are added together, finally converging in Acts 2! However we may view the presence of the kingdom during the earthly ministry of Jesus, these three most distinctive OT prophecies about the kingdom find their most natural and complete fulfillment in Acts 2. In Isaiah 2:2–4, the prophet speaks of a time when God promised to establish his mountain (kingdom) which was to be exalted above all other mountains (kingdoms). This momentous event was to take place in the last days, to include all nations and to begin in Jerusalem as the word of the Lord was sent out. In the second passage, Daniel (see especially 2:31–45) described a succession of four world empires culminating with the one we now know historically to be the Roman Empire. During the time of that awesome nation, God promised to set up a kingdom which would never be destroyed. And in Joel 2:28–32, quoted in Acts 2, the promise of a great outpouring of the Holy Spirit would mark the ushering in of the earth's new, and last, age.

The events of Acts 2 were in God's plan for mankind when the first man, Adam, was created. Thus the stage was set for changing the earthly destiny of nations and the eternal destiny of millions of souls!

Holy Spirit Baptism (Acts 2:1-21)

[1]When the day of Pentecost came, they were all together in one place. [2]Suddenly a sound like the blowing of a violent wind came from heaven and filled the whole house where they were sitting. [3]They saw what seemed to be tongues of fire that separated and came to rest on each of them. [4]All of them were filled with the Holy Spirit and began to speak in other tongues as the Spirit enabled them.

The significance of what happened on this momentous day can hardly be overstated. Holy Spirit baptism was to be a historical marker for the last stage of human history on this earth. The promise of Spirit baptism was first seen in the preaching of John the Baptist in Luke 3:16–17:

> John answered them all, "I baptize you with water. But one more powerful than I will come, the thongs of whose sandals I am not worthy to untie. He will baptize you with the Holy Spirit and with fire. His winnowing fork is in his hand to clear his threshing floor and to gather the wheat into his barn, but he will burn up the chaff with unquenchable fire."

The "baptism with fire" is a reference to a judgment against the unbelieving Jews. Some believe this refers to the destruction of Jerusalem in 70 AD. Others believe it refers to hell. The former is more probable. This impending destruction of their city was often mentioned in both the Old Testament and the New Testament.[1]

The "baptism with the Holy Spirit" is a reference to a blessing for the believing group. When the Spirit came, the apostles were promised that they would receive special power connected with their witnessing to the whole world (Acts 1:8). Acts 2 describes this "baptism" or "outpouring" of the Spirit. It is essential that we understand the exact definition of the baptism with the Holy Spirit. Acts 2:16–17 equates the "pouring out" of the Spirit with the "baptism" of the Spirit because pouring is from God's vantage point and baptism (a covering, or overwhelming) is from man's vantage point. For example, when water is poured over a coin in a glass, the coin is then covered or overwhelmed. Thus, pouring and baptism are both accurate terms to describe Holy Spirit baptism in Acts 2. The reason that this outpouring was called a "baptism" is because of the overwhelming nature of the Spirit's coming and subsequent availability. Before Spirit baptism occurred, the Holy Spirit was available only to a select few in the Old Testament (mostly the prophets). Once this baptism occurred, he was then available for everyone who became a Christian (Acts 2:38–40).

However, he did not do exactly the same work in everyone who received him. For example, the apostles could lay hands on people to give them the ability to perform miraculous works (Acts 6:5–6; 8:5–6, 14–19). Those with these gifts normally had only one or two specific gifts each (1 Corinthians 12:28–30). The need for the miraculous gifts ceased when the New Testament was complete in written form (2 Timothy 3:16–17, John 20:30–31).

Holy Spirit baptism, then, was the coming of the Spirit into the world in overwhelming measure. Through this onetime outpouring,[2] he became available for everyone who would receive him. A similar parallel may be made between Jesus' work and the Spirit's work in initial salvation. Jesus' death was for all (Hebrews 2:9), but only those who obey him receive the benefit of salvation (Hebrews 5:9). Similarly, the coming of the Spirit was for all, but only those who obey receive the Spirit (Acts 2:38–39, Galatians 4:6).

But what does the Spirit do for us today who live centuries past the miraculous age of the church? Plenty! Although this aspect of the Spirit's work is not the focus of this chapter, the connection between the Holy Spirit and the spread of God's message and movement to the lost world is unmistakable. Therefore, we must clearly understand at least the basics of how the Spirit helps us if we are to accomplish world evangelism as the Great Commission directs. This we will examine more closely when we come to the conclusion of this remarkable day of Pentecost.

The Heart of the Gospel (Acts 2:22-36)

22"Men of Israel, listen to this: Jesus of Nazareth was a man accredited by God to you by miracles, wonders and signs, which God did among you through him, as you yourselves know. 23This man was handed over to you by God's set purpose and foreknowledge; and you, with the help of wicked men, put him to death by nailing him to the cross. 24But God raised him from the dead, freeing him from the agony of death, because it was impossible for death to keep its hold on him."

The Crux of the Message

The centrality of the cross in the gospel message is too plain to miss. Just a few passages should establish this point clearly:

> For the message of the cross is foolishness to those who are perishing, but to us who are being saved it is the power of God. (1 Corinthians 1:18)

> For I resolved to know nothing while I was with you except Jesus Christ and him crucified. (1 Corinthians 2:2)

> For what I received I passed on to you as of first importance: that Christ died for our sins according to the Scriptures, that he was buried, that he was raised on the third day according to the Scriptures... (1 Corinthians 15:3–4)

> May I never boast except in the cross of our Lord Jesus Christ, through which the world has been crucified to me, and I to the world. (Galatians 6:14)

No question exists about the priority of the cross in the Bible; however, a question does exist about the priority of the cross in our teaching and preaching and in our individual hearts. How central is it to "our" religion, to "your" religion?

Martin Luther had a very unusual way of distinguishing between Gospel and Law. To him, it was not a distinction between Old Testament and New Testament but between promise and obligation. The Gospel was all about what God had done for us, while Law was all about what we must do for him. Although Luther's definition was flawed biblically, he understood the importance of proper motivation. An overemphasis on obedience and works, with a corresponding under-emphasis on grace, is sure to kill. Conversely, a "feel good" preaching diet will inevitably lead to an undisciplined, unspiritual life. But a "do or be damned" diet will paralyze and destroy, arousing more resentment than appreciation. After all, John did say: "This is love: not that we loved God, but that he loved us and sent his Son as an atoning sacrifice for our sins," and "we love because he first loved us" (1 John 4:10, 19).

Why do you do what you do for God? Is it more duty than desire? Many motivations have a part in causing us to follow God. We may well begin seeking him out of the fear of Judgment Day, and this stimulus has a place in prompting us to consider our ways. Proverbs 1:7 says as much: "The fear of the LORD is the beginning of knowledge." But while this type of fear may gain our attention initially, it cannot sustain us spiritually for long. The joy of Christian fellowship is deeply fulfilling. But if being in fellowship with people is our main motivation, then we will fall on very hard times spiritually whenever

Christians disappoint us. Our motivation must spring from a love and appreciation of Christ on the cross.

The key to a continual, sustaining motivation is in understanding both the utter sinfulness of our flesh and the grace of our God. The former keeps our hearts humble and the latter keeps them soft. When we have a clear picture of how short we really fall of Christ's example, whom we are to imitate (1 John 2:6), and of the infinite mercy of God toward us, then we are in position to grasp both how humbled and exalted we are as redeemed sinners, the objects of our Redeemer's great affection.

The Latin word for cross is *crux*, a word we use to show that something is absolutely central to the subject under consideration. Hence, the death of Christ on the cross for our sins is the central message of the Bible. Nothing is more important, in fact; and nothing can become more important in practice. The joy of salvation has always been the greatest motivator for evangelism (Psalm 51:12–13), and nothing else will suffice. Without question, the heart of the gospel is Christ on the cross, bearing your sins and mine. He bore the sins he did not commit in order that we might not bear the consequences of the sins we did commit. On the cross, he made up for all that you and I failed to do and to be. It was at Golgotha that God treated his own Son in harsh and unrelenting terms, as he must treat sin, in order that he might treat us as though we had never sinned (2 Corinthians 5:21). Let us make certain that this truth is never lost on us, as we love because he first loved us!

The Message of the Empty Tomb

But the gospel does not stop with the cross; it must include the empty tomb. The resurrection proved that Jesus was the Son of God (Romans 1:4) and removes, or greatly diminishes, our fear of death (Hebrews 2:14–15). 1 Corinthians 15:12–19 makes perfectly clear that modern theology's claim that a literal resurrection is not important is more than mere drivel—it is a Satanic lie! If Jesus did not raise bodily from the dead, then we are among the world's most foolish people for believing the Christian message, for it is the message of the empty tomb, the resurrected Lord.

Through the years, skeptics have tried inventing ways of discounting these fundamental truths of Christianity, but they cannot succeed. They are quite limited in their choices, for only four options exist: (1)

Jesus didn't die, but only passed out and later revived; (2) his enemies stole the body; (3) his friends stole the body; or (4) he rose from the dead.

The first option is ludicrous, for the Romans who killed him were professionals at the killing game. And besides, suppose that he wasn't dead and that he revived in the coolness of the tomb. What then? Where did he go? When did he die? Why would the apostles die for a lie?

The second option lacks motive, for the enemies wanted him in the tomb more than anyone. If they had illogically stolen the body, producing it would have silenced the early preachers in short order.

The third option also lacks motive, for the only thing that could have motivated those scared apostles who were hiding behind closed doors was a resurrected Master. Only then did they come to the faith and conviction for which they willingly died.

Yes, Jesus rose from the dead, and he promised that all of us would as well. You can bet your life on it! The enemies of the cross had their brief period of rejoicing as Jesus' body resided in the tomb, but their party was cut short on that Sunday morning when hell suffered its crowning blow. What seemed a certain victory for Satan's forces ended up being the very tool of defeat, for God uses stumbling stones to construct triumphal stairs which ascend into heaven itself. Revolutions do not succeed without miracles, and this miracle is the greatest of all. As we spread the message of Christ, it must be a message in which both the crucifixion and resurrection are central. It is time that we emphasize what the Bible repeatedly does, instead of often relegating these primary emphases to the status of honorable mention!

Good News! (Acts 2:37-41)

37When the people heard this, they were cut to the heart and said to Peter and the other apostles, "Brothers, what shall we do?"

38Peter replied, "Repent and be baptized, every one of you, in the name of Jesus Christ for the forgiveness of your sins. And you will receive the gift of the Holy Spirit. 39The promise is for you and your children and for all who are far off—for all whom the Lord our God will call."

Try to imagine what those in that Pentecost audience must have been feeling. At least some of them had fallen for Satan's lies about Jesus, believing the slander and rejoicing when he died. As Isaiah had prophesied in the long-ago, they "considered him stricken by God, smitten by him, and afflicted" (Isaiah 53:4). Now as Peter preached, the truth began to dawn suddenly and heavily about Jesus:

> But he was pierced for our transgressions,
> he was crushed for our iniquities;
> the punishment that brought us peace was upon him,
> and by his wounds we are healed....
> After the suffering of his soul,
> he will see the light of life and be satisfied;
> by his knowledge my righteous servant will justify many,
> and he will bear their iniquities. (Isaiah 53:5, 11)

What they had so smugly assumed about Jesus was shown to be 180 degrees mistaken—instead of crying for the destruction of a blasphemer of God Almighty, they had begged Pilate for the death of God's one and only Son! Unbelievable! Horrifying!

As they now beg Peter and the apostles for a remedy for their unthinkable sin, surely they must be feeling the human emotion of hopelessness. But because of who Jesus was and what he had done, their predicament was far from hopeless. Peter offers them hope and a future. He gives them two commands and describes for them two amazing blessings.

Repentance

Peter calls first for repentance. What does that mean? That we will never again sin? Hardly. The best of us is a mess, says Paul in Romans 1–3, and thus to claim sinlessness is to be a liar and make God out to be a liar as well (1 John 1:8–10). To repent is to have a godly sorrow about what you have done, wishing that you had not done it, believing that if you were in the same situation again you would say no, and determining not to say yes the next time you face that temptation. God does not merely look at what we do; he looks most closely at what we want to do. And if we want badly to do the right thing, he through the Spirit will enable us to enjoy that victory. We will give in to our ever-present sinful nature at times, but as we grow, we will fall less, fall less deeply and get up more quickly. And God will say, "Good. That's progress. Forgiven. New beginning."

Just how anxious are you to have your sins addressed and to be convicted of them deeply enough to prompt repentance? We can be like the parishioner of a traditional church who shook the preacher's hand as he was leaving the church building and said, "Preacher, you helped me to see myself as I have never seen myself before—and I'll never forgive you!" If we are blessed to hear strong biblical preaching, we had better respond to it wholeheartedly and immediately. Otherwise, we can be not only hardened to preaching, but by preaching. It is an embarrassment that religious leaders in our day are so unlike Peter in straightforward preaching, offering a message so different from his. They have nearly perfected the art of almost saying something as they preach their "feel-good" doctrine. In the large majority of churches, one who preaches the need for repentance as Peter preached it would likely be fired immediately, if not bodily assaulted!

Repentance is a topic, like the kingdom, that needs more attention in order to develop a greater understanding and appreciation of it. We know from reading Acts 3:19 that repentance is designed to be a very positive blessing, bringing times of refreshing. But too often the word is viewed in less than a positive light. A part of that viewpoint comes from our sinful nature not wanting to face the challenge of change, but another part of it comes from having a shallow understanding of the concept itself. The best book I know to recommend on the subject is one with just the simple title, *Repentance,* by Ed Anton.[3] It will help you clear up misunderstandings, and propel you to embrace repentance as the "friend" that it is.

Baptism

Hearing without obeying is hazardous to our spiritual health. In no uncertain terms, Peter told the people who were convicted by his message to repent and be baptized for the forgiveness of their sins.[4] The famous British scholar G. R. Beasley-Murray states plainly what is evident for scholars and nonscholars alike:

> Peter's response...to his conscience stricken hearers on the Day of Pentecost was not, "Repent and believe," but "Repent and be baptized!" (Acts 2:38). Naturally faith was presumed in repentance, but Peter's answer told the Jews how to become Christians: faith and

> repentance are to be expressed in baptism, and so they are to come to the Lord.[5]

Without such obedience, no forgiveness is obtained. Man cannot substitute his plan of salvation for God's. Again, can you imagine what would happen in most churches if the preacher boldly declared what Peter did about how to be saved? Sadly, this clear biblical teaching is directly resisted by the theologians of our day. You simply will not hear Peter's message preached in "evangelical" churches. Interpreting "salvation by grace through faith" in ways Peter and Paul never did, they have carved baptism for forgiveness out of the plan. But those of us who are determined to proclaim the biblical message can be neither bashful nor apologetic about teaching the same message as Peter preached. As Paul would later teach, baptism is a union with Christ in his death, burial and resurrection. It is that moment when the old man dies and the new man is raised up, justified by the blood of Jesus (Romans 6:1–4).

Baptism is, in words written later by Peter, "an appeal to God for a clear conscience" (1 Peter 3:21, Revised Standard Version).

By the end of the day we are describing, 3,000 people had made the decision to repent and be baptized in the name of Jesus. They responded wholeheartedly to God's gracious offer. Their lives were changed, and the floodgates of heaven were opened for them.

The Forgiveness of Sin

Through the prophet Jeremiah, God had promised that with the coming of the new covenant he would "forgive...wickedness, and remember...sins no more" (Jeremiah 31:34). Now the death of Christ was applied to each who gladly received the message and responded appropriately. Repentance and baptism were blessed by forgiveness and the gift of the Holy Spirit. The people in Peter's audience understood something of what baptism was, but even if they had not, they surely would have accepted it quickly, completely and gratefully. They had been deeply convicted of sin by an honest preacher, and they were not in an argumentative, bargaining mood. They were just grateful that forgiveness was available.

At the moment of baptism every sin we have ever committed is blotted out and remembered no more. We are justified. It is "just as if we had never sinned." But the news gets even better! From that moment on, the blood of Christ continues to cleanse us of sin, if we continue in our faith and keep coming into the light with our lives (Colossians 1:22–23, 1 John 1:7).

We sinners often think that we must have sinned away our allotment of God's grace this time; our sins must have finally reached the limit and exhausted the mercy of God. Have you never felt this? In fact, have you not often felt it? We all sin in many ways, in spite of our deepest desires to do otherwise, and we know that God is much more aware of these sins than we are ourselves. How could it be possible that his willingness to forgive never dims in the least? And yet, when we cry out in despair for the merest hint of another chance with him, he quickly replies, "Just repent."

The Gift of the Holy Spirit

When we are baptized into a saved relationship with Christ, the Spirit comes to indwell us (Acts 2:38, 5:32). We receive the Spirit as a gift. According to Galatians 4:6, he is sent into our hearts by God because we become children of God, thus signifying this new relationship. Several important truths are connected with this indwelling.

One, the Spirit is our seal (2 Corinthians 1:21–22, Ephesians 1:13). In the first century a seal was an official sign of ownership. When we become Christians, God stamps us as his property! The world may not be able to tell who is a child of God simply by looking, but the spirit world now can.

Two, the Spirit is the deposit of our inheritance (2 Corinthians 5:5, Ephesians 1:14). The deposit here carries the idea of earnest money put down for a purchase as a pledge that the full amount will be paid at the proper time. Therefore, the Spirit is God's deposit in us, guaranteeing our future blessings with him (Philippians 3:20–21).

Three, he strengthens us (Ephesians 3:14–21) and helps us to follow through with our convictions. Of course, he will not force us to do right against our will to do otherwise, but he will strengthen us to do what we really want to do for God. Once I was jogging a much longer distance than I ever had before, and near the end of the run I came to a formidable hill. When I was tempted to give up, a friend ran behind me with his hand in the middle of my back pushing me. Had I quit running, he could not have helped me, but because I was trying, he could assist me in completing the run. Similarly, the Spirit assists us to complete what we could not complete without his helpful and vital "push."

Four, he aids us in godly living. Just knowing that he dwells in me keeps me from wanting to sin (1 Corinthians 6:19–20), for where I go, he goes! Galatians tells us that we "live" by the Spirit in a number of ways: by refusing to gratify the desires of the sinful nature (Galatians 5:16–17); by being freed from a legalistic works orientation (5:18); by avoiding a life directed by the sinful nature (5:19–21); by developing the fruit of the Spirit (5:22–23); by crucifying the sinful nature (5:24); by keeping in step with the Spirit (5:25); and by maintaining loving relationships with our brothers (5:26). The Holy Spirit is vitally concerned about every aspect of our lives and needs. He loves us. He cares about how we feel. He intercedes for us (Romans 8:26–27) because he is an Encourager (Acts 9:31) and a Counselor to us (John 14:16–18).

Five, the Spirit acts providentially for us, often leading in ways that are very delightful to us: directly into the blessings of God. However, he also leads us into the desert of trials! (Matthew 4:1). Jesus was led into the desert right after he demonstrated his great commitment to God's will through his baptism by John. We need not be surprised when spiritual mountaintops are followed by some deep, dark valleys. Passages like Lamentations 3:38 inform us that everything that happens to us is either directly caused by God or at the least, allowed by him.

Douglas Jacoby makes a good point when he says that "being led by the Spirit is no different than being led by God or being led by Jesus."[6] Naive disciples are sometimes more influenced by religious writers about the Holy Spirit than they are by the Bible, and what they feel is "being led by the Spirit" becomes a better-felt-than-told experience for them. This is dangerous. The purpose of the Spirit in our lives is not to make us feel good; it is to make us fruitful in carrying out the mission to seek and to save the lost. In Acts 9:31 we read:

> Then the church throughout Judea, Galilee and Samaria enjoyed a time of peace. It was strengthened; and encouraged by the Holy Spirit, it grew in numbers, living in the fear of the Lord.

When people are being "led" to feel good without being effective in the mission of the Holy Spirit himself, they are being led by a different spirit than the one we are reading about in the book of

Acts! Let's be sure that we are those willing volunteers whose hearts beat with passion for the salvation of those for whom Christ died. This business of following the Christ is emphatically not a nice, little, "touchy-feely" project; it is an all-out "lay down your life" endeavor. When our lives are focused on the Great Commission, we are truly being led by the Spirit in the footsteps of Jesus and those who knew him best, and that same Spirit will help us to be fruitful.

Promise, Not Obligation

This message is called a "promise" in Acts 2:39. It was not obligation; it was opportunity. Although it was stated in the form of a command, it is overwhelmingly a promise in its effect. God is once again vowing to bless us infinitely beyond what our faith response deserves. How little we do for him at our most, and how much he does for us at his least (to use a figure of speech)!

When Paul wrote in Ephesians 2:8 that we are saved by grace through faith, he was in no way putting faith on the same level with grace. It is not man's part (fifty percent) plus God's part (fifty percent) that equals salvation; it is man reaching up in faith to accept from God the otherwise unreachable and inexplicable blessings that we in no way deserve. If you look at the commands of God as demanding and burdensome, you are blinded by your own lack of humility and gratitude. Wake up! Repent—with deep appreciation.

Whatever commands you are contemplating, rest assured that the element of promise far overshadows anything that you might be asked to do. The call to repentance and baptism represents a heavenly opportunity to accept the rare privilege of walking hand in hand with the God of the universe in the most exciting mission any man has ever imagined!

A New Family (Acts 2:42-47)

44 All the believers were together and had everything in common. 45 Selling their possessions and goods, they gave to anyone as he had need. 46 Every day they continued to meet together in the temple courts. They broke bread in their homes and ate together with glad and sincere hearts

The followers of Christ, as a group, are called by a number of designations in the New Testament ("church, kingdom, field, temple, body, vineyard," etc.), but my favorite is "family." The church is the family of God, and being his son or daughter makes us brother and sister to one another. However, in our society most families are dysfunctional to some degree, which makes the "family feeling" hard for many to fully grasp.

But our text teaches clearly that those in the church were devoted to Christ and to one another in remarkable ways. For example they were devoted to following leaders (v42). Submission and "followership" were readily embraced, for they knew that God has always appointed strong leaders through whom to work. They are like the older brothers and sisters in the family. Also, their devotion was seen in their dedication to assemblies. They met daily and felt privileged to be able to worship God as a big family. In fact, these assemblies were more like family reunions than what is generally seen in the denominational world. Certainly, attending church was not viewed as some religious duty, but as a blessing to be claimed and enjoyed. The first time we come into contact with a present-day church like the one described in Acts 2, our first thought may be that they meet too often and are too committed. But compared to the first church, this simply is not true. They met daily.

In verses 44–45, their devotion to one another included the use of their finances in a sacrificial way. Keep in mind that these thousands in Jerusalem had come from all over the world to observe the Pentecost feast. As brand-new converts, they were not at all equipped to go back to their homelands. They needed training as disciples and disciple makers, thus the need to remain in Jerusalem and the need to be supported while being trained. This prompted the occasion about which we read. Financial contributions today must be made with the same selfless and generous spirit, and for the same purposes. Understanding this principle makes the emphasis on sacrificial giving in our churches quite reasonable. We are supporting those who are being trained to take the gospel to the world and who are equipping us to take the gospel to those around us—wherever we may live.

As this early church lived out its mission as a spiritual family, the onlookers saw in action the love described in John 13:34–35 and longed to join (Acts 2:47). Carrying out the mission cannot be accomplished without the family relationships at the heart of it. Everyone is looking for love, whether they realize it or not, and when they see the real thing, they will be drawn to it.

Amazingly, whatever sacrifices must be made to follow Christ will be repaid a hundred times over, as Mark 10:29–30 states in these precious words:

> "I tell you the truth," Jesus replied, "no one who has left home or brothers or sisters or mother or father or children or fields for me and the gospel will fail to receive a hundred times as much in this present age (homes, brothers, sisters, mothers, children and fields—and with them, persecutions) and in the age to come, eternal life."

Relationships in the kingdom are designed to make up for those which have failed us in our physical families, and with the passing of a very small amount of time, they will be closer than physical family ties, even if those ties are strong. It is the plan of God, and those of us who have been in the kingdom for at least a year should certainly attest to this fact. If we cannot, something is clearly wrong and our kingdom relationships need immediate attention. When we accept Christ as Lord, God becomes our Father, and we become blood (of Jesus) brothers and sisters. And given the age differences, people like my wife and me are privileged to become dads and moms to hundreds. Praise God for his kingdom and glory and for the privilege of becoming his blood-bought family!

Questions for Further Study

1. Explain the view of Holy Spirit Baptism expressed in this chapter.

2. What do you think about that view?

3. The crux of the gospel message is really all about motivation to serve God—explain.

4. If you were talking to a person who seriously doubted the literal bodily resurrection of Jesus from the grave, what arguments would you use to try and convince them?

5. What does it mean to be hardened to preaching?

6. What does it mean to be hardened by preaching?

7. Acts 2:38 contains two commands and two promises. Explain each in three sentences or less.

8. In Acts 2:42–27, God's true spiritual family is described. In which area or areas do you believe that your congregation needs to grow, and why do you answer as you do?

Chapter Three

Love In Words And Deeds
Acts 3-4

Whe word "love" is not found in the book of Acts. However, the concept is found on just about every page. Love is not mainly a feeling, nor is it primarily verbal expression. It is something that you do. The apostle John put it this way in 1 John 3:18: "Dear children, let us not love with words or tongue but with actions and in truth." No one did this better than John's beloved Savior, who was the pattern for those described in Acts. We never have to look far to observe the ministry of Jesus being imitated by his early followers. They learned from him how to love in words and in deeds.

The Ministry of Jesus Continues (Acts 3)

[6]Then Peter said, "Silver or gold I do not have, but what I have I give you. In the name of Jesus Christ of Nazareth, walk." [7]Taking him by the right hand, he helped him up, and instantly the man's feet and ankles became strong. [8]He jumped to his feet and began to walk. Then he went with them into the temple courts, walking and jumping, and praising God.

The preaching and healing ministry of Jesus is described succinctly in Matthew 9:35–38, as his divine compassion was stirred mightily by those sheep who were harassed and helpless. As we look at his heart in action, physical needs of people drew him to them and drove him to help them. But ultimately, he was most concerned about their spiritual needs, as the context of Matthew 9 shows. All healed by him eventually died of some cause, and the same may be said of this man in Acts 3, healed by Peter and John. The social gospel, which consists of simply trying to help people physically, is a woefully inadequate attempt to bless lives. Without a relationship with God, those who are thus helped will still die lost.

Having said that, the converse is also true. Trying to minister spiritually without being ready to meet physical needs will also fail. James and John spoke to this situation most pointedly (James 2:14–16, 1 John 3:16–17). As important as doctrine is, people generally are not going to care how much you know until they first know how much you care. We should all be grateful for opportunities to serve the poor and needy through the various HOPE Worldwide projects, but how much serving are most of us really doing? Raising money, giving money and participating in a couple of projects each year is a very good thing, but that frequency and level of involvement is not quite what you see in the ministry of Jesus and the early church. All of us need at least a weekly way to reach out and help hurting people.

For most of us living in first world countries, that may appear to present a challenge. We are not oblivious to people's pain—we simply do not see it up close in our normal course of life. Therefore, we are going to have to start looking with a determination to find ways to serve. When we are looking, poor people, old people, sick people and incarcerated people are not hard to find. How many of us are even reaching out to those of our own number who face serious life challenges? Single moms need help from spiritual men in parenting their children, especially their sons who desperately need male role models. When we decide we really want to get involved, we can find plenty of ways to serve. We find not because we seek not.

How badly we need to serve people physically! When we get up close and personal with those needing help physically, it moves our hearts. As we meet these needs, it provides us with opportunities and the motivation to reach out spiritually. Many of us are not too good at feeling the spiritual pain of others, but if we start out by getting in touch with physical and emotional pain, it will provide training and perception for meeting spiritual needs. When people are thus served, they appreciate it. Their hearts are opened in ways that no other keys can unlock. Opportunities to preach the Word are provided by God in ways we would never anticipate when we open our hearts, our wallets and our schedules to those whose perceived needs are easily seen and felt. As a movement, we have made progress in this area—much progress. For that we have many to thank, but we must take our serving much deeper to keep the kingdom growing exponentially. Selflessness is one quality God stands ready to bless.

Notice in Acts 3 just how quickly the healing of the beggar led to a powerful opportunity to preach the gospel. Characteristically, Peter's message was a strong one, connecting sin to the betrayal of Jesus in order to bring his hearers to conviction. This emphasis was followed by the admonition once again to repent. Acts 3:19 reads:

> "Repent, then, and turn to God, so that your sins may be wiped out, that times of refreshing may come from the Lord."

At first glance, this passage seems to be different than what Peter preached in Acts 2, but it is not. Certainly Luke described various conversion messages in different terminology, but a closer examination of the texts in their contexts will show a remarkable uniformity.

For example, Acts 2:38 and Acts 3:19 are quite parallel. Repentance is first enjoined on the hearers in both accounts. Next, the baptism of Acts 2 and the turning to God in Acts 3 are equated. Then come the two results: forgiveness ("wiping out" of sins in Acts 3) and the gift of the Holy Spirit, whose indwelling presence brings us those "times of refreshing" (Acts 3:19). No one should ever assume that Peter's lack of specific mention of baptism in this passage eliminates its requirement as a part of the faith response whereby we receive forgiveness. Not only was Luke inspired as he penned these accounts—he was far from stupid. The apparent variations may very well have been purposely included by God to test hearts, to see if we want answers or excuses, explanations or rationalizations. We should be most grateful to have been baptized and forgiven, indwelt and refreshed!

Threatened But Not Silenced (Acts 4:1-22)

1The priests and the captain of the temple guard and the Sadducees came up to Peter and John while they were speaking to the people. 2They were greatly disturbed because the apostles were teaching the people and proclaiming in Jesus the resurrection of the dead. 3They seized Peter and John, and because it was evening, they put them in jail until the next day. 4But many who heard the message believed, and the number of men grew to about five thousand....

8Then Peter, filled with the Holy Spirit, said to them: "Rulers and elders of the people! 9If we are being called to account today for an act of kindness shown to a cripple and are asked how he was healed, 10then know this, you and all the people of Israel: It is by the name of Jesus Christ of Nazareth, whom you crucified but whom God raised from the dead, that this man stands before you healed."

The progress of persecution always follows a predictable pattern. It begins in mild forms and ends with violent forms, unless the preaching changes. Jesus himself was widely acclaimed and accepted in the early stages of his ministry. However, his life and teaching eventually prompted those in the darkness to kill him. Similarly, the early church experienced an early acceptance followed by increasing rejection. The favor they enjoyed in Acts 2:46–47 soon gave way to the persecution of the apostles in Jerusalem (Acts 4 and 5) and the persecution of other disciples in Jerusalem (Acts 8:1–3), and then in other parts of the world (Acts 17:5–8). Finally, it reached the point that Jewish leaders in faraway Rome said, "People everywhere are talking against this sect" (Acts 28:21–22).

The message of Jesus and his brand of discipleship is threatening to people, and their persecution of his messengers springs from this fact. Family ties are threatened by the call to put God first (Matthew 10:34–37); false teachers and false teachings are threatened by the proclamation of truth (1 Timothy 1:3–4, 2 Timothy 4:2–4); business and financial success are threatened by commitment to righteousness (Acts 19:23–34); and those pursuing worldly pleasures are threatened by those living a pure life (1 Peter 4:3–4).

The first reaction of the biblically ignorant who hear of the presence of persecution against a given group is shock and outrage. Being in the majority makes people assume that the majority is right! But it almost never is right—by definition. The way of truth is narrow, and most never find it (Matthew 7:13–14). Therefore, their conclusions about the way of the minority are going to be wrong. Christians must not be surprised when it happens (1 Peter 4:12–16). They must stay calm and rejoice in the anticipation of God's reward (Matthew 5:10–12). We cannot expect the world to view us positively, either as individuals or as a group. The public news media makes a living by producing sensational stories. Combine this motive with their lack of understanding about the spiritual realm, and you have the necessary elements to prompt misrepresentations on a broad scale.

Years ago, I remember reading adverse publicity about the churches who were devoted to discipling. Many of my friends and relatives reacted with alarm. My initial reaction was quite the opposite. The churches of which I had been a part for years attracted little attention from the world. In general, they were considered respectable and acceptable in their communities. I often wondered just why we were not viewed and treated like Jesus and the early church were. The answer should have been obvious: We were not hurting Satan's cause enough to prompt him to stir up the world against us. The presence of persecution does not prove that a person or group is of God, since it is possible to be persecuted for unrighteousness or for righteousness. But the absence of persecution makes a clear statement about the lack of godliness. In my case, adverse publicity caused me to take a closer look in order to determine the reasons behind the publicity. I knew it would be wrong to allow any man or group of men, no matter how "respectable," to do my thinking for me.

If Jesus and his early followers were misrepresented and slandered, we should not be taken aback when the same happens to us. Nor should we be shaken up when otherwise well-respected members of the community are the ones doing the damage. It was the Establishment who nailed Jesus to the cross and the religious leaders who demanded it. In our world of traditional religion, most people have been inoculated against the real thing. Therefore, the genuine article is going to be seen as strange and be treated accordingly. We must trust God and respond in harmony with his teachings on the subject. Even when the world thinks we are weird, God applauds our faith and our bearing of the cross. Relax, rejoice and keep preaching—it could be worse (and likely soon will be)!

A Truly Great Commission (Acts 4:23-31)

27Indeed Herod and Pontius Pilate met together with the Gentiles and the people of Israel in this city to conspire against your holy servant Jesus, whom you anointed. 28They did what your power and will had decided beforehand should happen. 29Now, Lord, consider their threats and enable your servants to speak your word with great boldness....

31After they prayed, the place where they were meeting was shaken. And they were all filled with the Holy Spirit and spoke the word of God boldly.

We often call the commission of Jesus in Matthew 28:18–20 the "Great Commission." Although the term is not expressly Biblical, it is a very good one. What cause could be greater than making disciples of Jesus all over the entire world? What could be more exciting than the sharing of Jesus' mission (a co-mission), as he works with and through us until the very end of the age? But if the commission is great, the carrying out of it is going to require greatness on many fronts. Not surprisingly, the book of Acts uses the term "great" numerous times as it describes the fulfillment of the Great Commission in a scant thirty years (Colossians 1:6, 23). The first instance occurs in Acts 4:29, and combined with the others, shows just what it took to accomplish that worldwide mission the first time. Obviously, we cannot succeed without the same ingredients.

- Great boldness (4:29)
- Great power (4:33)
- Great fear (5:5, 11)
- Great wonders and miraculous signs (6:8; 8:13)
- Great persecution (8:1)
- Great joy (8:8)
- Great numbers of people converted (11:21, 24, 26; 14:1)
- Great eagerness to hear the message (17:11)
- Great fervor on the part of Apollos (18:25)
- Great disturbance (19:23)
- Great humility (20:19)
- Great uproar (23:9)

These "great" things can be categorized under three headings: what the early preachers had, what they did and the effects on those who saw and heard them.

Great Leaders

Great leaders are those with great qualities. Notice those found in the leaders of the early church.

First, they had great boldness. They prayed for it and received it from the Holy Spirit (Acts 4:29, 31). Keep in mind that Peter and

John had just been released from being jailed for refusing to heed the warnings of the public officials to stop preaching. Now they are praying for the boldness to defy the authorities yet more! When we face any kind of persecution, we tend to pray that the persecution stop or that somehow we would be protected. These men had launched a mission that was more important to them than life itself, and it was a mission whose radical impact had to be greatly increased, not diminished. What are you praying for? Your answer must be great boldness to preach no matter what the consequences.

Second, these early ministers of the Word had great power as they preached Jesus and his resurrection. How did that power manifest itself? In the changed lives of the people. They became what they had not been formerly and did what they never would have done otherwise. Just look at that text in 4:32–37. These early disciples were in no way possessed by their possessions. Powerful preaching changes lives from the inside out, as hearts are cleansed of materialism and selfishness. But to be powerful, the focus must be on Jesus—not on man's obligations and duties. Take the time to look at the content of the sermons in Acts and at Paul's letters to the churches. The preaching was much more about what God had done than about what we must do. Frankly, our emphases are often different—too different. If your preaching and teaching does not make people fall more and more in love with God, his Son and his Spirit, it is not powerful. Loud it may be, but powerful it is not.

Preaching about giving money to meet needs and spread the Word is an excellent thing in the kingdom, if it is preached in proper relation to the good news (gospel) of what God has done for us. Correctly taught, it acts as a natural purifying agent to cleanse the church of stingy-hearted people. Unless they repent, they cannot go to heaven anyway, for Jesus clearly said in Luke 14:33: "So therefore, no one of you can be My disciple who does not give up all his own possessions" (NASB). The reaction people have to giving sacrificially to meet needs in the body and to spread the gospel is a good test of how powerful our preaching really is. But if our main focus is on man's duty instead of God's provisions in Christ, we are testing hearts the wrong way—with our own sin of a performance orientation!

Third, Apollos in Acts 18:25 taught with great fervor. He was also said to be a highly educated man in the Scriptures, but a boring lecturer he was not. The gospel is the most exciting message ever spoken, and none of us has the right to make it boring. Whether or not we are naturally gifted as communicators, Romans 12:11 tells us to "never be lacking in zeal, but keep [our] spiritual fervor, serving the Lord." Truthfully, few of us are born speakers, in either public or private settings. Communicating well is a learned process. But the more excited and enthusiastic we are about the contents of what we are sharing, the more effective we are in sharing it. Zeal and fervor are inseparably tied to our walk with God. How real is your relationship with him? How exciting is it? How anxious are you to share it with others? The answer to those questions will have a lot to say about your level of fervor. Can it be said of you that you, like Apollos, have great zeal? If the answer is no, then repent and change. Only one of the apostles was a Zealot, but rest assured that their walk with Jesus turned them all into zealots.

Fourth, Paul was a leader with great humility. In Acts 20 his humility is shown in several ways, including his willingness to serve day and night from house to house, preaching the whole will of God—complete with warnings. Perhaps the greatest indicator of his humility was his unashamed shedding of tears, which is mentioned three times (Acts 20:19, 31, 37). As has been said, our humility cannot be seen until our humanity is first seen. Jesus was a man of tears, and if we imitate him, our emotions will be shared openly and consistently. Men especially seem challenged with being real and vulnerable, but unless we conquer our sinful nature in this area, we will be neither humble nor great. Imitate Jesus. Imitate Paul. Let your humanity shine through, and then your humility will reap its rewards, for God resists the proud but exalts the humble (1 Peter 5:5–6).

Great Works

With these great qualities, the first-century leaders were able to do some great things. First, they did great wonders and miraculous signs.[1] We look at that accomplishment too lightly. Their faith fueled their ability to do these things, at least to an appreciable degree, for in Matthew 17:14–21 their inability to perform a miracle was due to their lack of faith. Even though they had a miraculous ability given by the Holy Spirit, it could not function without their faith. In 2 Timothy 1:6, Paul admonished Timothy to fan his gift into flame, and his gift was a miraculous one as an inspired evangelist. The point is that whether gifts of the Holy Spirit were of a miraculous nature or not, they still were gifts and had to be purposely and faithfully used. All of us have gifts. The question is whether or not we are using them powerfully. Using any type of gift from the Spirit is not automatic—it takes faith and hard work. Without these, no gift will ever be used to its full potential.

Second, these preachers in Acts converted great numbers. Even a cursory reading of Acts will demonstrate that God is into numbers. Every number represents a soul who will meet God in judgment, and he wants every one of them to have the opportunity to hear the message and respond with an informed choice. If a church is committed to the same mission that the early church had, that of evangelizing everyone in every nation (Matthew 28:18–20), then it will grow. In the Great Commission, Jesus said to go make disciples, and then he promised to be with us as we go. Rest assured that his presence with us in carrying out that co-mission will not be met with failure. If we do it his way, we will grow; if we are not growing, we need to reexamine our convictions, our focus and our actions. And that principle fits us individually as well as collectively. Look at the following list of verses and be encouraged to go do likewise!

- Acts 2:41—Those who accepted his message were baptized, and about three thousand were added to their number that day.
- Acts 2:47—...praising God and enjoying the favor of all the people. And the Lord added to their number daily those who were being saved.
- Acts 5:14—Nevertheless, more and more men and women believed in the Lord and were added to their number.
- Acts 6:1—In those days when the number of disciples was increasing, the Grecian Jews among them complained against the Hebraic Jews because their widows were being overlooked in the daily distribution of food.
- Acts 6:7—So the word of God spread. The number of disciples in Jerusalem increased rapidly, and a large number of priests became obedient to the faith.
- Acts 9:31—Then the church throughout Judea, Galilee and Samaria enjoyed a time of peace. It was strengthened; and encouraged by the Holy Spirit, it grew in numbers, living in the fear of the Lord.
- Acts 9:42—This became known all over Joppa, and many people believed in the Lord.
- Acts 11:21—The Lord's hand was with them, and a great number of

people believed and turned to the Lord.

- Acts 11:24—He was a good man, full of the Holy Spirit and faith, and a great number of people were brought to the Lord.
- Acts 11:26—... and when he found him, he brought him to Antioch. So for a whole year Barnabas and Saul met with the church and taught great numbers of people. The disciples were called Christians first at Antioch.
- Acts 12:24—But the word of God continued to increase and spread.
- Acts 13:49—The word of the Lord spread through the whole region.
- Acts 14:1—At Iconium Paul and Barnabas went as usual into the Jewish synagogue. There they spoke so effectively that a great number of Jews and Gentiles believed.
- Acts 14:21—They preached the good news in that city and won a large number of disciples. Then they returned to Lystra, Iconium and Antioch.
- Acts 16:5—So the churches were strengthened in the faith and grew daily in numbers.
- Acts 17:12—Many of the Jews believed, as did also a number of prominent Greek women and many Greek men.
- Acts 18:8—Crispus, the synagogue ruler, and his entire household believed in the Lord; and many of the Corinthians who heard him believed and were baptized.
- Acts 19:10—This went on for two years, so that all the Jews and Greeks who lived in the province of Asia heard the word of the Lord.
- Acts 19:20—In this way the word of the Lord spread widely and grew in power.

Third, Apollos gave great help to the believers in Achaia, having been sent by the brothers in Ephesus. Specifically, Acts 18:27–28 attributes this help to his vigorous refutation of the Jewish enemies of the church. Our world and our kingdom need more men like Apollos who are not afraid to have deep convictions and express them publicly, especially in the realm of morals and religion. It is not socially acceptable in our existential world to take dogmatic stands regarding right and wrong.

Several years ago, I talked to a young man who had become so enamored with academia that he had lost all touch with common sense. He objected to my "fundamentalism," which he defined as my insistence on the existence of absolute biblical truth and error. That seemed highly distasteful to him, for he had given up on the idea of absolute, infallible truth. As the conversation developed, it became apparent that he had reached an amazing philosophical conclusion: He was absolutely certain that no one could be absolutely certain! Am I an old moss-backed conservative, Bible-banging fundamentalist? Some would definitely describe me in those terms, but with brothers like Apollos and Paul, I am in pretty good company.

Great Effects

Finally, in looking at the "great" things in Acts, we come to the effects of great preachers and preaching. When God smote Ananias and Sapphira for lying, great fear came upon the whole church and on everyone else who heard about it. Obviously, God is serious about the commitment and righteousness level of those who do his bidding. Discipleship is serious business. Those who were serious enough to become disciples were filled with great joy that their names were written in heaven. The noble-hearted had great eagerness to hear Paul's preaching. Being neither suspicious nor naive, they checked out the message, but they desired to believe it. As Jesus described the faith process in John 7:17, he said in essence that we must have the will to believe before we will believe. Those without that receptive spirit will instigate great persecution, great disturbances and great uproars.

The Great Commission demands a great deal of us, but it delivers a great reward to those who first accept it and then pass it on to others. It takes great men and women of faith in any age to carry it out, but for that purpose we have been born, reborn and commissioned. Let's not fail in the only cause that survives this life. Never give up your life for anything that death can take away!

Unity Beyond Definition (Acts 4:32-36)

[32]All the believers were one in heart and mind. No one claimed that any of his possessions was his own, but they shared everything they had. [33]With great power the apostles continued to testify to the resurrection of the Lord Jesus, and much grace was upon them all. [34]There were no needy persons among them. For from time to time those who owned lands or houses sold them, brought the money from the sales [35]and put it at the apostles' feet, and it was distributed to anyone as he had need.

"All the believers were one in heart and mind." Who in modern society can even imagine such a thing? Such total unity today would bring to mind a host of non-endearing terms, and would undoubtedly arouse major suspicions! America became a nation as a direct result of disunity and rebellion, as did most other countries. From the tower of Babel forward, unity has been a scarce commodity, even in religious circles. The existence of hundreds of different churches in "Christendom" validates that point quite clearly.

Yet, Jesus staked the success of his movement on the ability of the church to be unified.

> "By this all men will know that you are my disciples, if you love one another." (John 13:35)

> "May they be brought to complete unity to let the world know that you sent me and have loved them even as you have loved me." (John 17:23)

Verses could be multiplied in which the purest kinds of unity are enjoined on believers.

The unity in our Acts 4 text included unity in the areas of finances and trusting leaders, two subjects which often strain unity. The need for leadership and the authority inherent in it exists in every group having any purpose to accomplish. In America, along with most of the rest of the world, society is bordering on chaos because of a breakdown of authority. The deterioration of homes and schools, former bastions for developing respect for authority, is nothing short of astonishing. However, no organization can survive and flourish without authority. God uses leadership in the church to lead his people to maturity and productivity (Ephesians 4:11–16).

The Bible wastes no time in showing us Satan's hatred of authority and his devious way of undermining it. He approached Eve (Genesis 3) by saying that God had forbidden her and Adam to eat from every tree in the Garden. Eve responded by essentially saying "No, it was really only one tree, but if we eat from it we will die." Satan pretty much replied, "Not true—God is lying to you because he doesn't want you to gain his knowledge." What was Satan doing here? He was undermining trust in the authority of God. He has not changed his approach one iota in the thousands of years since Eve ate the forbidden fruit. He hates every form of authority (except his own) and will continue his attempts to tear it down in every nation, society and family, and certainly in the church of the Almighty God!

We must be aware of his schemes and resist them fully if we are to be unified and accomplish the mission of God in our world. When suspicions or hurt feelings arise, we must "settle matters quickly" (Matthew 5:23–25). The salvation of the world depends on maintaining God's brand of unity. Although it nearly defies definition in the minds of ordinary men, it can simply be defined as our meeting on common ground beneath the cross of Christ for the purpose of accomplishing the mission of Christ.

Questions for Further Study

1. What were the two main components of Jesus' ministry, and how did Peter show his desire to carry on both of them?

2. Biblically, what are the main causes of persecution for disciples of Jesus?

3. In reading the section about the greatness of the Great Commission (our mission with and for Jesus), which things encouraged you most and which things challenged you most?

4. How can unity between all disciples be best built and maintained, and what are the greatest challenges to our unity?

Chapter Four

NO BOWL OF CHERRIES

ACTS 5:1-6:7

Life in the kingdom of God is a great life, to be sure, but it is no bowl of cherries. Acts 5:1–6:7 makes this fact abundantly plain. Two disciples were disciplined by God to the point of physical death. The apostles were arrested, threatened and beaten. The unity of the church was threatened by the hurt feelings of one class of Jews who thought their widows were being treated unfairly. Welcome to the church! God's divine plan for the church is perfect; those within the church are imperfect; those outside the church are sometimes just plain mean. There are always problems to be addressed. Jesus' words in John 16:33 were never more appropriate: "I have told you these things, so that in me you may have peace. In this world you will have trouble. But take heart! I have overcome the world."

Sin in the Camp (Acts 5:1-16)

[1]Now a man named Ananias, together with his wife Sapphira, also sold a piece of property. [2]With his wife's full knowledge he kept back part of the money for himself, but brought the rest and put it at the apostles' feet.

[3]Then Peter said, "Ananias, how is it that Satan has so filled your heart that you have lied to the Holy Spirit and have kept for yourself some of the money you received for the land? [4]Didn't it belong to you before it was sold? And after it was sold, wasn't the money at your disposal? What made you think of doing such a thing? You have not lied to men but to God."

[5]When Ananias heard this, he fell down and died. And great fear seized all who heard what had happened.

Many people reading this account for the first time may be reminded of similar OT stories in which God dealt directly and severely with sin. Thousands and thousands of people were killed as they rebelled and refused to submit to him and his leaders. As difficult as it may be for modern minds to grasp the reasons for what seems barbaric, if not somehow wrong, to read a similar story in the New Testament strains our sensibilities.

In the second century AD, a man named Marcion depicted the OT God as being different from the one described in the New Testament. To him, the God of the Old Testament was very harsh and vengeful, but the good God of the New Testament (Jesus) came to save us from the wrath of the former one. Marcion was rightly treated as a heretic, but if we tend to struggle with the idea of God in the OT period ordering wars, capital punishment and the annihilation of entire populations, then such doctrine may sound feasible or even appealing. But we cannot succumb to any doctrine which depicts God as varying in nature at different times. Jesus is the same yesterday, today and forever (Hebrews 13:8).

The sobering truth that we must accept is that God hates sin. Sin is not merely a misdemeanor; it is a flagrant thumbing of our noses at the Creator of the universe; it is an insistence on doing things our way in spite of what he is begging us to do. It is serious! Having said that, we must breathe a huge sigh of relief that he has made a way for us to be forgiven and to be strengthened against future offenses. Sure, we all sin and will always sin, but we cannot take it lightly. God says repeatedly, "Be holy because I am holy."[1] Holiness must be our aim and our pursuit. We have hurt the heart of our Father enough already, and we must dedicate ourselves to pleasing him through our diligence.

Let's return to the account of Ananias and Sapphira. What exactly happened with them, and why was their sin treated so severely? Acts 4 closes with the account of Barnabas selling a field and giving the money to the apostles to be distributed to the disciples who had needs. No doubt, he received deserved praise for such a generous sacrifice and may have received his new name, "Son of Encouragement," as a direct result of what he did. Ananias and Sapphira decided to do something similar, evidently desiring the praise that accompanied such a gift. Beyond this, they secretly agreed to give only a part of the money[2] and yet left the impression that they gave the entire proceeds from the sale to the church.[3] To us it might seem like simple exaggeration. To God it was blatant lying. During the infancy of the church, God used this event to graphically demonstrate the seriousness of sin, because sin unchecked destroys God's work and stops evangelism.

Their sin may not be as far from us as we like to think. Have you ever misrepresented what you have done or given? Have you ever pledged to give a certain contribution amount, given less, but tried to leave the impression that you had given the pledged amount? It is my conviction that many of us are concerned far too much with what people see and think about us and far too little with what God sees and thinks. We are tempted to create an impression that we have done more good things than we have and fewer bad things than we have. That is why the word "accountability" may be a negative one to us—we are concerned about how we will stack up in the minds of those who hear about our performance. Do we want to really be like Jesus, or simply appear to be like him? Please don't miss the lesson here! It may save your soul.

The effect of this "miracle"—Ananias' and Sapphira's deaths—on those who heard of it was swift and dramatic: Great fear seized them all (Acts 5:11). Church discipline, in any form, is often viewed as an unwelcome relic of "witch hunting" days. But without it, we cannot be the church of the Bible. The idea of religion being private and personal may be a popular one, but it is totally wrong on at least two counts. One, we are commissioned to make our faith public in evangelism with as many as possible. Two, we are to deal with the sins we see in the lives of fellow disciples. We are indisputably our brothers' keepers. Unrepentant sin in the lives of Christians must be dealt with in increasing intensity, beginning with a private setting and becoming increasingly public if need be (Matthew 18:15–18). The church must be protected and the individual sobered enough to repent.

Will those whom we are trying to convert be offended by our views of church discipline? Yes and no. Those with good hearts will be sobered but attracted, and those not interested in what God thinks on the subject will be repulsed. Strong teaching, preaching and high expectations will never harm those with seeking hearts. We may feel a bit tentative and anxious about how they will perceive it all, but we will end up learning a good lesson: Truth attracts, no matter how strong it may appear! Acts 5:13–14 provides proof positive of that fact:

> No one else dared join them, even though they were highly regarded by the people. Nevertheless, more and more men and women believed in the Lord and were added to their number.

Never give in to the temptation to be embarrassed about the truths of the Bible nor about the God who gave them!

Apostles in Jail (Acts 5:17-42)

[17]Then the high priest and all his associates, who were members of the party of the Sadducees, were filled with jealousy. [18]They arrested the apostles and put them in the public jail. [19]But during the night an angel of the Lord opened the doors of the jail and brought them out. [20]"Go, stand in the temple courts," he said, "and tell the people the full message of this new life."

[21]At daybreak they entered the temple courts, as they had been told, and began to teach the people.

This text is one of several in Acts (see also Acts 13:45, 17:5) that makes the roots of persecution from religious people quite plain—jealousy! Those who are afraid of losing control will make it seem as if they are concerned about protecting God's interests, but it is all a subterfuge. They care only about protecting their own interests, and no amount of smooth, educated rhetoric will camouflage their true intentions from spiritually perceptive people.

Back in Acts 4, only Peter and John were jailed, and they only had to endure a warning (which they quickly discounted). Now the ante is raised, as all of the apostles are arrested and will ultimately be flogged. The glory of leadership and kingdom growth is about to be mixed with some inglorious treatment, although that did not become immediately apparent. The punishment was postponed because an angel intervened and released them, but it did not take the Jewish leaders long to reclaim their prisoners. One can only imagine the consternation that their miraculous release caused their captors. They must have been filled with some serious unanswered questions about where God was in all of these strange events. Gamaliel definitely backed away from taking the route of more severe punishment (Acts 5:33–39, and the large number of priests who became disciples might have been influenced by this situation (Acts 6:7).

One also wonders how Luke knew about what occurred in the

Sanhedrin[4] with Gamaliel and his associates. Evidently, Paul, a star student of Gamaliel, told him about these inner proceedings. It does not take a great imagination to surmise that Paul's stories of his former ties in Judaism made for some exciting fireside chats during his travels! Gamaliel's advice spared the apostles more grief at the moment, but as advice, it was fairly mediocre. Numerous are the religious movements who are of human origin and yet flourish for centuries. Of course at the Judgment Day they will be brought to ruin, but that is not what Gamaliel had in mind on this occasion. But he was right in saying, "If it is from God, you will not be able to stop these men; you will only find yourselves fighting against God" (Acts 5:39).

Acts 5 closes with one of the most encouraging responses to persecution in the entire book:

> 41The apostles left the Sanhedrin, rejoicing because they had been counted worthy of suffering disgrace for the Name. 42Day after day, in the temple courts and from house to house, they never stopped teaching and proclaiming the good news that Jesus is the Christ.

They were not taken aback by intense resistance because they understood the nature of the radical Cause in which they were engaged. They had watched what happened to the Master as he had faced the same, and they felt honored to carry their cross of persecution in his name. We can never long for a nice little church to make us feel good and in which we can be comfortable. We are called to neither of these selfish ends. We have joined a spiritual army, and it is a be-faithful-to-the-death campaign we have embraced. Anything less is not the Christianity of the Bible.

Humanness in the Church (Acts 6:1-7)

1In those days when the number of disciples was increasing, the Grecian Jews among them complained against the Hebraic Jews because their widows were being overlooked in the daily distribution of food. 2So the Twelve gathered all the disciples together and said, "It would not be right for us to neglect the ministry of the word of God in order to wait on tables. 3Brothers, choose seven men from among you who are known to be full of the Spirit and wisdom. We will turn this responsibility over to them 4and will give our attention to prayer and the ministry of the word."

People are people are people—in any century. Sometimes we allow ourselves to be unsettled when problems arise in the church. The church is a divine organization in its design, but it is human in its membership. The wonder of it all is that we handle misunderstandings, hurt feelings and conflicts among ourselves, in very different ways than the world does (including the religious world). Some groups try to solve the problems by employing strong-arm tactics, with no room for questioning the status quo. Most simply refuse to face the issues at all, resulting in divisions of huge proportions over the centuries. Protestantism was splintering before its leaders died, and four hundred years later, the divisions number in the hundreds. Catholicism boasts of unity, but "unity in diversity" is a kind way to describe its membership. "One in heart and mind" it is not.

In Acts 6, the problems were addressed quickly and spiritually by the leaders of the church. The apostles refused to let distractions, even pressing ones, stop them from advancing the mission of Christ. They handled the "tyranny of the urgent" decisively and enlisted the help of other spiritual leaders to administer the responsibility of feeding the widows. They were not "too good" to serve in this way; they simply had been commissioned to direct the attack on Satan's forces, and they refused to do otherwise. Administration is a good thing, and all church leaders are going to have to do some of it. But in a complicated, red tape society like ours, it can stifle us unbelievably in carrying out the mission.

One of the greatest needs we have is getting more and more disciples involved in important but peripheral duties in the church, not in order to keep them from their personal mission of seeking and saving the lost, but to spread these duties widely enough to keep none of us from being distracted. If we do not meet this challenge, a clergy/laity organization is bound to ensue. At least two of those chosen in our present text were later seen as well-known evangelists. These seven chosen servants were not distracted from their mission of evangelism, but they were able to remove some scheduling burdens from the apostles, thereby allowing them to further "prepare God's people for works of service, so that the body of Christ may be built up" as it "grows and builds itself up in love, as each part does its work" (Ephesians 4:12, 16).

When we allow relationship problems in the church to fester, growth will slow down and ultimately stop. Unity, as mentioned previously, is a key ingredient in the evangelism of the world. On the other hand, when we face and solve these kinds of problems God's way, he will bless us with remarkable growth. Immediately after the solution of the widow situation in Acts 6:1–6, we read these words in verse 7:

> So the word of God spread. The number of disciples in Jerusalem increased rapidly, and a large number of priests became obedient to the faith.

If our church or church group is not growing, we should examine first our unity. Peaceful coexistence is the world's best shot at unity, but it cannot be ours.

Until the church is taken up to heaven and the kingdom of God reaches final fulfillment, there will be problems. Some will come from the inside and some from the outside. However, with unity of purpose and of heart, and with the help of God, they can all be overcome. One mind, one heart, one soul, one mission is the standard of Christ.

Questions for Further Study

1. Why do you think God resorted to an OT type of direct punishment in the case of Ananias and Sapphira and did not continue to do so in the rest of the New Testament (as far as we know)?

2. What does this situation have to teach us about the subject of church discipline generally?

3. Look up the following NT key passages on church discipline, and list the various reasons for administering church discipline: Matthew 18:15–17; Romans 16:17–19; 1 Corinthians 5:1–13; 2 Thessalonians 3:6, 14–15; Titus 3:9–11.

4. Was the advice of Gamaliel based on truth historically? Explain.

5. What do you learn from the situation regarding the widows (Acts 6) about leadership in the church?

Chapter Five

STEPHEN: A DEFINING MOMENT
ACTS 6:8-7:60

History is sprinkled with events that are seen in retrospect as defining moments. That is to say, the future of that group or culture was radically and permanently affected by that event. The emergence of Stephen into the limelight of God's movement was brief in its duration but monumental in its impact. It was, without doubt, a defining moment ordained by God to catapult the cause of Christ out of the narrow confines of Jerusalem's Judaism into the farthermost expanses of Rome's vast dominion. Stephen was the first Christian martyr, but he was far more. His death likely accomplished more for the spread of the gospel than any other—besides that of Jesus himself. Truly, he was a hero among heroes.

Stephen is Seized (Acts 6:8-15)

8 Now Stephen, a man full of God's grace and power, did great wonders and miraculous signs among the people. 9 Opposition arose, however, from members of the Synagogue of the Freedmen (as it was called)—Jews of Cyrene and Alexandria as well as the provinces of Cilicia and Asia. These men began to argue with Stephen, 10 but they could not stand up against his wisdom or the Spirit by whom he spoke.

11 Then they secretly persuaded some men to say, "We have heard Stephen speak words of blasphemy against Moses and against God."

12 So they stirred up the people and the elders and the teachers of the law. They seized Stephen and brought him before the Sanhedrin. 13 They produced false witnesses, who testified, "This fellow never stops speaking against this holy place and against the law. 14 For we have heard him say that this Jesus of Nazareth will destroy this place and change the customs Moses handed down to us."

15All who were sitting in the Sanhedrin looked intently at Stephen, and they saw that his face was like the face of an angel.

Stephen was one of the seven chosen to administer the food provisions for the Grecian widows. Their names indicate that all seven were themselves Grecian—a lesson in itself. Interestingly, after their appointment, which included having the apostles' hands laid on them, Stephen and Philip emerge as two who performed great miracles. Prior to this time, only the apostles were said to have worked miracles, but now those on whom their hands were placed were able to do the same. This fits the pattern that we see throughout the New Testament, in that only the apostles were used by God to confer to others the ability to exercise miraculous gifts. (See also Acts 8:14–19, 19:1–7 and Romans 1:11 in this connection.)[1]

The charges against Stephen did reasonably reflect the essence of what he must have taught: that the temple would be destroyed and that a new covenant would replace the old. Once the temple was destroyed, biblical Judaism was finished, for animal sacrifices were a major component of it. However, the charges were inaccurate in two key details. One, Jesus did not say that he was going to destroy the temple. He said that it would be destroyed by heathen armies (Matthew 24, Mark 13, Luke 21).[2] Stephen's enemies were trying to use the name of Jesus in the worst way possible at this point, and no greater animosity could have been promoted than to accuse Jesus of plotting a destructive act.

Two, they accused Stephen of speaking against the Law and changing the customs handed down by Moses. Yet Jeremiah, whom they accepted as a prophet of God, pointed forward to the replacement of the Mosaic covenant with a new one (Jeremiah 31:31–34), and Malachi, another accepted prophet, spoke of the destruction of Jerusalem (Malachi 4:1–6). Thus, Stephen was not speaking against the Law, but only relating what the prophets of God had taught on these specifics. Their contrived charges against him, nonetheless, stirred up their wicked hearts into an intense desire for vengeance.

The visage of Stephen at this point captured the attention of all who saw him, as his face appeared like that of an angel, whatever that may have been! Perhaps it was that look of conviction, confidence, love and peace whose image haunted Saul and which he (as Paul) related to Luke. Such a demeanor would not have been easy to deal with, even by those whose hate was stirred beyond measure, for fighting with someone who will not fight back can be quite unsettling. Yet their bitterness drove them to procure false witnesses and to enlist the aid of other leaders.

But now it was Stephen's turn to give his own witness to the issues at hand. This man who had only recently come into the forefront as an evangelist was destined to leave an indelible mark on sacred history. His speech is the longest recorded in Acts.[3] No preacher could imagine a better way to meet God than Stephen experienced—in his "swan song" message, pouring his heart out to a people whose need for it was exceeded only by their resistance to it, while Jesus stood watching from heaven, awaiting the arrival of the soul of his first Christian martyr. What a glorious ending to a life totally immersed in the Cause of Christ!

Stephen Speaks (Acts 7:1-53)

51 "You stiff-necked people, with uncircumcised hearts and ears! You are just like your fathers: You always resist the Holy Spirit! 52 Was there ever a prophet your fathers did not persecute? They even killed those who predicted the coming of the Righteous One. And now you have betrayed and murdered him— 53 you who have received the law that was put into effect through angels but have not obeyed it."

As he began to testify, Stephen followed the customary approach of Jewish speakers by recounting the salient facts of their glorious history. However, as subtle as it may have appeared at first, he was departing from this approach by including some of their inglorious history as well. An analysis of his speech shows that he was emphasizing three key points: (1) the presence of God was never confined to Jerusalem nor the temple; (2) the Jews had a long history of rejecting their leaders, which had now culminated in their rejection of the Messiah himself; and (3) in spite of all of the detours caused by man's sin, God was painstakingly moving history toward a promised goal. It would have been a priceless experience to have been able to watch the faces of the audience as different ones began to get the picture as his message unfolded. And certainly for the slow minded, Stephen brought it all to a conclusion that no one could miss in verses 51–53!

In several parts of his speech, Stephen showed that God's

presence was not tied to a specific location, which the Jews no doubt understood intellectually. But they still could not conceive of true worship outside the temple structure. He highlighted four stages of Israel's history—Abraham in Mesopotamia and Haran, Joseph in Egypt, Moses in Midian (with its "holy ground" mentioned in Acts 7:33), and David and Solomon. Though David and Solomon were in Jerusalem, David was forbidden by God to build the temple and Solomon, when he built and dedicated it, stated:

> "But will God really dwell on earth? The heavens, even the highest heaven, cannot contain you. How much less this temple I have built!" (1 Kings 8:27)

Stephen's point was well made, and by now some in his audience were likely starting to catch his drift!

Next, he demonstrated the unmistakable pattern of Jewish rejection of their key leaders. Joseph, Moses and Jesus shared in common the initial rejection of their brothers. Stephen was a good imitator of Jesus in stressing this line of reasoning, as seen in passages like Matthew 5:11–12, 23:29–37 and parallels. Jesus and Stephen both began with less strident teaching and progressed to the more blunt and pointed preaching as the resistance to it increased. Jesus' strongest words were in Matthew 23, but they had been preceded by similar teaching in the Parables of the Tenants and of the Wedding Banquet in Matthew 21:33–46 and 22:1–14.

Finally, Stephen drove home the point that God was indisputably in control of history, moving it to his desired conclusions. When the time was perfectly ripe (Galatians 4:4), with all of the elements of God's plan and world circumstances in place, he entered human history in the person of his Son. Jesus did not come because people were prepared in righteousness, but to move history in the direction required to accomplish righteousness. In simple terms, it was not because of the Jews that Jesus was sent, but in spite of them! With or without the cooperation of those who claim to be his people, God will get his work accomplished. He made sure that Jesus came the first time to lay the groundwork for the establishment of the kingdom, and he will make sure that Jesus comes a second time to deliver the kingdom up to him at the end of time (1 Corinthians 15:24). He is in control, and that point is unmistakably made in Stephen's speech.

Stephen Is Stoned (Acts 7:54-60)

[54]When they heard this, they were furious and gnashed their teeth at him. [55]But Stephen, full of the Holy Spirit, looked up to heaven and saw the glory of God, and Jesus standing at the right hand of God. [56]"Look," he said, "I see heaven open and the Son of Man standing at the right hand of God."

[57]At this they covered their ears and, yelling at the top of their voices, they all rushed at him, [58]dragged him out of the city and began to stone him. Meanwhile, the witnesses laid their clothes at the feet of a young man named Saul.

[59]While they were stoning him, Stephen prayed, "Lord Jesus, receive my spirit." [60]Then he fell on his knees and cried out, "Lord, do not hold this sin against them." When he had said this, he fell asleep.

Stephen's stoning must have made an indelible impression on Saul. The intensity of his later persecution exceeded that of his fellow Jews. Certainly, he never forgot that he was the chief of sinners because of his persecution, and perhaps his intensity traced back to this interaction with Stephen.[4] Without doubt, just as the death of Jesus made its impression on those who stood by (Luke 23:47), that of Stephen must have done the same. Dying with a prayer on your lips for those who are murdering you could not leave those who heard it unfazed.

It is most significant that Stephen saw Jesus "standing at the right hand of God" as he was being stoned. All other New Testament references to Jesus in heaven have him sitting at the right hand of God (Matthew 26:64, Mark 14:62, Hebrews 1:3, 8:1, 10:12 and 12:2). When the first martyr in this spiritual revolution died, Jesus was standing to welcome his disciple who remained "faithful, even to the point of death" (Revelation 2:10).

Acts 7, in conclusion, shows the remarkable similarity between Stephen and Jesus in their dying moments. Actually, in many ways Stephen was like his Savior. He condemned hypocrisy and hard-heartedness bluntly and pointedly, and as he died, he prayed for the Lord to receive his spirit and to forgive those who were killing him. Now Stephen had not been discipled by Jesus directly, but rather by those who had been. Jesus told the apostles that all who were baptized should be taught to imitate him (Matthew 28:18–20), which unquestionably had been done in Stephen's case. Properly done, discipling makes us like Jesus, no matter what spiritual generation we are in. The chain of discipling is not weakened by the passing of time, even the passing of centuries, for the teaching and the character of Jesus, which are to be transferred by the discipling process, are in the Book awaiting our correct use. Therefore, as we imitate him, the results are predictable: a Christlike spirit and an evangelized world. Discipling works, and without it the evangelization of the world will never be completed. Embrace it, as did Stephen, and your life will accomplish far more than would seem possible.

Stephen's sermon and death was a defining moment in at least two ways: (1) It served notice to the world that Jesus was not the only one willing to die for the gospel and became the inspiration for a whole generation of radical Christians; and (2) it laid the theological foundation for a ministry to the Gentiles and then propelled the church outward toward the realization of that ministry. After Stephen, the gospel in Acts is always moving out from Jerusalem on to the rest of Judea, on to Samaria and on to the rest of the world (8:1, 11:19–20). The church "after Stephen" was never the same.

Who are the "Stephens" in our day? I think of those bold disciples who have stood up and preached publicly in the marketplaces in large African cities. I think of those who have carried the gospel into the tough neighborhoods of America's inner cities. I think of those who are risking their safety and their freedom by making Jesus known in China and the Middle East. These and others are opening up new frontiers of evangelism and church building. Many more are needed with their spirit. Will you be a "Stephen"? Will the church that comes "after you" never be the same?

One man in the first or the twenty-first century can set in motion the call that awakens his generation.

> One man awake, awakens another.
> The second awakens his next-door brother.
> The three awake can rouse a town,
> By turning the whole place upside down.
> The many awake can make such a fuss,
> It finally awakens the rest of us.
> One man up with dawn in his eyes—multiplies!

Questions for Further Study

1. What were the accusations against Stephen, and did they have any truth in them? Explain your answer.

2. Explain the progression of Stephen's speech and why he followed the line of reasoning he used.

3. In what ways was Stephen like his Lord?

4. List the ways in which this whole incident was a defining moment for the movement in its early stages.

Chapter Six

Stage Two: The Mission Advances

Acts 8

For Christ's mission to succeed, it must be able to advance under all kinds of circumstances and move past all types of detours. The improbable must be made probable and the impossible, possible. God's first-century mission was carefully planned, but the details were known only by him. His missionaries were probably just like us in designing a way to carry out his plan, but he always delights in doing things his way—in spite of our best planning. Those first disciples were constantly asked to face the unexpected and to continue walking by faith into unknown territory. As we attempt to accomplish what they accomplished—world evangelism—we are blessed to be able to learn from them and follow in their steps where appropriate. But God will never change his approach of keeping most of the plan's specifics secret, for the advance of the cause will forever come as we follow the path of faith.

The Advance Through Persecution (Acts 8:1-4)

[1]On that day a great persecution broke out against the church
at Jerusalem, and all except the apostles were scattered throughout
Judea and Samaria. [2]Godly men buried Stephen and mourned deeply
for him. [3]But Saul began to destroy the church. Going from house to
house, he dragged off men and women and put them in prison.
[4]Those who had been scattered preached the word wherever
they went.

While Stephen's death seemed to the eyes of men a terrible defeat for the church, it was in the eyes of God a necessary step in carrying out his plan for world missions. Soon after Stephen's spirit met God, the reason God allowed such an atrocity became plain. Persecution would catalyze the next stages of Jesus' plan for world evangelism: moving out from Jerusalem to Judea and Samaria and the ends of the earth (Acts 1:8).[1] Stage two, the advance into Judea and Samaria, was about to begin. But those who had just lost a hero had to do what humans always do: weep when pain comes. Up until this point, God had intervened and spared the apostles on more than one occasion. Now, however, he allowed Satan to have his day. Just why God intervenes on some occasions and does not on others will remain a mystery to us who can never see fully from heaven's perspective. We simply have to work though our grief and leave the rest to God.

Death is never easy to accept for us time-bound humans, and it is always accompanied by pain. We may not, in the words of Paul, "grieve like the rest of men, who have no hope" (1 Thessalonians 4:13), but grieve we do. Those who buried Stephen "mourned deeply." Yes, the Psalmist's words are true: "Precious in the sight of the LORD is the death of his saints" (Psalm 116:15). And, yes, it is "better by far" to "depart and be with Christ" (Philippians 1:23). But those who are left will feel the loss deeply, and thus must mourn.

No sooner is Stephen buried than Saul erupts with a volcanic hatred toward the disciples. Unlike his teacher Gamaliel, he believed that this new movement could not be tolerated under the guise of peaceful coexistence. Radicals like Stephen would not stop preaching even under threats of death. For Saul it became an all-out war. His entire life became dominated by one purpose: Stamp out the movement of this Messianic usurper. The violence forced many of the Christians to leave Jerusalem, but being disciples meant that nothing could deter them from their mission, hence they preached as they went. Saul, who may have felt elated by the initial effects of his vengeful activities, would soon realize that God was working through it all to spread the Word.

As we take the gospel to every country, every city and every village, we will hear stories of great victories, but we will also hear of setbacks. As the message is taken to countries where religious zealots will despise the message of Jesus and hate those who carry that message, there will surely be men and women who will follow in Stephen's footsteps. When that happens, we, too, will mourn our fallen heroes. However, we must never forget that God is in control and that he is still the God who turns defeats into victories. Jesus said it: "I will build my church, and the gates of Hades will not overcome it" (Matthew 16:18).

The Advance in Samaria (Acts 8:5-25)

5Philip went down to a city in Samaria and proclaimed the Christ there. 6When the crowds heard Philip and saw the miraculous signs he did, they all paid close attention to what he said. 7With shrieks, evil spirits came out of many, and many paralytics and cripples were healed. 8So there was great joy in that city.

9Now for some time a man named Simon had practiced sorcery in the city and amazed all the people of Samaria. He boasted that he was someone great, 10and all the people, both high and low, gave him their attention and exclaimed, "This man is the divine power known as the Great Power." 11They followed him because he had amazed them for a long time with his magic. 12But when they believed Philip as he preached the good news of the kingdom of God and the name of Jesus Christ, they were baptized, both men and women. 13Simon himself believed and was baptized.

Philip, one of the seven chosen in Acts 6, now emerges from the pack to shine as a new star of the movement. A problem in the church had prompted the appointment of Hellenistic leaders, and now a problem outside the church prompted their departure from Jerusalem. God's hand in all of this soon became obvious. The Hellenistic leaders, with their broader worldview, were not so reluctant to leave the narrow confines of traditional Jewish audiences in spreading the message. Philip began preaching in Samaria, an area whose inhabitants were despised by the Jews. The response was dramatic. Samaritans were baptized in the name of Jesus just as their Jewish brothers had been. Now Samaritans and Jews shared a common name in Christ.

Bad blood had existed for a long time between Jews and Samaritans, dating back to the Northern Kingdom's fall to Assyria in 721 BC, when exiles from many nations settled Samaria (Ezra 4:9–10). Josephus tells us that later the Samaritans were refused the opportunity to participate in the rebuilding of the temple in Jerusalem, at which time they built their rival temple on Mt. Gerizim. By the first century, Jews traveling between Judea and Galilee would cross to the east of the Jordan to avoid going through Samaritan territory. Even James and John wanted to call down fire on the Samaritans (Luke 9:52–55). Remember this as you read of John being chosen to go with Peter to welcome the Samaritans into the church. The "Son of Thunder" went to lay hands on them that they might share with the rest of the church needed spiritual gifts. Grace is indeed transforming! (And God indeed has a sense of humor!)

The degree of change in John should not be overlooked: from the harsh youth to the friend of Samaritans to the aged "Apostle of Love." There is a powerful lesson here. Once I was talking to a minister of another church who was a critic of the discipleship-partner concept. His main criticism was that the use of many young leaders will lead to mistakes of harshness. I spoke to him of Luke 9 where we have the example of young leaders wanting to burn down a city. Talk about a new brand of harshness! What did Jesus do with these two, James and John? He believed in them, discipled them and kept pointing them to righteousness, which ultimately changed them into highly successful leaders whose lives affected thousands for the good. The apostles were likely all fairly young. Most of those willing to go against the grain of accepted values are. The older Establishment is normally more concerned with keeping the status quo than turning worlds upside down (or right side up). All young leaders have lessons to learn, but they have to be given the opportunity and shown the patience necessary for them to develop.

The impact of Philip's preaching and miracle working was remarkable. Even Simon the magician, who had fooled everyone except himself and God, was baptized. However, his sinful nature was residing just beneath the surface, and it did not take long for it to reappear. When he tried to buy from Peter and John the ability to pass on miraculous powers, which was not for sale at any price, Peter strongly rebuked him. Note Peter's evaluation of his spiritual condition in Acts 8:23: "For I see that you are full of bitterness and captive to sin." The nature of the bitterness we are not told, but it likely was based on envy of those who had been uniquely blessed of God, namely the apostles. How do you view those who have been given more by God than you in role or ability?

Peter's direction to him was to repent and pray (v22). In Acts 2:38, to those who had not been baptized, Peter said to repent and be baptized, but to Simon he said, "repent and pray." A good lesson ensues from this comparison. Both baptism and prayer are connected with forgiveness, but one is for initial forgiveness, as we come into a relationship with God, and the other is for continuing forgiveness once we have made this initial step. It is wonderful and necessary to pray for forgiveness (1 John 1:9), but it will not suffice to get a lost person saved. Praying the "Sinner's Prayer," as some call this denominational doctrine, will at best move God to send a preacher to teach and baptize you (as in the case of Cornelius in Acts 10).

We are not told if the magician worked out his problem with God. On this point, dogmatism either way is unwarranted. But the process he was told to follow is simple and helps us to better understand continual forgiveness. Forgiveness is a gracious act of God which we in no way deserve. Our performance is not what saves us—it is Christ's performance. But we by faith must accept it, and then trust it. Repentance and baptism for the non-Christian, or repentance and prayer for the Christian, are simply conditions of accepting God's mercy. We must trust his grace, not our conditions of acceptance. In view of that principle, is it not strange that many feel much more saved when they are baptized for forgiveness than when they pray for forgiveness as a Christian? Something is amiss in our understanding of grace, and an in-depth study of Romans is perhaps the best antidote for this malady![2]

This section of our text closes with the return of Peter and John to Jerusalem, preaching to Samaritans as they went (8:25). They were not the ones used by God to preach first to Samaria, but they were disciples of Jesus, always willing to learn and willing to change. The breadth of the gospel's intended target was preached by Peter through inspiration in Acts 2:39, but he came to understand his own words only in stages. God is patient with our sluggish hearts and minds, leading us step by step into seeing fuller pictures of his will. Soon, Peter would be called to another stage in God's plan—one much harder to accept than the entrance of the Samaritans. To make that step, he would need a miraculous vision directly from God.

The Advance in a Desert (Acts 8:26-40)

[26]Now an angel of the Lord said to Philip, "Go south to the road—
the desert road—that goes down from Jerusalem to Gaza." [27]So he
started out, and on his way he met an Ethiopian eunuch, an important
official in charge of all the treasury of Candace, queen of the Ethio-
pians. This man had gone to Jerusalem to worship, [28]and on his way
home was sitting in his chariot reading the book of Isaiah the prophet.
[29]The Spirit told Philip, "Go to that chariot and stay near it."

[30]Then Philip ran up to the chariot and heard the man reading
Isaiah the prophet. "Do you understand what you are reading?" Philip
asked.

[31]"How can I," he said, "unless someone explains it to me?" So he
invited Philip to come up and sit with him.

"God moves in a mysterious way, his wonders to perform." That stanza from a well-known hymn powerfully expresses the lesson Philip was about to learn. He was preaching to hundreds of people, maybe thousands, and now God was sending him out to a wilderness place that was virtually devoid of humans. While early church leaders were led by God to grasp the wisdom of making key cities a base of mission operations, Philip was going to see that God still delights in working powerfully in seemingly insignificant places. The lesson: Never put God in a box. Stay open to his leading. If we only allow him to lead in ways that we understand, we will never be led very far. From the multitudes to the desert—that was the direction given to this evangelist in Samaria. In the city or in the desert, under bright lights or in the shadows, with loud fanfare or with whispers, God moves—often mysteriously.

The conversion of the eunuch in the desert teaches many lessons about evangelism.

1. From God's vantage point we see his interest in the salvation of every individual. If any person really wants to know God, he will be found by him. In Matthew 13:44–46, two kinds of seekers are described in two brief parables. One was actively looking for the pearl of great price, and he found it. In this case I believe that God will make sure someone gets to him with the message, as he did with the eunuch and with Cornelius. The other parable describes

a person who was not looking but stumbled onto the treasure hidden in the field. In this case, such a person is going to have to see it first before his interest is aroused. Most who end up in the kingdom are in the second category.

What is the lesson for us? Simply this: The seeker will be found, period, but the "stumbler" will not be found unless we are diligent in doing our best to carry out the mission. Hence, Jesus said in Luke 14:23 to "go out into the highways and along the hedges, and *compel* them to come in, that my house may be filled" (New American Standard Bible, emphasis added). Never be guilty of assuming that if you miss an opportunity to influence someone for Christ, he will still find the kingdom. The majority of lost people are not seeking, and we therefore must be! Why else would Paul admonish us to be "making the most of every opportunity"? (Ephesians 5:16). God wants every person to be taught, and the story of the eunuch must convince us of that.

2. The disciple must be interested in the salvation of every person of every type. In the Mosaic system, eunuchs were forbidden to worship in the temple (Deuteronomy 23:1), but Isaiah 56:3–5 foretold an end to that prohibition. A worldly minded preacher would have been perturbed about having to leave the masses to teach one person, but in this setting, he would have been more perturbed to preach to a eunuch. Philip, however, was neither worldly minded nor prejudiced. Are you? Which types of people do you not enjoy reaching out to or teaching? What are your prejudices? I once heard a speaker affirm that, although he had once been prejudiced, he was now one hundred percent prejudice-free! I am grateful for his growth, but neither he nor anyone else is totally devoid of prejudice; nevertheless we must strive to be with all of our hearts if we are to be imitators of Christ and evangelize everyone for whom he died.

   Prejudice works in ways we do not even understand. We can be evangelistically prejudiced against very talented, very successful people. Philip was sent by God to convert an opinion leader, the treasurer of an entire nation. This is the first of many such instances in the book of Acts, and the accounts are included for a highly significant reason: Opinion leaders are usually more difficult to convert (obviously not always), but without such conversions, the mission will ultimately fail. These people have a following with whom they have great influence, and they can soon be fruitful—abundantly fruitful. Just as important, they can rise up quickly to become leaders. If you want to build a ministry that is sure to fail, convert only non-opinion leaders. I have seen denominational churches do it time and time again. It is not the plan of God, as may be seen in this and numerous accounts. According to tradition, this eunuch went back to his home country and built quite a church.

3. Bringing people into the kingdom is hard work, and at times "dirty" work. We should not be surprised when God calls us to run along some "dusty roads." We sometimes long to have Philip's experience, meaning that we want to find someone with an open Bible and an open heart who will quickly come to Christ. Keep in mind that quickly in this passage did not equate with easily. Look at a map and see where Gaza is located. From Samaria, it was a long way just to Jerusalem, and then Gaza was far south of that. Do you really want Philip's experience? Are you willing to pay that price? Most of us are not nearly as fruitful as we could be because of one character quality, which needs to be eradicated: laziness!

4. From the eunuch's vantage point, becoming a disciple required a large dose of humility. Yes, he was religiously minded and he knew the Bible. Many like this never become true disciples. His humility was the key that turned the lock in the door of salvation. He was a "big shot" politician but willing to listen to a dusty, sweaty "nobody" (as far as he initially knew). He was willing to admit that, although religious, he had a lot to learn and was anxious to be taught by anyone who was willing to teach. Then when he was taught, he wanted to humble himself before God and the preacher and get all wet in some presumably muddy water. There is no protest from him. He does not argue: "Do I really have to be baptized to be saved?" It was just, "Look, here is water. Why shouldn't I be baptized?" (Acts 8:36).

5. Baptism into Christ is always proclaimed in biblical evangelism.

When Philip told the eunuch the good news about Jesus (Acts 8:35), that gospel message included the faith response of baptism. This is the only way this man could have possibly known the right question to ask. Philip preached exactly the same message about salvation that Peter had preached in Acts 2, as did all Spirit-inspired preachers. And by being open to God's leading, he found an amazingly open man characterized by the godly quality of humility. When we have a heart like Philip's, we will find those with open hearts like the eunuch had. The heart of the issue is the heart, and the issue of the heart is the issue!

After this baptism, both men went on their way rejoicing, one to Ethiopia and one to Caesarea. The Greeks viewed those living in Ethiopia as being on the edge of the world, which means that Jesus' words were being carried to the ends of the earth. Philip made his way along the coast preaching in all the towns and no doubt sharing the story of this exciting conversion. Some twenty years later, we find him still in Caesarea, now blessed with four single daughters who were also known for preaching the Word (Acts 21:8). The Cause of Christ advanced mightily in the space of one short chapter, for God's truth was marching on!

Questions for Further Study

1. What are the main points and lessons found in Acts 8:1–4?

2. What are the main lessons that stand out to you in the conversion of the Samaritans?

3. What are the five main lessons learned from the account of the Eunuch's conversion?

PAUL: WHAT A BLIND MAN SAW

ACTS 9:1-31

The conversion of Saul is one of history's most remarkable stories. It is difficult for us to conceive just who this man Saul was in Judaism and the immense improbability of his conversion to Christ. His baptism ranks among the greatest miracles in the Bible. God's master plan begins with his Son being born in a stable. It continues as God picks a fierce hater of Christians to carry the message to the populous Gentile world.

With his own words, Paul opens the curtain for us to see "Saul" before he became Paul.

> If anyone else thinks he has reasons to put confidence in the flesh, I have more: circumcised on the eighth day, of the people of Israel, of the tribe of Benjamin, a Hebrew of Hebrews; in regard to the law, a Pharisee; as for zeal, persecuting the church; as for legalistic righteousness, faultless. (Philippians 3:4–6)

> I was advancing in Judaism beyond many Jews of my own age and was extremely zealous for the traditions of my fathers. (Galatians 1:14)

> "I am a Jew, born in Tarsus of Cilicia, but brought up in this city. Under Gamaliel I was thoroughly trained in the law of our fathers and was just as zealous for God as any of you are today." (Acts 22:3)

In rabbinic Judaism of the first century, two famous past rabbis had developed schools of thought which had held sway for many years, namely Shammai and Hillel. Gamaliel, the most influential rabbi of the first century, was the head of the Hillel party at this time.[1] Saul was likely his star disciple, being trained by Gamaliel to take his place as the leading scholar in conservative Judaism. Before Saul's conversion, if a poll had been taken among Jewish leaders to determine the last person likely to ever become a Christian, Saul's name would have headed the list. By his own later admission, he was a "blasphemer and a persecutor and a violent man" (1 Timothy 1:13). Even the apostles were afraid and suspicious of him after his conversion, fearing that he was using the old Trojan horse ploy to infiltrate their ranks (Acts 9:26).

When Jesus appeared to him on the road to Damascus, he was struck blind, but in his blindness he "saw" some things that changed him and the course of human history forever. What opened the eyes of his heart? First and foremost, a resurrected Christ.

A Resurrected Christ (Acts 9:1-9)

1Meanwhile, Saul was still breathing out murderous threats against the Lord's disciples. He went to the high priest 2and asked him for letters to the synagogues in Damascus, so that if he found any there who belonged to the Way, whether men or women, he might take them as prisoners to Jerusalem. 3As he neared Damascus on his journey, suddenly a light from heaven flashed around him. 4He fell to the ground and heard a voice say to him, "Saul, Saul, why do you persecute me?"

5"Who are you, Lord?" Saul asked.

"I am Jesus, whom you are persecuting," he replied. 6"Now get up and go into the city, and you will be told what you must do."

With Saul on his way to a foreign city for the express purpose of opposing followers of Jesus, one can only imagine the shock that he experienced in seeing and hearing Jesus. Everything in his training and experience convinced him that Jesus was a pseudo-Messiah, and yet now Jesus had invaded his world in an overwhelming manner. "Who are you, Lord?" Saul asked. The words "I am Jesus" must have landed on him like tons of rock. Those were the last words he expected to hear. The three-day fast that ensued was probably needed just for him to overcome the shock to his system. Why would God allow

Paul's persecution of the church to continue as long as it did, and why would he supernaturally intervene to convert him, when the normal mode of preaching the Word had not done it? Why indeed? The only answer we can come up with is to hold on to faith and trust God, for he is the only one who knows the answers—and he's not telling! Of course he ultimately did it to bless the world through Paul's ministry. We must trust and leave it at that.

Paul's conversion is described in three different accounts in Acts: chapters 9, 22, and 26, of which the latter two are in his own speeches.[2] A comparison of them raises further questions and provides additional insights.[3] Acts 22 gives the fullest description of his baptism, and it also lists the most questions that were asked—one by Christ, two by Paul and one by Ananias. A consideration of these questions helps us better understand the conversion process.

The first question was asked by Jesus himself: "Why do you persecute me?" Although Paul was directly persecuting the church, all who do not accept Christ are enemies of his through their sins. He takes sin personally, as may be seen in a number of passages like Matthew 25:41–45. Whatever we do wrongly (or fail to do rightly) to others, it is done to Christ. In Matthew 12:30 he stated, "He who is not with me is against me, and he who does not gather with me scatters." No one will ever come to Christ until and unless he is convicted seriously of his sins against Christ. Saul was unquestionably convicted and offered absolutely no rationalization about what he had done.

The second question, asked by Saul, was "Who are you, Lord?" The word translated "Lord" is the normal word for "Sir," but I think Paul had more in mind than that. This was a divine voice from the sky, not a whisper from behind a rock. But the question is a necessary one for all of us. Who is Jesus? A man? Yes. God? Yes, Immanuel ("God with us"). All God and all man at the same time. Is that confusing? Sure, but it is biblically true. (Wouldn't you be concerned if we humans could totally understand the nature of God?) Study these passages in the gospel of John (in the order listed) about what it means to be the "Son of God," and you will be convinced of his deity: John 20:30–31; 1:1–3, 14, 18; 5:18; 8:56–59; 10:27–33; 14:6–9; 20:24–31. (When the Jews started picking up stones to kill him, they did so because they understood that he was claiming to be God in the flesh!)

Saul was a trained rabbi who had cut his teeth while reciting the Shema: "Hear, O Israel: The LORD our God, the LORD is one"

(Deuteronomy 6:4). No one believed in the one God more than he, and yet no one described the deity of Christ and the Trinity better than he.[4] Surely much of that conviction found its anchor in that Damascus road experience. Was it hard for Paul to believe that Jesus was God in the flesh? Certainly, but in the face of compelling evidence, he came to have that faith.

Question three, asked by Saul, was "What shall I do, Lord?" Another appropriate question for those in any generation. Modern theologians often seem ill at ease or even embarrassed about questions regarding doing something to be saved. Influenced more by Martin Luther and John Calvin than Jesus Christ, they want to focus on "What shall I believe?" Luke was not reluctant to use the word "do" in describing man's response to God. (See Luke 3:10, 12, 14; 10:25; 18:18; Acts 2:37; 10:35; 16:30.)

Jesus was not hesitant about insisting on obedience, as Luke 6:46 shows: "Why do you call me, 'Lord, Lord,' and do not do what I say?" Of course, we are not to trust in the obedience but in the One who commands it, a point also made clear by Jesus in Luke's gospel:

> "So you also, when you have done everything you were told to do, should say, 'We are unworthy servants; we have only done our duty.'" (Luke 17:10)

In Paul's case, Jesus told him to ***"get up and go into the city, and you will be told what you must do"*** (Acts 9:6, emphasis added). What he would hear would include being baptized to have his sins washed away, as he called on the name of Jesus (Acts 22:16). Only one plan of salvation exists. It is totally centered on Jesus, but it includes the one baptism of Ephesians 4:5.[5] Nothing is in the water itself. Everything is in Jesus. But it is God's plan for us to come to Jesus by getting in the water. Paul did that, and he went on to preach it.

Question four, asked by Ananias, was, "And now what are you waiting for?" (Acts 22:16). After Paul had fasted and prayed for three days he was ready to be baptized. Actually, this was the longest period of waiting for baptism that we see in the book of Acts. Those three thousand in the Pentecost audience (Acts 2) were baptized the same day; the eunuch in Acts 8 was baptized as soon as he was taught; the jailer in Acts 16 was baptized at the same hour of the night. They were blessed by not having to unlearn false brands of Christianity, as is most often the case today. But no matter what error has to be dismantled first, the urgency to get right with God must be present.

However, urgency must be balanced with the understanding of and decision to be a committed disciple (Luke 14:25–33). Otherwise, repentance is incomplete. Repentance is not only turning away from the bad things we have been doing; it is turning to the good things which we have not been doing. Success in the mission is not about "getting baptisms"—it is about "making disciples." One builds a flimsy foundation whose building will eventually collapse, while the other builds a spiritual army against which the gates of hell cannot prevail. We must build wisely, which is to say, biblically.

Everything about Paul becoming an apostle was abnormal. As already noted, it was most unusual that he became a Christian at all. As a result, of course, he did not meet the qualifications laid down in Acts 1 for the apostle who would take Judas' place. He was not with Jesus during his earthly ministry from his baptism to his ascension (Acts 1:21–22). He, almost certainly, was not in the throng on Pentecost when the Spirit was poured out, equipping the apostles to not only perform miracles, but to have the ability to lay hands on others in passing the miraculous gifts to them. Yet, by the grace of God he became an apostle—one "abnormally born" into that role (1 Corinthians 15:8). If it took some special help from Barnabas to convince the apostles and disciples in Jerusalem that Paul was in fact a Christian, it must have taken much more for them to warm up to the fact that he was also an apostle, soon to become one of the two most influential on earth (and in most minds, number one)!

A Call to Suffer for Christ (Acts 9:10-19)

[15]But the Lord said to Ananias, "Go! This man is my chosen instrument to carry my name before the Gentiles and their kings and before the people of Israel. [16]I will show him how much he must suffer for my name."

[17]Then Ananias went to the house and entered it. Placing his hands on Saul, he said, "Brother Saul, the Lord—Jesus, who appeared to you on the road as you were coming here—has sent me so that you may see again and be filled with the Holy Spirit." [18]Immediately, something like scales fell from Saul's eyes, and he could see again. He got up and was baptized, 19and after taking some food, he regained his strength.

From the outset, Jesus made it clear that Paul's mission would include a focus on the Gentiles. Considering how entrenched in Judaism Paul was, compared to the Galilean gang of apostles, this choice is intriguing. In Acts 26:16–18 we find a longer account of Jesus' initial words to Paul, and they included this Gentile mission. Like most speeches in Acts, which had "many other words" not recorded (Acts 2:40), the Acts account of Jesus' talk with Paul was abbreviated. Paul departed from that talk knowing that he had "been entrusted with the task of preaching the gospel to the Gentiles, just as Peter had been to the Jews" (Galatians 2:7).

This "blind man" also saw that his call would involve suffering for Christ. Likely his understanding of the theology behind this would have developed only with time. His assumption must have been that if he preached what had once stirred him to brutal persecution, then others would respond in kind to him. By the time he was writing his letters to the churches, he had come to understand much more fully the power found in persecution and to appreciate the value of redemptive suffering. Paul would later write 2 Corinthians 4:7–12, one of the most important passages in helping us understand the nature of such suffering:

> But we have this treasure in jars of clay to show that this all-surpassing power is from God and not from us. We are hard pressed on every side, but not crushed; perplexed, but not in despair; persecuted, but not abandoned; struck down, but not destroyed. We always carry around in our body the death of Jesus, so that the life of Jesus may also be revealed in our body. For we who are alive are always being given over to death for Jesus' sake, so that his life may be revealed in our mortal body. So then, death is at work in us, but life is at work in you.

This passage points out how suffering affects us (in moving us to rely on God) and also how it affects others. The life of Jesus is most apparent in us at the precise times when his death is most apparent in us. His life, with its impact on hearts, shines brightest through us when we have Christlike attitudes while suffering. The essence of those attitudes is our willingness to suffer that others might be drawn to him. In Philippians 3:10–11 Paul gives us more insight into how this works:

> I want to know Christ and the power of his resurrection and the fellowship of sharing in his sufferings, becoming like him in his death, and so, somehow, to attain to the resurrection from the dead.

Knowing Christ and his resurrection power demands our sharing in his sufferings and becoming like him in his death. The deepest communion with Jesus can never be enjoyed until we have imitated him in redemptive sufferings. My favorite passage in this vein is Colossians 1:24:

> Now I rejoice in what was suffered for you, and I fill up in my flesh what is still lacking in regard to Christ's afflictions, for the sake of his body, which is the church.

At first reading, it seems incredible that Paul would claim something was lacking in Christ's afflictions. Did not Jesus say on the cross, "It is finished"? Do not the Scriptures affirm repeatedly the all-sufficiency of his suffering on Calvary? Yes, to both questions. However, Paul's words are not at all ambiguous: Something was lacking! What was that "something"? It ties in with the principle of the church being the fullness of Christ, just as Christ in the flesh was the fullness of God (Colossians 2:9–10). Just as no one could fully understand God until they saw him in human form, neither can they understand Christ fully until he is seen in our flesh as the church. The world must see us loving and serving as did Jesus during his earthly sojourn, but more is needed. If it took a cross to draw the world to Jesus originally, it will still take a cross to draw them, and we are the ones who must bear that cross.

Do you grasp the magnitude of what it means to deny self, take up the cross daily and follow Jesus? The implications are staggering! We have the obligation as disciples to imitate the extraordinary life of Jesus and to take his message all over the world. But we also have the obligation to take his death all over the world in our bodies—we must demonstrate his cross to the world by being lifted up in our suffering, and when death to self becomes a reality in our lives, then and only then can the life of Jesus be demonstrated in our mortal bodies. Suffering by Paul was redemptive in his life, in that it drew others to Christ, and it must do the same in ours.

Deep Conviction (Acts 9:20-31)

[20]At once he began to preach in the synagogues that Jesus is the
Son of God. [21]All those who heard him were astonished and asked,
"Isn't he the man who raised havoc in Jerusalem among those who
call on this name? And hasn't he come here to take them as prisoners
to the chief priests?" [22]Yet Saul grew more and more powerful and
baffled the Jews living in Damascus by proving that Jesus is the Christ.
[23]After many days had gone by, the Jews conspired to kill him,
[24]but Saul learned of their plan. Day and night they kept close watch
on the city gates in order to kill him. [25]But his followers took him by
night and lowered him in a basket through an opening in the wall.
[26]When he came to Jerusalem, he tried to join the disciples, but
they were all afraid of him, not believing that he really was a disciple.
[27]But Barnabas took him and brought him to the apostles. He told
them how Saul on his journey had seen the Lord and that the Lord had
spoken to him, and how in Damascus he had preached fearlessly in
the name of Jesus. [28]So Saul stayed with them and moved about freely
in Jerusalem, speaking boldly in the name of the Lord. [29]He talked and
debated with the Grecian Jews, but they tried to kill him. [30]When the
brothers learned of this, they took him down to Caesarea and sent
him off to Tarsus

Paul quickly became a man of deep conviction about Jesus. He was warned about the dangers inherent in his mission, and his experience soon verified those warnings. Just days after his baptism, the opposition became so fierce and the danger so great that he had to escape in a basket through an opening in the wall of Damascus! His Jewish brothers were in no mood to listen to this turncoat. Though he had to leave to preserve his life, we soon learn that his boldness was undiminished. He was fully convinced of the reality of his experience with Christ.

We do not know what all he felt upon returning to Jerusalem. Did he expect to be welcomed as a new convert and brother in Christ, or was he expecting the chilly reception he got from the fearful disciples who knew of his history? Whatever he was thinking, he survived—thanks to Barnabas—and soon was found in the city out sharing his faith with more people who then wanted to kill him. Once again, he had to leave in order to live. This passage teaches us several lessons:

1. We will not survive without a personal encounter with Christ that produces in us deep conviction. The nature of that encounter may be quite different than what Paul experienced, but its effect must be the same.
2. We must be ready for attacks from the world and even questions from our brothers and sisters. "In fact, everyone who wants to live a godly life in Christ Jesus will be persecuted" (2 Timothy 3:12).
3. We need to both be like Barnabas and appreciate the "Barnabases" God puts in our lives. Encouragement is a wonderful commodity, without which sustained spiritual growth cannot occur.
4. We must make the decision to be a disciple and then follow through immediately by doing what disciples of Jesus are to do, to the best of our ability at that time. It all boils down to a matter of conviction. Paul began preaching immediately because he had deep convictions, convictions he was willing to die for, not because he was well-trained and experienced in public speaking. Abilities void of heart are useless at best and dangerous at worst. Paul could never be accused of being apathetic about the lostness of people or the love of Christ. He grew more and more powerful, as always happens when we use our gifts and opportunities.

A final word about deep convictions is in order, because they are difficult to develop and even more difficult to maintain over the long haul. Satan works tirelessly to deceive us about the level of our conviction. Biblically, it is quite possible to think that you are alive spiritually while you are dead (Revelation 3:1–2), and rich spiritually while you are lukewarm (Revelation 3:15–17). Those who allow their convictions to mellow and who become comfortable may well end up in the state of numbness often called apathy. It has been observed that the opposite of love is not hate but rather, apathy. Anyone who has done much marriage counseling will likely agree. Mates who can still muster up a bit of hate have some deeper feelings underneath that can, with help and desire, be rekindled. Once one partner reaches the point of apathy, it is much more challenging to pull the marriage out of the fire.

Disciples desperately need to understand the horrific damage that apathy to the mission produces. One of the most chilling passages in the Bible is this one: "One who is slack in his work is brother to one who destroys" (Proverbs 18:9). Whether a cause is destroyed after it has been built, or never been built in the first place, the end result is exactly the same. When we are not building as God has commanded, we have thrown our lot in with the very enemies of the cross who are set on destroying God's movement!

Let's open our eyes and see what this "blind man" saw centuries ago. Let's imitate him who imitated his Master so very well. When we see what he saw, we will do what he did—with the same intensity and results. We cannot afford to remain blind to any part of the battle that rages, for it all weighs heavily on the scales of eternity. Arise and advance!

Questions for Further Study

1. Read Appendix 3 and list any lessons you discover from comparing the three conversion accounts of Paul.

2. What lessons do you learn from the questions found in the Acts 9 conversion account?

3. When Paul was converted, he was called to a life of suffering. How does this differ from the current concepts of what being a Christian in America is all about?

4. Being asked by a young minister (who was sensitive about his youth) what it was that people really respected about a leader, I answered "Convictions." Why do you think I answered with this word?

Chapter Eight

Stage Three: The Gentiles

Acts 9:32-11:18

In Acts 1-7 the church was contained in Jerusalem. In chapter 8, it spread throughout Judea and into Samaria. Now in this section the stage is being set for the message to go to the ends of the earth, but it must begin with the fisherman who has been given the "keys of the kingdom." Hence, we find him traveling about the country to minister to those who had been scattered from Jerusalem or converted by those who had. If he took the trip by a revelation from God, the text does not state it. God was most likely working through the choices of man to get his will accomplished. That approach seems always the favorite one of God because it contains the greater miracle—the Almighty using the un-mighty; the Infallible using the fallible. But it all began when Peter took time for the "little" people.

Time for the "Little" People (Acts 9:32-43)

[32]As Peter traveled about the country, he went to visit the saints in Lydda. [33]There he found a man named Aeneas, a paralytic who had been bedridden for eight years. [34]"Aeneas," Peter said to him, "Jesus Christ heals you. Get up and take care of your mat." Immediately Aeneas got up. [35]All those who lived in Lydda and Sharon saw him and turned to the Lord.

[36]In Joppa there was a disciple named Tabitha (which, when translated, is Dorcas), who was always doing good and helping the poor. [37]About that time she became sick and died, and her body was washed and placed in an upstairs room. [38]Lydda was near Joppa; so when the disciples heard that Peter was in Lydda, they sent two men to him and urged him, "Please come at once!"

Lydda was about twenty-five miles northwest of Jerusalem, and Joppa was another ten miles or so northwest of that, on the coast. While in Lydda, Peter healed a paralytic, which led to the conversion of many who saw him healed.

Following that, he was summoned to Joppa to do a greater miracle in raising Dorcas from the dead. The account is reminiscent of Jesus' miracle in Mark 5:22–43 in which he said to the dead twelve-year-old, *"Talitha koum,"* meaning "Little girl, I say to you, get up!" (Mark 5:41). Jesus had his *"talitha"* and Peter his Tabitha, both of whom were raised from the dead in the presence of weeping family members and/or friends. This miracle by Peter had a similar result to his earlier one in Lydda, in that many were brought to faith through it.

Who Is Important?

Dorcas was an older woman who was known for her work as a seamstress, for doing good and helping the poor. Why is her story in the Bible? She was not a high-profile leader and certainly not a big financial contributor. From man's perspective, she was not all that impressive, but she appeared to have impressed God and her circle of widow friends. Jesus often talked of widows and held a number of them up as great spiritual examples. His brother James had this to say:

> Religion that God our Father accepts as pure and faultless is this: to look after orphans and widows in their distress and to keep oneself from being polluted by the world. (James 1:27)

How do you think widows feel in our fellowship: appreciated and useful, or fairly unimportant? Why don't you ask them? The answer may prove to be revealing.

Obviously, the importance of the mission to evangelize is paramount. But we still may be missing something, namely an appreciation of the church as a "body." That is about the most commonly used word describing the church in the New Testament. We are not just a body of people when we gather to worship together; we are the body of Christ responsible for revealing him to the world. Paul said that corporately we are the fullness of Christ, and when people behold the church functioning as it should, they see Christ in action—but no one of us is his fullness.

Every member is important, even though we do not all have the same gifts (maybe especially because we do not all have the same gifts). Study through Romans 12 and 1 Corinthians 12. 1 Corinthians 12:22 states that "those parts of the body that seem to be weaker are indispensable." Is that really how we feel about weaker members or older members or sicker members? We have a lot to learn about the value of different kinds of people with different types of gifts, and how they all contribute to the effectiveness of our mission.

What Is Important?

Do we value the little things that people do for God and for others in his name, or do we only see the more obvious kinds of impact that are being made? It's a good question, isn't it? Sometimes it appears to me that some are afraid to commend people for the little things, as if that will lower the emphasis on evangelism. Everything that falls under the definition of "good" is important and, done properly, has some place in carrying out our overriding mission of reaching the world with the message of Christ. He who gave the Great Commission—and died for it—had this to say about the matter: "I tell you the truth, anyone who gives you a cup of water in my name because you belong to Christ will certainly not lose his reward" (Mark 9:41).

In the church we have many unsung heroes who serve in a multitude of different ways behind the scenes. We have too many of them—not because they should not serve in these ways, but because they should not remain unnoticed and unsung. God can open hearts in quite ordinary ways. Once my wife called a woman to try to study the Bible with her, but she happened to be ill that day and was not too interested in studying anyway. Theresa made a chicken pie (yes, from "scratch"!) and drove a long distance in a snowstorm to deliver it. The woman (who got right with God) attributed her heart change to that act of kindness. Oh sure, it is the word of God that brings people to faith, but the Word must be read in the lives of people just as surely as in the "Good Book."

Every disciple is special, and all of us are going to have to learn to make each other feel special. Those of us who are parents have hopefully figured out the absolute necessity of building up our children and helping them to view themselves as God views them. And we have learned that our less talented youngsters need it the most. Now we must learn the same lessons in dealing with God's kids—all of them—especially the weaker ones. Peter had been with Jesus too long not to have time for the "little people." And because he had this heart, God used these kindnesses to get Peter in just the right place at the right time to use those "kingdom keys" once more.

From God-Fearer to Disciple (Acts 10:1-48)

1At Caesarea there was a man named Cornelius, a centurion in what was known as the Italian Regiment. 2He and all his family were devout and God-fearing; he gave generously to those in need and prayed to God regularly. 3One day at about three in the afternoon he had a vision. He distinctly saw an angel of God, who came to him and said, "Cornelius!"

4Cornelius stared at him in fear. "What is it, Lord?" he asked. The angel answered, "Your prayers and gifts to the poor have come up as a memorial offering before God. 5Now send men to Joppa to bring back a man named Simon who is called Peter. 6He is staying with Simon the tanner, whose house is by the sea."

You cannot read this account without being drawn to this centurion[1] named Cornelius. He led his family spiritually, and evidently, the soldiers under his charge as well. He was generous with his money, and prayer was a part of his daily life. His prayers and gifts were a memorial which moved God to send a preacher to him. He was one of the "God-fearers,"[2] a rather large group of Gentiles who were attracted to the morals and spirituality of Judaism but who never became full-fledged proselytes. To become proselytes, among other things, the men had to be circumcised, which would suggest that more women than men made this decision! The presence of God-fearers all over the Roman Empire helps to explain how the church was able to be established quickly and strongly in city after city. This group, along with the Jews who were prepared by prophecy for accepting their Messiah, provided a leadership base of considerable proportions. Paul planted churches and then was able even to appoint elders in short order (Acts 14:21–23).

Cornelius was a very good man, but he was a lost man. In our present age of biblical ignorance, a man like him would be accepted in just about any church as a star member. But by the time he sent for Peter, he had no such illusions about his spiritual state before God (see Acts 11:13–14). Being good and doing good are important things, but they cannot save anyone. In comparison to Jesus, there is "no one righteous, not even one...there is no one who does good, not even one" (Romans 3:10, 12). We can be too intimidated by those religious people who seem to be good and do good. Yet, we have to see them as Peter saw Cornelius and his family—in need of biblical obedience. Cornelius and his family had to hear the Word, accept it and be baptized into Christ (Acts 10:47–48). Peter had not changed his doctrine since Acts 2. Everyone, Jew or Gentile, must follow the same steps into the kingdom.

This account is unusual in at least one respect: The Holy Spirit came on these unsaved people before they had been baptized so that they were able to speak in tongues as the apostles had done on Pentecost. In fact it happened as Peter began to speak (Acts 11:15). Regardless of how this event is explained, in the end it must be viewed as a most unusual occurrence with no other account like it in Acts. However, the text makes it clear that the miracle was not to convince Cornelius and his group. It was to convince the Jews, who had quite a hurdle to clear when thinking about Gentiles being brought into God's kingdom. (Note the wording of Acts 10:46 and Acts 11:17–18.) It happened so Peter would have no hesitation about baptizing Cornelius and his family, even though they had never become Jews.

Prior to the conversion of Cornelius, the Jewish Christians, including Peter, had not grasped that the gospel was for Gentiles. Since the Old Testament did foretell the inclusion of Gentiles in some sense, perhaps the Jews assumed that they would first become Jewish proselytes. They had either forgotten or totally misunderstood that God declared through Isaiah that the coming light would be for the Gentiles (Isaiah 42:6; 49:6; 49:22) and that Jesus had been run out of his home town for teaching that God loved the Gentiles (Luke 4:24–29). Prejudice runs deep, and they evidently assumed that going into all nations meant simply reaching the Diaspora, the scattered Jews all over the world. By inspiration Peter preached the truth in Acts 2:39, but it took the visions described in Acts 10 for him to understand it.[3] Paul was told that his mission included the Gentile field, but God did not send him out to carry out that mission (Acts 13) until after Peter was sent to Cornelius. Leaders must stay open to learning. Peter was still used by God, even though he was ignorant in some key areas for a long time. Isn't it encouraging to know that God can use us even when we have much to learn?

A Serious Prejudice Test (Acts 11:1-18)

[1]The apostles and the brothers throughout Judea heard that the Gentiles also had received the word of God. [2]So when Peter went up to Jerusalem, the circumcised believers criticized him [3]and said, "You went into the house of uncircumcised men and ate with them."

Peter began and explained everything to them precisely as it had happened.

The prejudice of the Jews, even Jewish Christians, now comes to the forefront. The circumcised believers back in Jerusalem who were not witnesses of the events in Caesarea were not simply in a questioning mode; they were in a critical mode. The nominal reader of the New Testament would have a difficult time assessing the seriousness of the inclusion of the Gentiles into the church and how it affected the church for decades. It took someone like Paul, with his trained rabbinic style of argumentation and presentation, to deal with such a broad and complex subject. Much of what he wrote in the New Testament was in reference to the Jew/Gentile controversy. It arose immediately upon the conversion of the first Gentiles, and it lasted for decades. When you have been trained for centuries to hate a group to the point of thinking of them as dogs, changing your attitudes and practices is not an overnight phenomenon.

The issues were not philosophical and doctrinal; they were practical and social. Peter was criticized for going into Gentile homes and eating with them. And even though the brothers ended up praising God over the salvation of Cornelius (Acts 11:18), the issue was far from over. It later became so heated in Antioch that Paul rebuked Peter in front of the church (Galatians 2:11–14). That didn't seem to surprise Paul as much as the fact that even Barnabas, his former discipler in Antioch's early days, fell prey to the same hypocrisy. Before it all was reasonably settled, it took a church conference in Jerusalem with the movement's key leaders (Acts 15). (We will look at this in Chapter 11.)

The pressing question for the Jews revolved around what the Gentile men would be required to do to receive full membership in the church. The more rigid ones thought (and taught) that they would have to do essentially the same thing to become Christians as they formerly would have had to do to become Jewish proselytes:

be circumcised in accordance with the Law of Moses (Acts 15:1). Interestingly, the Jewish disciples were not asking questions about their own Jewish practices. They still practiced much of Judaism as a matter of national custom. Paul took a vow (Acts 18:18) and was open to James' suggestion in Acts 21 that he go into the temple with four Jewish Christians who had taken a vow to assist them in their purification rites. Read Acts 21:20–25 carefully. It is quite clear that the Jewish disciples in Jerusalem were still keeping the Mosaic Law at this time. That may seem surprising to us, or even alarming, but it is clearly a fact.

However, Paul was careful not to make anything in the Law a matter of necessity for salvation. It could be practiced by Jews as a matter of expediency and custom, but never bound upon Gentiles as a matter of required righteousness. Thus, Paul would circumcise Timothy (Acts 16:1–3) because he was half Jewish and would be received more easily by the Jews that they were evangelizing. But he would under no circumstances allow Titus, a Gentile, to submit to circumcision (Galatians 2:3–5).

What we see in these years is a transitional period allowed by God for the Jewish disciples to gradually extricate themselves from their Jewish thinking. Hebrews 8:13 describes that period in these words: "By calling this covenant 'new,' he has made the first one obsolete; and what is obsolete and aging will soon disappear." The old covenant became obsolete at the cross, but it was not going to disappear until Jerusalem was destroyed in 70 AD, forever ending the sacrificial system. By then the church was no longer seen as a group under the umbrella of Judaism but as a separate religion. The persecution had reached the point that Jewish Christians had become outcasts from their race.

The years between Cornelius' conversion and the destruction of Jerusalem were filled with some tense times that would strain tolerance and reveal prejudice in many disciples on both sides of the fence. That the church survived those tests is a testimony to the power of the cross and the strength of their commitment to the mission. If we hang on to our relationship with Christ and stay in the battle, we can maintain the unity necessary for accomplishing the mission. Those who band together in a common cause against a common enemy are not prone to brandish their swords against each other. May our own hang-ups always remain subjugated to the larger issues, for this is all a part of denying ourselves and taking up our crosses. Bear in mind that our mission as world changers is carried out by all kinds of people for all kinds of people.

Questions for Further Study

1. What does the story of Dorcas teach us about a person's value before God?

2. What important lessons can we learn from the conversion of Cornelius and his family?

3. Why do you think that there were so many "God-fearers" in the first century?

4. What is meant by the Jews having a "transition" period between the cross and AD 70? Explain it well—it's very important to an understanding of the New Testament!

Chapter Nine

Prelude To Conquest

Acts 11:19-12:25

While God was using the persecution connected to Stephen to expand the movement into Samaria, he was also using it to send the Word to "the ends of the earth." Acts 11:19 picks up where Acts 8:4 left off.

No sooner was Samaria evangelized, than the first Gentiles were converted by God through Peter. And even while that was happening, men were moving toward Antioch, which was to become the stronghold of Gentile missions and the second "pillar church" of the young movement. God's plan may be known only by him, but he can work with many people, apparently moving in many directions yet having all of them moving in his direction. This section of Scripture makes plain the entire plan of Gentile missions, for when Paul arrived in Antioch the pieces were all in place.

Antioch: A Pillar Church (Acts11:19-30)

[19]Now those who had been scattered by the persecution in connection with Stephen traveled as far as Phoenicia, Cyprus and Antioch, telling the message only to Jews. [20]Some of them, however, men from Cyprus and Cyrene, went to Antioch and began to speak to Greeks also, telling them the good news about the Lord Jesus. [21]The Lord's hand was with them, and a great number of people believed and turned to the Lord.

[22]News of this reached the ears of the church at Jerusalem, and they sent Barnabas to Antioch. [23]When he arrived and saw the evidence of the grace of God, he was glad and encouraged them all to remain true to the Lord with all their hearts. [24]He was a good man, full of the Holy Spirit and faith, and a great number of people were brought to the Lord.

> [25]Then Barnabas went to Tarsus to look for Saul, 26and when he found him, he brought him to Antioch. So for a whole year Barnabas and Saul met with the church and taught great numbers of people. The disciples were called Christians first at Antioch.

Antioch Planted

Antioch was a free city, with a population third only to Rome and Alexandria in the Roman Empire. It was certainly one of the most cosmopolitan cities of its day, making it the most likely place to start a large church characterized by diversity. Since it is presumed that the scattering was comprised mostly of Hellenistic Jews, God was clearly using their broader worldview to open the kingdom gates to both Samaritans and now Greeks. For whatever reasons, the disciples from Cyprus and Cyrene were more daring in preaching to non-Jews, and they met with instant success.

Just as the Jerusalem church sent Peter and John to Samaria when they had accepted the gospel, now they sent Barnabas.[1] They picked the right man. Barnabas was a man who lived up to his name. He was a mighty encouragement to the church. Whether he was giving money sacrificially for the needy brothers (Acts 4:36–37) or seeing the best in the newly converted Saul of Tarsus (Acts 9:26–28) and now the Greeks, he shows us what a powerful quality encouragement really is and how it moves the church forward. Encouragement is listed in Romans 12:6–8 as a spiritual gift from the Holy Spirit (obviously non-miraculous), and while all do not have this gift, all have the responsibility (1 Thessalonians 5:11). Those with the special gift, such as Barnabas, serve as role models for the rest of us to imitate. No doubt many became much more effective encouragers by watching and imitating our brother Barnabas (Paul being the most stellar example of this process).

Barnabas was not only a great leader; he was a very humble leader. (Actually, no leader is great in God's eyes if he is not humble, although he may appear great in men's eyes before his pride brings him down.) His humility is seen especially in his willingness to share the limelight of leadership with another, in this case another whose impact would soon eclipse his own. He had already seen great numbers brought to the Lord by his ministry, but he wanted to go from the "more fruit" stage to the "much fruit" stage. His greatest desire was to advance the kingdom as rapidly as possible, and he sensed that Paul was the most powerful leader available to help with that lofty goal.

At this time Paul was back in his home area of Tarsus. By comparing the Galatians chronology and Paul's comments in Philippians 3:8, it seems likely that he had gone back home to preach his new faith and was disinherited in the process. All we know for sure is that when Barnabas found him, he was willing to come to Antioch to help. Many are the times when God "rescues" us from one failed dream with the exciting opportunity for another. Paul was about to enter the most fruitful ministry he had yet experienced and one that would determine his direction for years to come.

In Acts 11:26, we find the first mention of the term "Christian" for it was in Antioch that the term was first used to describe disciples. Almost everyone agrees that this designation for the followers of Christ was applied first by those outside the church. The next mention is clearly from the mouth of an unbeliever, King Agrippa, in Acts 26:28. The third and final use of the term in the New Testament is in 1 Peter 4:16, as Peter encourages his readers to view and endure persecution righteously: "However, if you suffer as a Christian, do not be ashamed, but praise God that you bear that name." This passage makes it clear that while the term originally was used by outsiders in a derogatory manner, disciples were to wear the name without embarrassment. In our age, the word "Christian" has come to mean many things to many people, but generally it is used in ways quite foreign to the Bible's definition of what it means to be a follower of Christ. Because of this, it is often more helpful to use the word "disciple" in clarifying what is actually involved in following Christ.

A Visit with Dual Purposes

At the end of chapter 11, a prophet named Agabus alerted the disciples in Antioch that a famine was in the offing, which led to their decision to send their brothers in Judea some financial assistance. The fact that Barnabas and Saul left their ministry to deliver the funds personally is interesting. It almost certainly suggests that, as top leaders, they wanted to show as much support as possible. It may also suggest that those back in Judea might have remained a little dubious about the Gentile mission, and Barnabas and Saul were anxious to personally alleviate those doubts.

The mention of Paul's trip to Jerusalem, when compared to his comments in Galatians, raises some questions. Galatians 1:13–2:14 speaks of two trips to Jerusalem that were separated by a number of years. According to Galatians 1:18, Paul did not go to Jerusalem until three years after his conversion, which means that Acts 9:26 occurred later than might have been assumed by reading the Acts passage alone. Galatians 2:1 then informs us that his next trip was fourteen years later. The question is which Acts trip is being described in Galatians 2:1: this text at the end of Acts 11 or the Jerusalem Conference trip of Acts 15? Good arguments have been presented for both, and scholars seem fairly evenly divided. The whole issue is not highly consequential.

Given the fact that God was about to send Barnabas and Paul on the first mission trip, their visit with the elders in Judea (assumedly Jerusalem, Acts 12:25) likely proved vital in preparing the church for what was about to take place. The entire church had been Jewish in the early years, and at this point, it was still mostly Jewish. Because of Paul's mission to the Gentiles, the church would become more and more Gentile in character, which would strain the tolerance levels of Jewish brothers for years to come. But God no doubt used many situations to prepare the older brothers for the inevitable changes that lay in the future, and this brief trip was one of them.

The Mission Reigns Supreme (Acts12:1-25)

1 It was about this time that King Herod arrested some who belonged to the church, intending to persecute them. 2 He had James, the brother of John, put to death with the sword. 3 When he saw that this pleased the Jews, he proceeded to seize Peter also. This happened during the Feast of Unleavened Bread. 4 After arresting him, he put him in prison, handing him over to be guarded by four squads of four soldiers each. Herod intended to bring him out for public trial after the Passover.

5 So Peter was kept in prison, but the church was earnestly praying to God for him....

21 On the appointed day Herod, wearing his royal robes, sat on his throne and delivered a public address to the people. 22 They shouted, "This is the voice of a god, not of a man." 23 Immediately, because Herod did not give praise to God, an angel of the Lord struck him down, and he was eaten by worms and died.

24 But the word of God continued to increase and spread.

A Glorious Death

We are left to guess why the story of Herod's[2] persecution and death is inserted at this point. It must have something to do with the preparation for the ensuing Gentile mission which occurs in the next chapter. At the end of their mission of mercy, Barnabas and Paul returned from Judea with John Mark, who was to become a part of the first missionary trip (and a focus of controversy before the second). Perhaps the Herod story is included to show that, while the focus was shifting to the Gentiles, God is still interested in, and working mightily in, the old Jewish mother church.

The martyring of the first apostle—James the brother of John—is described with much less fanfare than that of Stephen in Acts 7. However, we cannot doubt that the church was emotionally involved, as one of the three closest to Jesus gave glory to God in his death for the Cause. Herod gained glory from the Jews for his treacherous act, which motivated him to plan Peter's death next. However, God stepped in and delivered Peter in one of the more exciting deliverance accounts in the Bible. Why God intervened in the case of Peter and not of James is unknown to us. Why James was the first apostle to die and his brother John the last is also a mystery. No doubt many disciples and family members raised such questions, but they were left to walk by faith alone, as we all are during similar crisis points in our lives.

The story of Peter's miraculous release is an amazing one for several reasons. One, he was surrendered enough spiritually to be sleeping deeply, even while on death row. This is a powerful testimony to his faith and an example with which most of us have trouble identifying. Two, the brothers and sisters who were praying for him had a strange combination of faith and unbelief. They had the faith to pray as a group well into the night and yet could not quite accept that their prayers for his release had been answered. Three, the military personnel involved were both ruthless and highly professional; but God can make the ordinarily impossible quite possible. The soldiers who were responsible for guarding Peter were held responsible for his escape and executed as a result. (This account helps us understand another Roman jailer's intended actions later in Philippi—Acts 16:27). Four, it provides us with an insight into the common belief of that time that every person had their own angel who took on their appearance (Acts 12:15). We do know that saved persons have "guardian" angels of some sort (Hebrews 1:14), which is a comforting thought!

Pride and Destruction

Herod had his day in the sun (Acts 12:19–22), but God rules in the affairs of men and "brings princes to naught and reduces the rulers of this world to nothing" (Isaiah 40:23). God's laws in the spiritual realm are just as certain as those in the physical realm, although they are not as evident to those lacking spiritual perspective. However, on the day of his death Herod may have become as aware of the law of pride as he was of the law of gravity. The latter is more immediately demonstrable, but the former is no less certain. Indeed, "Pride goes before destruction, a haughty spirit before a fall" (Proverbs 16:18), for "God opposes the proud but gives grace to the humble" (1 Peter 5:5). Spiritual laws apply just as much to Christians as they do to non-Christians. We cannot expect some "law of compensation" to protect us from the consequences of sin in one area because of our righteousness in another. We may be highly involved in converting others, but if we neglect our own family in the process, they—and we—will suffer the terrible consequences. We may be highly effective in any number of ways, but if we are not really striving for righteousness in every area of our lives, we are in for some harsh surprises. A law of spiritual compensation simply does not exist. Whatever we sow, we will reap. The "harvest" may be a long time in coming, but come it will, for the law of sowing and reaping is in effect for one and all.

Herod's problem of pride is no stranger to any of us. For years I have openly admitted that pride and selfishness are at the root of just about all of my sins. Pride has caused me much heartache, and I am more fearful of it than of the plague. However, Satan absolutely loves this sin in our lives, and he works overtime trying to provide us with ways to rationalize it away. The oft-repeated statement, "Well, everyone has pride," does not excuse the problem; it only shows the magnitude of it and the effectiveness of Satan in helping us to make excuses for a sin that God absolutely hates![3]

The movement of God in Jerusalem could not be stopped by Herod or any other force. He became worm food while "the word of God continued to increase and spread" (Acts 12:24). As Barnabas, Saul and Mark set out for Antioch, they had little idea of the powerful events that lay just before them. Whether aware or unaware, those who are really following in the footsteps of Jesus are constantly being prepared for works of greater service. Few would have believed the magnitude of the impact these men were going to make, and few of us would believe the potential that we have for changing the world; but the God of Abraham, Isaac and Jacob was the God of Barnabas, Paul and Mark. And he is our God, fully prepared to do the same kinds of things with us as he has done with his people of centuries gone by. Let's not be guilty of studying these accounts as simply history, for God had many, many more reasons for recording these events than entertaining or even amazing us: We are to imitate their faith—and enjoy their results.

Questions for Further Study

1. When Samaria received the Word, the apostles in Jerusalem sent Peter and John to minister to them. When Antioch received the Word, they sent Barnabas—not one of the 12 (or 13) apostles. Do you think this choice could have been based upon his intention to work with Paul, and in what way would that have been especially helpful?

2. How would you define "pillar church"? What were the main ones in the Book of Acts?

3. Why was Antioch a great choice for becoming a pillar church?

4. What convicted you most in the section about your own pride (when studying Herod's example)?

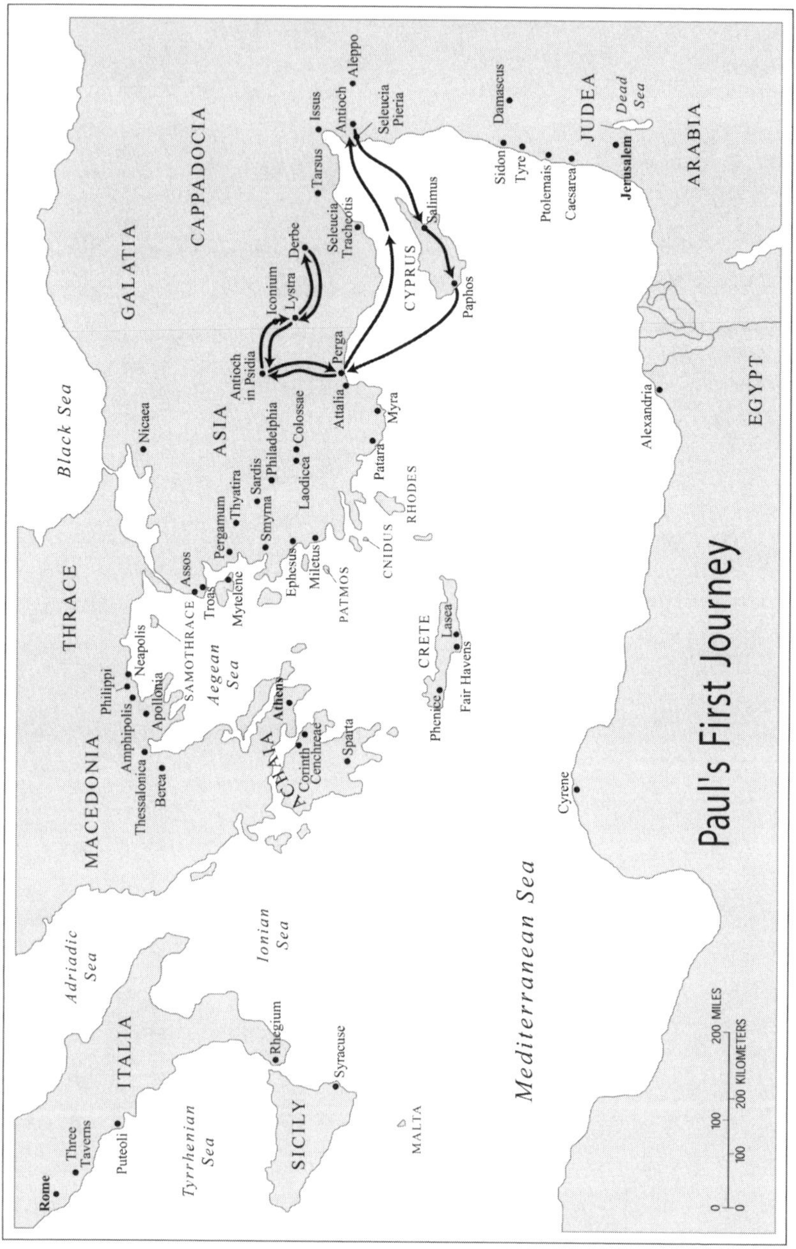

Paul's First Journey

Chapter Ten

Campaign One

Acts 13-14

This chapter begins what could accurately be called "The Book of Acts—Part Two: The Mission of Paul." Up until now, when we read of Paul, it was always "Barnabas and Saul." Before we read very far into Acts 13, we see that Paul is becoming the primary leader. As we read the remainder of Acts, we are made aware of another key shift: the elevation of Paul's leadership in the movement to at least an equal footing with Peter's, who had been the principal leader of the movement up until this point. Luke describes Paul's accomplishments in terms that are so reminiscent of Peter's that it can scarcely be accidental.

Therefore, as we move into Acts 13, the focus moves from Jerusalem and Samaria to faraway places, and from the original apostles to Paul and his coworkers. After James was martyred in Acts 12, none of the original apostles are again mentioned in Acts except Peter, and after the Jerusalem Conference in Acts 15, neither is he. As Paul's friend and traveling companion, Luke, Acts' author, was much more aware of Paul's life, but there is no doubt that God moved Paul to center stage in the unfolding drama of his redemptive intervention on planet Earth.

Spirituality and the Spirit (Acts 13:1-3)

[1]In the church at Antioch there were prophets and teachers: Barnabas, Simeon called Niger, Lucius of Cyrene, Manaen (who had been brought up with Herod the tetrarch) and Saul. [2]While they were worshiping the Lord and fasting, the Holy Spirit said, "Set apart for me Barnabas and Saul for the work to which I have called them." [3]So after they had fasted and prayed, they placed their hands on them and sent them off.

It was a critical time for the church. The opportunity was unprecedented. It was time for deep spirituality. Fasting is mentioned twice in this brief text, each time for a different purpose. The first was to seek the will of God, and the second was to accompany the appointment of Barnabas and Paul for their mission. This voluntary abstinence from food was a fairly common practice in the Old Testament, engaged in for a variety of reasons. One, it is described as a natural response to emotional situations. Hannah in her sorrow wept and did not eat (1 Samuel 1:7); Jonathan fasted when angered by his father's treatment of David (1 Samuel 20:34); and in grieving at the death of Abner, David fasted (2 Samuel 3:35). Two, fasting is seen in times of repentance (Joel 2:12–14, Jonah 3:4–10). Three, it was practiced in times of great spiritual significance, such as Moses' reception of the Law (Exodus 34:27–28), Daniel's seeing of a vision (Daniel 10:1–3) and the Jews' observation of the Day of Atonement (Leviticus 16:29–31). This special day was called "the Fast" in Acts 27:9. Four, fasting was done to seek God's aid and guidance (Ezra 8:21–23, Esther 4:15–16).

Obviously, it was in this latter connection that the first instance of fasting in Acts 13 occurred. Just why they specifically called a fast we are not told, but through the worship and fasting, they gained the Lord's attention and favor. A practical definition of fasting is called to mind in this case, namely "the willingness to give up something good for something better." Fasting has an unusual power to attract the strength and blessings of God. When his disciples were unable to perform a difficult miracle, Jesus told them that the particular kind of demon would come out only by prayer (Mark 9:28–29), but some manuscripts add the words "and fasting." Certainly prayer and fasting are a natural duo, as they focus faith on what is being sought in a highly effective way.

One of the greatest benefits of fasting is found in its effects on an individual's spiritual life and attitude, regardless of how God may intervene providentially in other ways. Years ago, when I was ministering with the church in San Diego, the leadership was seeking God's wisdom for our future plans as a congregation. I suggested a fast like the one described in Acts 13, having in mind a one-or two-day fast. The elders suggested a longer one, to be concluded by a devotional service and an all-night prayer session. Frankly, that scenario challenged both my faith and my flesh at the time. I envisioned the devo being a gathering of tired, cranky people with bad cases of halitosis! My eyes and heart were about to be opened to the power of fasting.

As a congregation, we fasted all day Wednesday, Thursday and Friday and then met in a high school auditorium Friday night for the devotional. The atmosphere was charged, as with electricity, and people seemed like they were almost floating off the ground a few inches! To say that we were "fired up" would not adequately describe what took place that night. Up until that point I had never experienced anything like it. Then we met in small groups and prayed through the remainder of the night, breaking our fast together at around daybreak the next morning.

For days afterward, I felt much more spiritually in tune than usual, with a noticeable emotional response when thinking about the goodness of God in my life and the blessings he had poured out on me. I remember driving alone to Sunday morning services after the fast, singing hymns with tears of gratitude streaming down my face. As I think back to that occasion and to others like it, I wonder why we don't fast more often. It has a power that far exceeds my ability to comprehend the dynamics at work within it. At Antioch, fasting led the Holy Spirit to initiate the most far-reaching mission thrust the world had ever experienced. Certainly he will do similar things through us when we imitate the example of that great mission church. It is a battle in which we are engaged, and fasting with prayer is one of the finest weapons in the disciple's arsenal.

The Advance to Cyprus (Acts 13:4-12)

[4]The two of them, sent on their way by the Holy Spirit, went down to Seleucia and sailed from there to Cyprus. [5]When they arrived at Salamis, they proclaimed the word of God in the Jewish synagogues. John was with them as their helper.

[6]They traveled through the whole island until they came to Paphos. There they met a Jewish sorcerer and false prophet named Bar-Jesus, [7]who was an attendant of the proconsul, Sergius Paulus. The proconsul, an intelligent man, sent for Barnabas and Saul because he wanted to hear the word of God. [8]But Elymas the sorcerer (for that is what his name means) opposed them and tried to turn the proconsul from the faith. [9]Then Saul, who was also called Paul, filled with the Holy Spirit, looked straight at Elymas and said, [10]"You are a child of the devil and an enemy of everything that is right! You are full of all kinds

of deceit and trickery. Will you never stop perverting the right ways of the Lord? [11]Now the hand of the Lord is against you. You are going to be blind, and for a time you will be unable to see the light of the sun." Immediately mist and darkness came over him, and he groped about, seeking someone to lead him by the hand. [12]When the proconsul saw what had happened, he believed, for he was amazed at the teaching about the Lord.

Previously, Barnabas appears to have been the lead person in his work with Paul, but on Cyprus, Saul becomes Paul. After this point, he is the unquestionable leader of the mission effort, and in verse 13, Barnabas is simply included in Paul's "companions." This rather remarkable change is a tribute both to Paul's power as an apostle and to the humility of Barnabas. It has been surmised that John Mark's decision to leave the first mission trip (Acts 13:13) might have been due to his inability to emotionally adjust to this reordering of the relationship between his cousin Barnabas and Paul. While that possibility is pure speculation, it is not speculative to assume the depth of humility that must have been evident in Barnabas himself.

The destructive miracle involving Elymas had the same purpose as the miracles with positive effects: to promote faith in those who observed them. This designed intent was certainly not lost on the proconsul, who in amazement believed the teaching about Christ. A question is raised in the minds of some readers about whether the proconsul only believed the basic facts Paul presented or actually became a saved disciple. I think he definitely became a disciple, since the Bible often uses such brief descriptions to denote that people became Christians. Of course at other times, more specifics of the obedient acceptance are given. The apparent discrepancies have caused some to assume that different methods of salvation were actually being taught in certain places at certain times. That assumption not only contradicts clear biblical teaching, but it also calls into question the Holy Spirit's inspiration of Scripture. The confusion is eliminated by understanding that the Bible uses the term "faith" in both a restricted sense and in a general comprehensive sense.

Many passages use the word "belief" as a type of mental assent, which would be the narrow or restricted sense. For example, Acts 18:8 states that "many of the Corinthians who heard him believed and were baptized." Something besides faith is mentioned, so faith here is used in the narrow sense. (Other similar passages are Acts 11:21, Mark 16:16, John 12:42 and James 2:19.)

The general or comprehensive use of "faith" is seen in passages like John 3:16, John 20:30–31, Romans 1:16 and Acts 4:4. This latter passage reads: "But many who heard the message believed, and the number of men grew to about five thousand." Acts 13:12, in the case of Sergius Paulus, also follows this broader usage.

A helpful further explanation is to realize that the Bible writers employed a common figure of speech called "synecdoche," in which a part is stated when the whole of something is intended. For example, Luke's version of the Great Commission (24:44–49) mentions that "repentance and forgiveness of sins will be preached." Since this says nothing about faith, it is obvious that repentance is used here for the whole response to the gospel which would certainly include faith (and baptism). Most commonly, faith is mentioned since it is the beginning point out of which the other conditions grow and the most central quality needed for continuing in the Christian life. Obviously, when the term "faith" is used in this manner, it is meant to include all other aspects of man's response, including both repentance and baptism.[1]

The conversion of Sergius Paulus is yet another example of the conversion of a prominent opinion leader. The numerous similar accounts in Acts can be viewed as nothing less than a divinely sanctioned pattern for church plantings. Both biblically and practically, the first people converted in new locations often became among the first leaders there. And if those with leadership abilities are not among the early conversions, then the planting is certain to struggle and falter. Establishing churches by converting a strong base of those with leadership gifts is the way of God, and anything less will hinder the mission. A classic example of the pattern is seen in 1 Corinthians 16:15–16:

> You know that the household of Stephanas were the first converts in Achaia, and they have devoted themselves to the service of the saints. I urge you, brothers, to submit to such as these and to everyone who joins in the work, and labors at it.

Whether Sergius Paulus became the leader of the church in Paphos we cannot know; but that he became a leader there would seem highly probable.

The Advance to Pisidian Antioch (Acts 13:13-52)

13 From Paphos, Paul and his companions sailed to Perga in Pam-
phylia, where John left them to return to Jerusalem. 14 From Perga
they went on to Pisidian Antioch. On the Sabbath they entered the
synagogue and sat down. 15 After the reading from the Law and the
Prophets, the synagogue rulers sent word to them, saying, "Broth-
ers, if you have a message of encouragement for the people, please
speak."...

42 As Paul and Barnabas were leaving the synagogue, the people
invited them to speak further about these things on the next Sab-
bath. 43 When the congregation was dismissed, many of the Jews and
devout converts to Judaism followed Paul and Barnabas, who talked
with them and urged them to continue in the grace of God.

44 On the next Sabbath almost the whole city gathered to hear the
word of the Lord. 45 When the Jews saw the crowds, they were filled
with jealousy and talked abusively against what Paul was saying.

46 Then Paul and Barnabas answered them boldly: "We had to
speak the word of God to you first. Since you reject it and do not con-
sider yourselves worthy of eternal life, we now turn to the Gentiles."

A Characteristic Sermon to Jews

Paul made use of every opportunity afforded him to preach the gospel, and one unique opportunity came via the synagogue practice of allowing qualified visitors to deliver a message. Jesus made use of this custom in Luke 4:16–27 to address the audience in his hometown of Nazareth. Paul's main mission was to the Gentiles, but he understood the reason that the gospel needed to go to the Jews first and then to the non-Jews (Romans 1:16). One of those reasons is made perfectly clear in Acts 13: The opportunity to address a ready-made audience in nearly every town was there for the asking. Obviously news of his conversion to Christ had not yet reached these places. Although his perspective regarding Judaism had changed tremendously since his conversion, he was still anxious to do all possible to reach as many of his Jewish brothers as possible. A big part of that readiness is seen in 1 Corinthians 9:20:

> To the Jews I became like a Jew, to win the Jews. To those under the law I became like one under the law (though I myself am not under the law), so as to win those under the law.

Paul's messages to Jews followed a characteristic line of reasoning, and this longest of such examples was no exception. The Jews were history buffs, but not in the ordinary sense. They were not concerned with history simply as history, but as it demonstrated God's special interest in them as a people over all the other people in the world. Paul used this interest to build rapport with them as he summarized some of the key points from their past. The consistent application was that Jesus was the Messiah of prophecy, and that although he had been rejected and murdered by the very ones to whom he was sent, God had raised him from the dead. Over and over these early preachers laid the prophecies and their fulfillments side by side and proved to all who were open-minded that Jesus was truly the Christ.

Interestingly, Paul concluded the message with a strong warning, not unlike Stephen had done back in Acts 7. Peter ended his classic sermon at Pentecost in a similar vein, as Acts 2:40 describes: "With many other words he warned them; and he pleaded with them, 'Save yourselves from this corrupt generation.'" Sermons that do not warn are not gospel sermons. Even with the biblically ignorant Athenians, Paul spoke of the Judgment Day (Acts 17:30–31). Having been raised personally in somewhat of a "fire and brimstone" setting, I know that such can be overdone if grace and love are not proclaimed to give proper balance. But we are far from overdoing the kind of preaching that puts the fear of God into rebellious and self-centered hearts. Our society's lack of respect for authority and irreverence for all things spiritual has affected nearly all of us to some extent, and often to an alarming extent. It is time to return to the apostolic preaching method of Acts. We are out to make disciples of Jesus, not to ease people into the baptistery.

Hearts Are Exposed

Paul's sermon ended with the audience wanting to hear more, which was arranged for the next Sabbath. When that day dawned, "almost the whole city gathered to hear the word of the Lord" (Acts 13:44). The religious leaders with closed hearts did what religious leaders of this nature always do: "They were filled with jealousy and talked abusively against what Paul was saying" (Acts 13:45). The same reaction is described specifically in Acts 5:17 and 17:5. Naive non-Christians and young Christians are often unsettled by those who appear and sound rather pious as they assault the true way, but we must learn from Acts that the religious Establishment are those who are usually the worst persecutors. After all, they have the most to lose by their members being converted. Never forget who insisted Jesus be nailed to the cross. It was not the Zealot renegades or the sinful masses whose sins were being condemned; it was the "respectable" Jewish leadership of Israel, the ones most hardened by sin.

It is easy for us to play the part of judges and to decide who will be most closed and most open to the gospel. However, we are not assigned that role by God, nor are we really that perceptive about open and closed hearts. We would tend to think that the morally upright, religious people of Jesus' day would have been the most open, but they decidedly were not. Conversely, we would tend to think that the immoral and dishonest (prostitutes and tax collectors) would have been the most closed, but they were not. Some of my biggest disappointments and positive surprises in trying to reach out to friends and relatives have fallen along similar lines. We can never know the nature of hearts until the word of God is applied to them, for only that application can expose hearts for what they really are.

Hearts are always responsible for the choices that they make. However, in Acts 13:48, we find these potentially confusing words:

> When the Gentiles heard this, they were glad and honored the word of the Lord; and all who were appointed for eternal life believed.

Does this wording suggest a Calvinistic type of predestination? No, for those thus described were also said to have honored the word of the Lord. They were "appointed" in the sense that God determined from the beginning that those with "a noble and good heart" (Luke 8:15) who accept the Word will be saved. On the other hand, those who will not accept the Word are appointed for damnation. But it is a matter of an individual making a free moral choice about how they are going to respond to God. Whether we accept or reject, we are totally responsible. Acts 13:46 provides a clear example of the personal responsibility involved in the rejection process:

> Then Paul and Barnabas answered them boldly: "We had to speak the word of God to you first. Since you reject it and do not consider yourselves worthy of eternal life, we now turn to the Gentiles."

The last section of Acts 13 contains a valuable lesson. After the ministry of Paul and Barnabas had produced much fruit, the persecution heated up to the point that they were expelled from the region of Pisidian Antioch. However, the disciples who were left behind "were filled with joy and with the Holy Spirit" (Acts 13:52). When Paul was run out of town after town, the disciples who so quickly lost their spiritual leaders still remained strong and faithful. It took deep convictions developed in a brief span to produce this amazing result. New disciples were not shallow in their faith, which meant that the leaders had tied the people's hearts tightly to Christ and not to themselves. Our task in disciple making is to convert people to Christ, not simply to the church with its leaders. Both the church and its leaders are essential in the plan of God, but if Christ is not the supreme devotion of the disciple's heart, the disciple is shallow and in danger of falling away quickly. Hence, there is a need to teach much about God, Christ and the Holy Spirit. Our faith must be deeply grounded in Deity, not just in the directives given by Deity! This is a fundamentally important point—ponder it.

To Iconium and Beyond (Acts 14:1-20)

1At Iconium Paul and Barnabas went as usual into the Jewish synagogue. There they spoke so effectively that a great number of Jews and Gentiles believed. 2But the Jews who refused to believe stirred up the Gentiles and poisoned their minds against the brothers. 3So Paul and Barnabas spent considerable time there, speaking boldly for the Lord, who confirmed the message of his grace by enabling them to do miraculous signs and wonders. 4The people of the city were divided; some sided with the Jews, others with the apostles. 5There was a plot afoot among the Gentiles and Jews, together with their leaders, to mistreat them and stone them. 6But they found out about it and fled to the Lycaonian cities of Lystra and Derbe and to the surrounding country, 7where they continued to preach the good news.

The purpose of miraculous spiritual gifts in the early church is once again made clear in verse 3: God confirmed the message by these gifts. Obviously, the miracles did not force anyone to believe, for many who saw them rejected the message and the messengers. But those with any openness of heart were influenced to believe.

God never overwhelms man into believing if man does not have the disposition to accept. Even in the natural revelation of God, physical creation, he gives plenty of good evidence that he is Creator, but not evidence that interferes with our free will. Many look at the creation and say that it is all a product of godless evolution. Similarly, the Bible contains many self-authenticating evidences, but some look at it and pronounce it a book of man's invention rather than one of God's revelation.

As Paul and Barnabas made their way to Lystra, they encountered a highly unusual reception. The people saw Paul heal a crippled man and judged that Paul and Barnabas were gods who had come down in human form. Local legend in that area had it that these two gods, Zeus and Hermes, had visited the area earlier. Thus, the people did not want to offend them by not offering them a suitable reception. Since the people were speaking in the Lycaonian language, Paul and Barnabas were not able to determine what was being done for quite a while. After the crowd was deterred from their intended actions, Jews from Antioch and Iconium came and quickly turned the crowd against Paul. Perhaps their disappointment in finding that this apostle was not a god made them more open to being persuaded that Paul was dangerous.

The stoning of Paul in Lystra left him all but dead.[2] After he revived, he went back into the city until he left for Derbe the following day. Where would you have spent the night? Paul was a man of immense courage. As may be seen in several texts, he was not without fear, but courage is the quality of character that allows one to do what is right, and even do it boldly, in spite of fears. Spreading the gospel in any culture in any age is never easy, for opposition is always predictable (John 15:18–20). Paul was not theorizing when he wrote in 2 Timothy 3:12 that "everyone who wants to live a godly life in Christ Jesus will be persecuted." The mission of Christ is neither for the fainthearted nor the tentative. The cost must be counted in advance, and those who still volunteer for heaven's earthly army must be willing to pay the price.

Reporting All That God Has Done (Acts 14:21-28)

21They preached the good news in that city and won a large number of disciples. Then they returned to Lystra, Iconium and Antioch, 22strengthening the disciples and encouraging them to remain true to the faith. "We must go through many hardships to enter the kingdom of God," they said. 23Paul and Barnabas appointed elders for them in each church and, with prayer and fasting, committed them to the Lord, in whom they had put their trust. 24After going through Pisidia, they came into Pamphylia, 25and when they had preached the word in Perga, they went down to Attalia.

26From Attalia they sailed back to Antioch, where they had been committed to the grace of God for the work they had now completed. 27On arriving there, they gathered the church together and reported all that God had done through them and how he had opened the door of faith to the Gentiles. 28And they stayed there a long time with the disciples.

As Paul and Barnabas returned to Lystra, Iconium and Pisidian Antioch, they strengthened and encouraged the disciples by reminding them that life in the earthly kingdom includes many hardships before we enter the heavenly kingdom. Being a disciple is the most rewarding life possible, but it is not an easy one. An inherent danger in trying to convert people in the "me" generation is that they may be attracted mainly to the benefits found in the kingdom rather than to its mission. Luke 14:25–33 is included in the Bible for the purpose of avoiding this mistake. Preaching is not about "getting people saved"; it is about persuading them to deny self, take up their crosses and to willingly accept the suffering that goes with the territory. We are disciples of Jesus, not self-seeking and indulgent church members who demand to be served. The latter mind-set may well permeate modern society's view of religion, but it is nowhere close to what Jesus demands. He will not tolerate anything less than biblical discipleship. The adage to "go anywhere, do anything and give up everything" is not simply a cliché—it is God's expectation.

In Acts 14:23 we see elders being appointed very quickly in the new churches. A prepared pool of leadership came into the church from the synagogue setting, including mature Jews, proselytes and God-fearers. But even though they had been prepared in some good ways, their appointment was accompanied by prayer and fasting. They had to be left to carry on what Paul and Barnabas had started, in the midst of the hostile atmosphere that had been produced by their work. All of the disciples in these churches, especially those who were assuming leadership roles, had no doubt counted the cost well, understanding that the hardships in the kingdom were directly connected with the persecution. Many hardships are part and parcel of life on earth, but those of disciples go far beyond these. Their hardships are inseparably connected to the Man whose name they wear and to the mission they share with him. The victories reported back at the home base of Antioch were reports of the advancement of a radical mission—the mission from God, by God and for God.

Questions for Further Study

1. What are your thoughts about, and experiences with, fasting? Describe.

2. Explain the differences in the use of faith in a restricted, narrow sense, and in a comprehensive sense.

3. How important are these differences in studying with those from a religious background? Explain.

4. What would you say about Paul's "balance" in his preaching approach?

5. Describe the different instances of persecution in this section covered that Paul received?

6. How willing are you to receive persecution from strangers, friends and family? (Explain your answer)

Chapter Eleven

TROUBLE IN PARADISE

ACTS 15

Racial tensions have always been pervasive in our world. The early church was not immune to these, and in some form they existed in the church almost from its inception. The Judeans on Pentecost had noticed the Galilean accents of the apostles (Acts 2:7), not simply because the accents were different, but because Galileans were seen as inferior by those residing in Jerusalem. Galilee, while better than Samaria in Judean minds, was still viewed with some disdain, especially when it came to religious leadership. Anyone who was anyone in Judaism did not stray far from the hub of Jerusalem. God was definitely striking a blow at prejudice by having his Son brought up in Galilee and then by having him choose the twelve apostles from that area as well.

In Acts 6 we hear of hurt feelings that arose among the widows of the Grecian Jews. Generally, Hellenistic (Greek-speaking) Jews were regarded as being inferior by the Hebraic Jews. Whether the Hebraic Jews in the church felt this way or not, the Hellenistic group most likely held this self-image from past experiences. Once Stephen was killed and many scattered from Jerusalem, the persecution died down some, causing many Bible scholars to think that the dispersion was mainly comprised of Hellenists. Something along these lines must have been true or else the apostles could not have remained in Jerusalem (Acts 8:1), for in times of persecution, the leaders are the most vulnerable to it. Because the apostles were able to remain in Jerusalem, the above explanation seems quite plausible.

Next in Acts came the inclusion of the Samaritans, which no doubt strained the tolerance of the more rigid Jews. The Samaritan woman at the well was genuinely amazed that Jesus would even speak to her, for in John's comments about the interaction, he accurately stated that "Jews do not associate with Samaritans" (John 4:9). One can only imagine the types of conversations that took place among the onlooking, nonbelieving Jews. Surely even some in the church had to deal with their emotions as the Samaritans were being invited into the one body of believers. Since deeply ingrained prejudices are never cast off easily, we are not assuming the improbable.

But now we come to the big issue in the church. Compared to the Jew/Gentile issue, the prejudices just described pale in comparison. It may be difficult to imagine the level of prejudice residing in Jewish hearts, but Luke included one account that helps the modern reader to grasp the magnitude of the problem. When Paul was recounting his conversion experience to a Jerusalem crowd, they listened well until he said that God had told him that he was to be sent on a mission to the Gentiles. Then a hellish fury was immediately unleashed, as Acts 22:22 describes:

> "The crowd listened to Paul until he said this. Then they raised their voices and shouted, 'Rid the earth of him! He's not fit to live!'"

The following verse says that this outburst included "shouting and throwing off their cloaks and flinging dust into the air" (v23).

Certainly the disciples in the church were far above these kinds of attitudes by now, but it would be unrealistic to think that centuries of nursing such prejudices would not leave its impact in their heart of hearts. Whatever rationalizations were used by the disciples from among the more rigid Jews, they were dealing with prejudice, pure and simple. Some had doctrinal concerns—concerns that actually grew out of a misunderstanding of the gospel. Those concerns had to be addressed and bad theology had to be corrected, but we are naïve if we don't realize that there was prejudice there that had to be weeded out.

Jesus staked the effectiveness of the mission on the maintenance of unity among believers (John 17:20–23), and if the fledgling church was to permeate and conquer the evil empire, the issue had to be addressed forcefully and quickly. This Paul did, pushing it to the forefront of the movement's attention, and for the only time in Acts, a church council convened with all of the top leaders present. Obviously, God was not taking the situation lightly in any way, and he moved his leaders to be of the same mind and heart in the matter.

The First Church Conference (Acts 15:1-21)

1Some men came down from Judea to Antioch and were teaching
the brothers: "Unless you are circumcised, according to the custom
taught by Moses, you cannot be saved." 2This brought Paul and Barn-
abas into sharp dispute and debate with them. So Paul and Barnabas
were appointed, along with some other believers, to go up to Jerusa-
lem to see the apostles and elders about this question. 3The church
sent them on their way, and as they traveled through Phoenicia and
Samaria, they told how the Gentiles had been converted. This news
made all the brothers very glad. 4When they came to Jerusalem, they
were welcomed by the church and the apostles and elders, to whom
they reported everything God had done through them.

5Then some of the believers who belonged to the party of the
Pharisees stood up and said, "The Gentiles must be circumcised and
required to obey the law of Moses."

6The apostles and elders met to consider this question.

A Crisis Stage Is Reached

There was strong teaching being spread from Jerusalem that the Gentiles could not be accepted as part of the church unless they were circumcised and began to keep the law of Moses. In other words, they would have to become Jews before they could be considered Christians. Paul and Barnabas were not involved here at a theoretical level, for they had converted those who were now being told they were second-class citizens of the kingdom—if even that. The words "sharp dispute" and "debate" are strong words describing the atmosphere produced by the Judaizing teachers. The issue was out in the open and the battle lines had been drawn. This had to be settled, no matter what measures had to be taken. The decision was made to send a group of leaders to Jerusalem to meet with the apostles and elders to work out the conflict and to come to righteous solutions. At this time, Jerusalem was still the leading church in the movement, with a full complement of leaders, which included apostles, elders and the Lord's brothers.

The influence of elders in the Jerusalem church is seen in this passage. One of the Lord's brothers, James, appears to have been one of the elders (Acts 21:18) and evidently the key leader of the Jerusalem church. (In Galatians 2:9, the "pillars" of the Jerusalem church were said to be James, Peter and John—in that order.) He certainly seems to have been the key spokesman at the council meeting, as will be seen later in Acts 15. Typically, evangelists planted churches and then raised up and appointed elders to shepherd the flock. But the evangelists continued to lead churches who had elders; Paul's later letters to Timothy and Titus establish that point very clearly. However, the experience and maturity of both elders and evangelists would have played a key role in how they related as they led together. 1 Timothy 5:17 and Acts 20:28 demonstrate that elders were very much involved in leading the church also. Practically speaking, evangelists focus more on evangelistic outreach, while elders focus more on shepherding the flock, but elders and evangelists must be vitally concerned and involved with both outreach and maturation.

As Paul and his associates were en route to Jerusalem, they reported the great things that God had been doing among the Gentiles (Acts 15:3). This showed that they had not lost any confidence in what God had commissioned them to do, no matter what the opposition had been. It also showed that they did not allow church problems to deter them from the mission at hand. Sometimes it does not take much to distract us from the mission of seeking and saving the lost. We can too easily be pushed off course by simple distractions such as the ordinary cares of life, to say nothing of what happens when deeper problems arise. From these early brothers we must learn to stay about our purpose even in the midst of significant problems. If we are only diligent about evangelism when the church is hitting on all cylinders, so to speak, then we will be very ineffective in making a real impact for eternity. Let's imitate these disciples who were constantly focused on helping others see Jesus and the life he offers.

The Failure of Rigid Religion

Rigid religion is a hazardous spiritual condition, one difficult to perceive by those caught in its deceptive web. It can be rooted in bad motives, but also in bad theology—as seems to be the case here in Acts 15. The gospel is based on God's grace because man simply cannot save himself. Any effort to establish a relationship with God based on law keeping and a performance model is doomed to failure. The letter to the Romans builds upon that premise in a profound manner. "The best of us is a mess," and "we all need grace" are the twin messages of this crucial biblical book. However, the most rigid of Jews, the Pharisees, had a difficult time in accepting this message. They pursued righteousness "not by faith but as if it were by works" (Romans

9:32). This erroneous mind-set led, as it always does, to rigid religion. Those Jewish Christians with a Pharisaic background apparently accepted Jesus as the Messiah without understanding the very nature of his gospel. They believed that Gentile believers would have to submit to certain Jewish works to secure their salvation. Hence, Peter strongly reminded them that salvation is by grace through faith and not by works:

> "He made no distinction between us and them, for he purified their hearts by faith....We believe it is through the grace of our Lord Jesus that we are saved, just as they are." (Acts 15:9, 11)

Lest we be tempted to look at these early brothers self-righteously, we had better do some self-examination. The performance model is drilled into us from birth by friends and enemies alike. We learn to feel great when our performance is great and bad when it is flawed. "What's wrong with that?" you may be thinking. "Isn't that how we are driven to keep improving?" The problem is that we easily slip into spiritual legalism. We begin to feel saved when our performance is great and feel lost when it is flawed. The difference between the two concepts may seem subtle, but the impact on our hearts and lives is enormous.

A religion based on performance can yield only two results, nearly opposite in some ways but both disastrous in the end. One, we may become discouraged, defeated and guilt-ridden disciples. Those in this category will likely fall away from God at some point, unless they have a huge tolerance for emotional pain. Two, we may attempt to solve the tensions of failure by codifying our religion into manageable tenets. In other words, we reduce our walk with God to obeying the things we deem most important and basically ignoring the rest of his teachings. We invent our own checklist and glory in checking things off, rather than glorying in God. Outward obedience becomes exalted far above issues of the heart. Read Matthew 23 with this in mind. When we disciple people more urgently about what they fail to do than what is in their heart, we are falling prey to this same tendency to overemphasize performance. Given time, it will result in a legalism not unlike that which Peter was condemning.

In Acts 15:5, the seriousness of rigid religion exposes itself for all to see. While the brothers were still rejoicing over the salvation of the Gentiles, the uptight Pharisaic believers interjected their complaints. Before we proceed further, it should be noted that these former Pharisees had made the courageous decision to accept Jesus in spite of opposition from their relatives and colleagues. However, it is obvious that they still carried a good deal of baggage from their past experiences. From reading Galatians we know that some of them unquestionably went to dangerous extremes of rigid religion, which was diametrically opposed to the whole tenor of the gospel.

Rigid religionists can never really enjoy the blessings of the kingdom, for they are burdened with their duties as "watchdogs": They must ever be on guard against the intrusions of falsity into their pious presence. People with such mind-sets, then and now, follow predictable patterns of behavior with predictable results. In Matthew 12:43–45 Jesus described such people as those who swept out their houses, making sure that no evil was present, but then failed to fill themselves with good things. The result was that the demons found plenty of ways to fill the unoccupied houses (hearts and lives).

Godly religion is focused primarily on what is right instead of on what is wrong. Sure, the sin in our lives has to be eradicated, but this is the means to an end (being filled with the righteousness of Christ), not an end within itself. The message of Paul in passages like Colossians 3 is that we must put off the sinful attitudes and practices in order to put on the good things of Christ. It is far more effective to fill our lives with the good, thereby crowding out the bad, than to focus on the "don'ts." Repentance, which is always mandated by God before he can establish a covenant relationship with us, is a very positive thing. When we repent, we stop the behavior that harms us emotionally and spiritually (and often even physically) and replace it with behavior that only blesses.

Having been immersed in a rigid religious setting for most of my life, I can attest to the damage it does to the individuals involved, to say nothing of the destiny of the churches. Most of my peers have long since rejected these types of churches, if not religion generally. Most of those groups of which I was once a part are diminishing both in numbers of congregations and in membership. Where young marrieds once gathered with youngsters in tow, only older marrieds now gather. Those like me found the atmosphere irrelevant at best and terribly stifling at worst.

While the Jew/Gentile problem that we find here in Acts 15 is not likely to reappear, we must recognize that legalistic religion can reappear in any age. When it does, we must have the conviction to face it head on and once again lift up the cross of Christ as the only way to God. Any other avenue could aptly be called a "yoke" which none can bear (Acts 15:10).

A Decision Is Reached (Acts 15:22-35)

[22]Then the apostles and elders, with the whole church, decided to choose some of their own men and send them to Antioch with Paul and Barnabas. They chose Judas (called Barsabbas) and Silas, two men who were leaders among the brothers. [23]With them they sent the following letter:

The apostles and elders, your brothers,
To the Gentile believers in Antioch, Syria and Cilicia:

Greetings.

[24]We have heard that some went out from us without our authorization and disturbed you, troubling your minds by what they said. [25]So we all agreed to choose some men and send them to you with our dear friends Barnabas and Paul—[26]men who have risked their lives for the name of our Lord Jesus Christ. [27]Therefore we are sending Judas and Silas to confirm by word of mouth what we are writing. [28]It seemed good to the Holy Spirit and to us not to burden you with anything beyond the following requirements: [29]You are to abstain from food sacrificed to idols, from blood, from the meat of strangled animals and from sexual immorality. You will do well to avoid these things.

Farewell.

The Decision-Making Process

This passage gives us a record of the decisions made, but it also gives us insight into how those conclusions were reached. Several verses are key to understanding the process used. In verse 2, the brothers chosen and sent from Antioch were "to go up to Jerusalem to see the apostles and elders about this question." Verse 6 states that the "apostles and elders met to consider this question." Then in verse 22 we read:

> Then the apostles and elders, with the whole church, decided to choose some of their own men and send them to Antioch with Paul and Barnabas. They chose Judas (called Barsabbas) and Silas, two

men who were leaders among the brothers.

The sequence here is very important. The leaders from Antioch were sent specifically to meet with the top leaders of the Jerusalem church, namely the apostles and elders. This they did, and it was in this setting that the issues were discussed and decisions reached. Then, the whole church was brought in and informed of the discussions and the decisions, and their involvement was sought in deciding how to disseminate the decisions.

The church is a kingdom, not a democracy, which means that leaders are responsible for deciding the weightier issues. Sometimes the idea is advanced (often based on a misunderstanding of this passage) that everyone in the church should have an equal vote. Now that may sound very American, but it does not sound very biblical! Just imagine what would have happened at the Red Sea if Moses had left the decisions up to a democratic vote. The Israelites did have a vote of sorts in Numbers 13, as ten spies "outvoted" Joshua and Caleb. The result was disastrous, leading to forty years of wandering around in a desert while a couple of million funerals were held. Pilate asked for a vote from those assembled before Jesus, and they voted to murder God in the flesh. Majority rule in the world has never been righteous rule, because the majority are always on the wrong path (Matthew 7:13–14). Even among God's people, in the Old Testament or New Testament, God never instituted a one-vote-per-person process of decision making. Leaders must do exactly that—lead. And the rest of us must follow that leadership. Judges 5:2 describes the happy occasion when leadership and "followership" work together correctly: "When the princes in Israel take the lead, when the people willingly offer themselves—praise the Lord!"

However, let me also hasten to add that the church must be involved in the decision-making process at appropriate levels. In this Acts 15 passage, they were brought in and informed in a way that they appreciated, and they were involved in deciding how and by whom the decisions would be spread. Back in Acts 6, another decision was made in a similar manner regarding how to meet the needs of neglected widows. The apostles decided just how the problem would be solved, and then they asked the congregation to select the men to carry out their plan.

Respect of followers for leaders and leaders for followers must be present in our hearts, expressed in our words and put into actions as we labor together. We are all a part of the one body described in 1 Corinthians 12, in which none are superior and none are inferior. Different roles we do have, but different value as children of God we do not have.

The Specific Decisions Reached

The decisions of the council were fourfold: The Gentiles were to abstain from food sacrificed to idols, blood, meat of strangled animals and sexual immorality (Acts 15:20, 29). Two common questions are often raised by the mention of these four items from which the Gentiles were to abstain. One was their exact identification, and the other is the question of application to us today. As to their identification, if they are all judged to be of a moral nature, then two are related to idolatry, one to murder (blood) and the other to basic immorality. If they are to be viewed as ceremonial, one would be meat sacrificed to idols, two would have to do with Jewish dietary laws, and the immorality would perhaps reflect the prohibitions of Leviticus 17–18, which were often practiced by Gentiles but were especially odious to Jews. Scholars differ on what they believe was being described, based on what they think the Jews were most likely to be perturbed about.

The issue of application to us today is by far the bigger question that gets raised. Many people have attempted to go to the OT setting (out of which these issues come) to determine various good and bad practices today. From the Old Testament, you can forbid tattoos (Leviticus 19:28), the wearing of clothes woven of more than one kind of material (Leviticus 19:19), having marital sexual relations during the time of the wife's monthly period (Leviticus 20:18) and the eating of many types of food. I have heard the Old Testament called in as an authority on these and many other similar issues, but perhaps the food requirements are most touted. It may be that pork and catfish are not the best foods to eat, but when Jesus "declared all foods 'clean'" (Mark 7:19), that ended the issue for me. If the purpose of the Bible was to give us health instructions, then Jesus could have taught many things that would have prolonged the lives of countless millions, but the fact remains that he did not do such.

However, does the mention of these food-related items in Acts 15 thus bring them into the New Testament as binding teaching? Obviously, sexual immorality is wrong in any age, but what about the other three items? Is it wrong to eat "nonkosher" meat with too much blood in it? Even on the issue of eating food sacrificed to idols,

Paul later modified this teaching by saying that you could eat it if you didn't know it had been sacrificed in an idol temple, and in fact, you should not ask (1 Corinthians 10:25–30). My opinion on these requirements is that they do not apply unless taught elsewhere in the New Testament. These stipulations were for this unusual period in history while the transition was being made from the old covenant.

The food requirements were temporarily needed to relax the tensions between the Gentile Christians and the Jewish disciples who had the more rigid background and resultant ultrasensitive consciences. Not that I have any intention of eating blood pudding (popular in some cultures), mind you, but I will still enjoy many other foods forbidden in the Old Testament. If your conscience is different than mine on these matters, then heed it until such time as it changes, and in the meantime, do not attempt to bind your opinions on others (Romans 14).

In any age, issues will arise that seem highly important to us. We could put these in three categories: (1) issues that the Bible addresses explicitly; (2) issues that the Bible addresses less thoroughly; and (3) issues about which the Bible says nothing directly. In the first case, the issue is easily settled (for example, sex outside marriage is always wrong). In the second and third cases, biblical principles have to be determined and applied, which obviously requires more human judgment. An example of the second category would be deciding how the food laws mentioned in Acts 15 apply to us. Abortion would be an issue in the third category. We must be willing to examine any issue that seems important, but one thing is sure: We cannot allow ourselves to be distracted by issues and become issues oriented. Many "people of the Book" through the centuries have done exactly that. We must learn from examples such as those in Acts 15 and stay focused on the advancement of the kingdom. Any issue that we allow to move us away from our primary mission of seeking and saving the lost has become for us a stumbling block.

I have seen well-intentioned people become intrigued by good things that became bad for them, be it studies of grace or the Holy Spirit (two thus commonly misused). My question for them is simple: Is this subject that captivates you making you more enthused about saving the lost and more effective at it? If the answer is no, then you are issues oriented and being deceived by Satan in your emphasis on what otherwise might be a wonderful subject. That's the proof of the pudding. Paul was focused on carrying out the mission for which

Christ died, and nothing in heaven or on earth was going to deter him from that task, even "trouble in paradise." How about you?

Paul and Barnabas Part (Acts 15:36-41)

36Some time later Paul said to Barnabas, "Let us go back and visit the brothers in all the towns where we preached the word of the Lord and see how they are doing." 37Barnabas wanted to take John, also called Mark, with them, 38but Paul did not think it wise to take him, because he had deserted them in Pamphylia and had not continued with them in the work. 39They had such a sharp disagreement that they parted company. Barnabas took Mark and sailed for Cyprus, 40but Paul chose Silas and left, commended by the brothers to the grace of the Lord. 41He went through Syria and Cilicia, strengthening the churches.

No sooner is one issue of potential disunity solved, with much time and effort, than another arises. This time, two powerful leaders who had been totally united on the previous issue now have a sharp disagreement and end up parting company over it. The inclusion of such an account in this record of God's great plan of evangelizing the world should convince us that the Bible is indeed a Spirit inspired book. Since both Paul and Barnabas went on to do great things, and all parties remained in fellowship, God could have chosen not to include this story showing the foibles of his most outstanding leaders. But he always deals with reality in a truthful, open manner. The Bible describes David as the man after God's own heart (Acts 13:22), but it also tells us of his sins of adultery and murder, with the horrendous consequences thereby brought on his family. Great leaders like Eli and Samuel failed as fathers with their children. Such examples are many, because God inspired a Book with the "dirty laundry" laid out openly for all to see. Men do not write such accounts about their own heroes. They normally slant the truth to portray the weaknesses of their characters in the best possible light—to the point that the light is artificial!

Paul and Barnabas left the Jerusalem Conference triumphant, only to have their worst conflict ever, as far as the inspired record informs us. What happens when leaders cannot agree? Do they, like those in the world, become bitter enemies from that time forward? Not if they are true disciples. But the truth remains that they did part company without coming to agreement. How are we to explain this?

Who was right in the situation, and who was wrong? Very good questions are these! One lesson that jumps off the page is that there may be times, however rare, when leaders do not agree and must agree to disagree until such time that God clarifies the situation further.

In 1 Corinthians 16:12, we read of a somewhat similar dynamic between Paul and Apollos:

> Now about our brother Apollos: I strongly urged him to go to you with the brothers. He was quite unwilling to go now, but he will go when he has the opportunity.

This example involved mostly a disagreement about timing, in that Apollos was willing to do what Paul asked but not at the time he asked. Neither this passage nor Acts 15 can be used to justify being unsubmissive to leaders. In both cases, we are looking at two highly influential leaders and how they relate when each has strong but differing opinions. Paul may not have agreed with either of his leader brothers, but he did respect their rights to follow their own consciences, for these were conscience issues. None of us should violate our consciences, but all of us should be very willing to be persuaded.

I have observed specific modern leaders with a great deal of responsibility in similar situations, and they followed exactly the same approach as did Paul. They strongly expressed their judgments about directions they thought were best, but when other key leaders could not be convinced one way or the other, they did not try to force the issue further. On the one hand, they did not want to push the other leaders beyond their own faith, knowing that the venture would fail without that faith. And on the other hand, they did not want to force anyone to violate their own consciences. Righteous leaders always must lead within these restrictions and boundaries.

However, we who follow their leadership must not be self-willed and difficult to convince. In Hebrews 13:17, we read about righteous submission in these terms: "Obey your leaders and submit to their authority." The word translated "obey" carries the basic idea of being willing to be persuaded. The burden is not on the leader to convince, but on the follower to be convinced. Once a very prominent leader was trying to persuade several of us about the validity of a certain point. Two of us were having some difficulty agreeing with the point, but we kept talking and worked through it. Later, in describing the situation, the key leader paid me a compliment. He said that I gave more evidence of wanting to be convinced than did the other brother. That seems clearly to be the right posture to take in light of the Hebrews passage—and the posture all of us must assume.

But what of Paul and Barnabas: Who was right? Actually, the text does not say, although it does say that "Paul chose Silas and left, commended by the brothers to the grace of the Lord" (Acts 15:40). It says nothing of such commendation for the mission of Barnabas and Mark. This was perhaps God's way of saying that Paul made the better decision, or it could be simply saying that Paul was thought by others to have made the right decision. We do not know for sure.

Barnabas and John Mark were cousins, raising the likelihood of sentimentality in their relationship. From Mark's perspective, Barnabas believed in him, stood up for him and stuck with him, which appeared to be ultimately beneficial. When Paul was old and near death, he wrote "Get Mark and bring him with you, because he is helpful to me in my ministry" (2 Timothy 4:11). At some point, Mark worked through his immaturity and weaknesses, but whether he had worked through them by Acts 15, we cannot know. Barnabas apparently thought he had, but Paul was not certain enough to take a chance on bringing him along on the second mission trip. As with the disagreement between Paul and Apollos in 1 Corinthians 16, timing was the key issue. This text does not force us to the conclusion that Paul was down on Mark after his failure and untimely departure from the first mission trip, but, at the very least, he felt that too much was at stake to try him again so soon.

In the final analysis, God can still work through everyone involved if they keep their hearts and attitudes right. All four of these men remained in fellowship and later worked together in some capacities, being used by a God who knows how to work with sinful humans (praise Jesus!). Even when the Jerusalem gathering chose two men to deliver the decisions to Antioch, God was working through them, because Silas was one of these men. Paul was able to get to know him, and when he needed a new partner, he sent back to Jerusalem for Silas.

God has what would appear to us as contingency plans, but since he sees the end from the beginning, they are simply his one plan for the ultimate spiritual conquest of a lost world. Differences of opinion, even those accompanied by sharp disagreements, can be worked into the successful plans of God for us—if (and this is a big "if") we are determined to stay in the battle for souls and not be derailed from

Christ's Great Commission. Distractions and personality challenges will come our way, but if we keep our backs together as we face the enemy, ungodly division and failure will be thwarted. Let's keep our eyes on Jesus and his purpose for us, and in the end God's plan will reign triumphant!

Questions for Further Study

1. How was Paul's refusal to be distracted from his mission demonstrated in this section?

2. What types of distractions affect you most in carrying out your mission for Jesus?

3. What are the characteristics of a "performance-based religion"?

4. Do any of these show up in your life with God? Explain.

5. What did you learn from Acts 15 about the decision-making process of the church and its leaders?

6. What do you think were likely the main issues in the sharp disagreement between Paul and Barnabas?

Paul's Second Journey
Black Sea
THRACE
MACEDONIA
GALATIA
CAPPADOCIA
ASIA
ACHAIA
CYPRUS
CRETE
JUDEA
ARABIA
EGYPT
ITALIA
SICILY
SAMOTHRACE
PATMOS
CNIDUS
RHODES
MALTA
Aegean Sea
Adriadic Sea
Ionian Sea
Tyrrhenian Sea
Mediterranean Sea
Dead Sea
Rome
Three Taverns
Puteoli
Rhegium
Syracuse
Thessalonica
Berea
Amphipolis
Apollonia
Philippi
Neapolis
Athens
Corinth
Cenchreae
Sparta
Assos
Troas
Mytelene
Pergamum
Thyatira
Smyrna
Sardis
Philadelphia
Ephesus
Miletus
Laodicea
Colossae
Nicaea
Antioch in Psidia
Iconium
Lystra
Derbe
Perga
Attalia
Patara
Myra
Tarsus
Seleucia Tracheotis
Issus
Antioch
Seleucia Pieria
Aleppo
Salimus
Paphos
Sidon
Tyre
Ptolemais
Damascus
Caesarea
Jerusalem
Alexandria
Cyrene
Phenice
Fair Havens
Lasea
0 100 200 MILES
0 100 200 KILOMETERS

Chapter Twelve

CAMPAIGN TWO
(Part One)
ACTS 16

When we come to Acts 16, we see how God's missionaries dealt with closed doors and events that did not unfold as they had planned. Life's path is strewn with roadblocks and obstacles of many types. Disappointments, with their accompanying frustrations and hurt feelings, begin to invade our lives from the earliest ages. We can grow up focusing more on closed doors than open ones, more on failed opportunities than successful ventures. Who of us does not have many thoughts of the past in which "it might have been" is ringing in our ears? This sometimes painful struggle encapsulates a lot of what a life of faith is all about: Once we figure out biblically that God is in control of all that happens to us, whether he directly causes it or allows it to occur, then the challenge of disappointments can loom larger than ever in our thinking. Then we do not simply wonder what might have been; we wonder why God did not orchestrate it as we had envisioned it.

I can remember asking God why he did not answer previous prayers according to my requests—or questioning him about why he had allowed certain situations to occur in my life that were very hurtful. We do tend to struggle with God over such issues, and that is not a bad thing—if we handle our questioning and struggling like David did in the Psalms. He was open and honest with God about his feelings, but then he always worked it through, coming out with faith for the future. Someone said that doubt is a great shovel if it is used to dig for faith. No matter what the pain or disappointment, we must end up surrendering to God's plan for our lives. Even if we cannot understand what he is doing or allowing, he is still a perfect, loving Father who will never make a mistake or be unloving toward us (nor will he be sentimental!).

I also can remember a select group of prayers in which I thanked God for not answering previous prayers. As the country song says, "I thank God for unanswered prayers." Hindsight is usually 20/20. We so often can look back and see that God has given us what we needed rather than what we wanted. In this sense, the past is the key to the future. "Count your many blessings, name them one by one, and it will surprise you what God has done." And hopefully, it will cause you to trust him more as you face the future, for he who has guided our feet into the paths of peace will not forsake us now. As Paul put it to Timothy:

> That is why I am suffering as I am. Yet I am not ashamed, because I know whom I have believed, and am convinced that he is able to guard what I have entrusted to him for that day. (2 Timothy 1:12)

Paul's experiences in the early part of the second mission tour helped him have faith whenever he faced future suffering. Closed doors to him came to mean not disappointment, but excitement, as he awaited something better. He learned well that man's extreme challenges are indeed God's opportunities. No matter what Satan did to block his way, God would come along to lead him through the blockades or to lead him in an even better direction. If we can learn that lesson in life, thus extinguishing our disappointments and doubts in God and in ourselves, then he will be able to use us through the changing times and seasons of life. Then it will no longer be closed doors equaling disappointments; it will be closed doors equaling open hearts—through the exciting guidance of God through his Spirit!

When God Says No (Acts 16:1-10)

6 Paul and his companions traveled throughout the region of Phrygia and Galatia, having been kept by the Holy Spirit from preaching the word in the province of Asia. 7 When they came to the border of Mysia, they tried to enter Bithynia, but the Spirit of Jesus would not allow them to. 8 So they passed by Mysia and went down to Troas. 9 During the night Paul had a vision of a man of Macedonia standing and begging him, "Come over to Macedonia and help us." 10 After Paul had seen the vision, we got ready at once to leave for Macedonia, concluding that God had called us to preach the gospel to them.

Raising Up Leaders

When God decides to say no to us, we must decide to say yes to his decision. Therein lies one of man's greatest spiritual challenges in life. Disappointments are never easy to accept, but when they come via the hand of God, it takes a seasoned faith to see the silver lining in the clouds. Paul had such a faith. He was disappointed in how things worked out with John Mark, but he looked for an alternate and found him in young Timothy (Acts 16:1–3). Evidently, he always included in his entourage men at various stages of training. He had more mature leaders like Silas and Luke with him, but he knew that leaders had to be raised up continually if the world was to be evangelized. Hence, Timothy was invited along and would later become one of Paul's most trusted associates in the ministry.

What we see here is a clearly distinguishable pattern of raising up and training leaders. Jesus called men to be with him and then to be sent out to preach (Mark 3:14), and the apostles followed this pattern. The work of Paul and Barnabas in Antioch resulted in many leaders being raised up (Acts 13:1, 15:35). As Paul traveled on his preaching tours, he continually called men to be with him for further training. Sometimes these disciples were simply called his "companions" (Acts 13:13), and sometimes their names were mentioned. Timothy was trained and later sent out with Erastus to preach in Macedonia (Acts 19:22). Still later, he would be sent out to preach in Ephesus (1 Timothy 1:3). Paul was always looking for leaders and potential leaders to be with him and then be sent out. He pulled in Gaius and Aristarchus from Macedonia (Acts 19:29), perhaps leaving Timothy and Erastus in their place. Acts 20:4 mentions a number of other disciples: Sopater, Secundus, Tychicus and Trophimus. Leaders were constantly being trained in practical ministry in Paul's company and then sent out to lead churches.

This type of approach in providing practical training of leaders was certainly the example of Christ, but being who he was, the apostles received more in-depth Bible training than we can imagine. That has led to a question regarding leadership training in our day: Should we focus on a classroom type of instruction or on practical on-the-job (OTJ) training? Answer—*yes,* to both. This is one of many areas where some tend strongly in an either/or direction, but in this and many other areas a both/and approach provides the best solutions.

God next said no to Paul's plan to preach the Word in the province of Asia (Acts 16:6). Asia (the western side of "Asia Minor" or the area we know today as Turkey) was a very influential portion of the Roman Empire, and spreading the gospel there seemed absolutely essential. But God said no. Next, Paul and his group tried to enter Bithynia, to which God again said no. Amazing!

Paul's experiences call to mind my decision to try to enter the ministry many years ago. I reached the point when I said, "Here am I, send me," assuming that God would open some wonderful doors of opportunity quickly. I started looking into schools for further training and found one that seemed ideal. After being assured that support to attend would be readily available, we were ready to pack our bags and make our great move of faith. God seemingly slammed the door in my face and broke my heart. For months I was in shock and despair. In my mind, I had said yes to God, and he had said no to me. The book of Job became a familiar friend. I was hurt, but I had to cling desperately to God anyway. That was one of the most difficult times in my life. I did not understand what God was doing, and I struggled valiantly to maintain faith. Some months later, in a matter of hours, a series of events occurred that left my head spinning and my young family of three on the road to another type of school with full (though meager) financial support. Sometimes God is saying yes but with a built-in pause.

Keep On Keeping On

Asia was still on God's mind, and he would send Paul there on the next mission trip where he would establish in Ephesus one of the most effective beachheads ever for the furtherance of the mission. However, the first order of business was for Paul to receive the "Macedonian Call" which would yield fruit from multiple cities. The element of perseverance in faith is tremendously important to God, to us and to the mission. There are weeks, sometimes months (sadly), when I seem to be woefully ineffective in evangelism. But I cling to God. How much does that clinging really count in his eyes? I think probably much more than we think. Oh sure, I believe that if I do not become strong enough and convicted enough to repent and get my evangelistic juices flowing again, I will eventually dry up and die spiritually (even if I remain in the "visible" church). But I still think that our perseverance through the times of challenge and failure makes a significant statement to both God and to the enemy. A very close elder friend once made a statement that I have never forgotten. It went something like this: "To God, probably our best way of saying 'I love you' is simply to persevere year after year with faith, no matter what the circumstances or challenges." I think he was right on target. We have all been impressed with a new convert who is extremely fired up and perhaps initially very effective in evangelism, only to see him fall away in a matter of weeks or months. We may not be as impressed with a brother or sister who has been around fighting the battle for years, but who has never found their way into the spotlight. However, I think God may be much more impressed with that person than we are, for they are clinging to faith even though they do not receive the public recognition that others do.

It is wonderful and essential that highly talented people are reached and raised up as leaders. But it is also wonderful and essential that the family of God include those who are not the five-talent people and who may in fact struggle with weaknesses for a painfully long time. Paul said in 1 Corinthians 12:22 that "those parts of the body that seem to be weaker are indispensable," but we do not generally leave the impression that we feel the same way. To us, the weak seem more of a burden than a blessing. How do we feel about those who struggle just to hang in and not lose faith?

Honestly, I think our theology on producing fruit has at times been shallow in the past, if not totally flawed. Some taught that being evangelistically fruitful within a time period determined by man was inseparably connected with personal righteousness. In other words, if we were not fruitful in evangelism in a certain "man defined" time frame, then sin in our lives must be keeping God from blessing us with conversions. If true, then it would seem logical that the opposite also must be true—that productivity demonstrates that God is pleased to bless our righteousness. However, I know of ministry leaders whose ministries have been very effective while at the same time their personal lives were full of sin (as came to light later). I also know individuals who were very fruitful at the precise time that they were committing and hiding major personal sins. What is the lesson? God can and does use those whose lives are not where they ought to be, but if they are not moved to repentance by his kindness (Romans 2:4), at some point he will expose their sins and deal with them quite directly.

Let me hasten to say that sin in our lives certainly can block fruitfulness and often does. I remember a single brother who was not a highly talented brother, but after becoming a disciple, consistently shared his faith for years—with no visible results. Some might assume that he must have had a hidden sin problem which was prohibiting God from blessing him with fruit. I think he was simply a good-hearted disciple who had a lot of growing to do in his social skills. But he persevered like the persistent widow until a rather amazing thing happened. After those years of ineffectiveness, he saw eight people whom he had personally met and shared with baptized into Christ in one year, as I recall. Now we're all impressed, aren't we? But God was impressed all along, because he appreciates those who refuse to give up and give in, even though for them outward success seems quite elusive.

Because Paul handled with faith the times when God said no, he was guided to some very open doors of opportunity. He also encountered other doors closed for a time. The lesson is that we must keep going and keep persevering, for this kind of faith will keep the movement of God moving, as he ultimately will bring fruit from and into your life.

Keep On Singing (Acts 16:11-40)

11 From Troas we put out to sea and sailed straight for Samothrace, and the next day on to Neapolis. 12 From there we traveled to Philippi, a Roman colony and the leading city of that district of Macedonia. And we stayed there several days.

13 On the Sabbath we went outside the city gate to the river, where we expected to find a place of prayer. We sat down and began to speak to the women who had gathered there. 14 One of those listening was a woman named Lydia, a dealer in purple cloth from the city of Thyatira, who was a worshiper of God. The Lord opened her heart to respond to Paul's message. 15 When she and the members of her household were baptized, she invited us to her home. "If you consider me a believer in the Lord," she said, "come and stay at my house." And she persuaded us.

Down by the Riverside

To this city of rivers and jails Paul and his company came in response to his vision from God. First came the river where the brothers met Lydia and her household. This incident tells a lot about the nature of Philippi. The Jews were scattered all over the empire, and synagogues existed in large numbers of cities. However, it was necessary to have ten Jewish men to have an official synagogue and no synagogue was to be found in Philippi, a Roman colony whose government was modeled quite closely on that of Rome. Philippi was a retirement center for military people. This probably explains the small number of Jews living there. In such places the Jewish residents would congregate on the Sabbath at locations like a river, here designated as "a place of prayer."

Lydia was obviously a rather high-powered business woman, which may explain why she was in Macedonia. In this area the independence of women was notable, for they were given special rights to conduct legal transactions on their own. Again we see Luke's emphasis on the conversion of opinion leaders and one of the reasons why this was vital. She was converted, and through her influence so were those in her household (which most likely would have included those who worked for her). That she possessed a strong personality was evident, for she was able to persuade the apostle Paul to accept her hospitality (Acts 16:15)!

Note in Acts 16:14 that God opened her heart to respond to his message. That does not mean that God opened a heart that was otherwise unreceptive, thus overriding her free will. It does mean that the conversion process is led and blessed by God. Thus, conversion cannot be seen as primarily a human endeavor, but as a divine one. When we begin to look at the success of the mission in humanistic ways, we are going to experience failure, with its accompanying frustration. In such a case, the failure is a failure not of effort, but of faith in God's power. It involves our mind-set and heart-set. Fruitfulness is not dependent on our abilities and efforts, but rather on God using our abilities and efforts. The difference in the two may seem subtle, but everything depends on our understanding it and living by faith, not by sight.

An Earthquake Is Coming!

In the next events in Acts 16, leading up to Paul and Silas being arrested, the Holy Spirit shows us something of Paul's humanness. He went about the city for many days with a possessed slave girl following him and shouting the purpose of his mission before he had an opportunity to begin preaching. Can you imagine how that would try one's patience? Finally, he reached the limits of his patience, and with a troubled spirit, cast out the demonic spirit in her. Her owners were then motivated by a loss of income to do what Paul's preaching had not caused them to do. Negativity and hatred did what they always do—attract people who know little but shout much. After a severe flogging, Paul and Silas were jailed and placed in stocks. Can you imagine how that would try one's faith in God and love for mankind?

Faith may be tested when God says no to our plans, but that test does not compare to the one brought about when God says yes to Satan's plans to wound us! What do you think you would have done if you had been in Paul's place? Most of us would have been very mad at the men who had mistreated us and very questioning toward God (if not indeed angry at him, too). "God, I've tried to do the right things and serve you, and then you stand by and let me get beaten to a pulp and don't even intervene to help!" In similar circumstances, these might well be our sentiments. Not Paul. He seemed not to doubt that God was in complete control of everything that happened and that God had a plan to glorify himself in every situation in which his servants remained faithful. Maybe it was this occasion that molded his theology expressed later in these words:

> And we know that in all things God works for the good of those who love him, who have been called according to his purpose. (Romans 8:28)

Instead of moaning and groaning in misery, these two men of pristine faith sang and prayed joyfully in anticipation of discovering God's plan to bless them. Incredible! It staggers the imagination to think about what they really faced and how they responded. (It also staggers the imagination to think about what God would have been able to do in our lives had we responded to all of our challenges with similar faith.) The statement in Acts 16:25 that "the other prisoners were listening to them" may be one of the book's biggest understatements. I would think that the others were absolutely shocked by such behavior and may have wondered what these missionaries had been drinking! God never overlooks an opportunity to bless such faith, and that blessing did not tarry long. It came, of course, in the form of an earthquake. When the earthquake struck and the cell doors flew open, the jailer awoke in a panic, assuming that all of the prisoners had escaped. That was not a bad assumption, but surprisingly, it turned out to be wrong. Had it been correct, he would have been judged responsible and likely lost his life, as similarly occurred in Acts 12:19. Probably the reason that the prisoners did not escape is that Paul and Silas detained them. Given the highly unusual circumstances surrounding the imprisonment of these two men, the prisoners were evidently awed enough to do what they were asked. More than one miracle occurred that night!

The jailer's question in Acts 16:30, "Sirs, what must I do to be saved?" has generated much discussion. What was he asking? Simply to be saved physically, as some allege? Paul and Silas had been preaching in the city for a number of days by this time, and the jailer may have even heard them or at least heard about them. Further, he was surely aware of what charge had been lodged against his prisoners, and he may have heard them singing and praying earlier. The point is that he knew enough already to be asking about spiritual salvation, even if it was a hazy concept for him.

The answer given by Paul and Silas was as basic as the man's question: "Believe in the Lord Jesus, and you will be saved—you and your household" (Acts 16:31). Amazingly, many in various denominations turn to this passage in an attempt to prove a "faith only" doctrine. If I believed what they do about salvation before baptism, I would avoid this passage at all costs. Multiple reasons are obvious right from the text as to why their doctrine cannot fit into the passage.

First, "believe in the Lord Jesus" is the introduction of Paul's message to a pagan man who needed to start at square one. That statement is Paul's topic sentence, but its meaning must be spelled out before there can be a response.

Second, faith is predicated on hearing and responding to the Word, for Romans 10:17 states that "faith comes from hearing the message, and the message is heard through the word of Christ." Until the jailer and his family had heard the message, they could not believe. Therefore, Acts 16:32 informs us that the next order of business was to preach that message. ("Then they spoke the word of the Lord to him and to all the others in his house.")

Third, after they did hear the message of who Jesus was and what a response to him would involve, they were urgent about baptism. With the dust not yet settled from an earthquake, they were baptized "the same hour of the night." A remarkable statement! What more could one need to understand that baptism into Christ is right at the center of conversion? Delay cannot be tolerated when it comes to baptism. Once I was studying with an older couple who were baptized years before in a church about which I knew nothing. So I asked them if their church ever had baptisms after midnight, to which they replied, "No." Their church had special baptismal services twice annually. From that response, I was sure that they had not been baptized as Scripture teaches, for churches that wait until a "baptismal service" once or twice a year to baptize certainly do not connect it with the forgiveness of sins and initial salvation.

The jailer heard the message, believed it, repented (shown by washing the wounds of the preachers, among other things) and was baptized—all after midnight. When were he and his family saved? They were saved when they, in faith, accepted and responded appropriately to the message. The promise made back in Acts 2:38–39 was indeed for the Jews on Pentecost and for these Gentiles—"all who are far off." After baptism one could rejoice in forgiveness and the gift of the Spirit. Acts 16:34 provides us with a wonderful summary as it describes the entire faith process in these words:

> The jailer brought them into his house and set a meal before them; he was filled with joy because he had come to believe in God—he and his whole family.

The "believe" in verse 31 is defined in verses 32–34, and it quite obviously includes baptism rather than excludes it! Studying specific verses in their own context eliminates most of the errors based on them in the first place.

Covering All the Bases

Acts 16 ends with Paul boldly asserting his rights as a Roman citizen.[1] Read verses 35–40 and you will not fail to see the humor involved. Because of what we know of Paul's character, we must assume that he made his appeal, not to somehow obtain some personal satisfaction or a measure of vengeance, but to protect the disciples left behind. Luke apparently remained there to minister to the new church, which we surmise by the terminology in the last two words of the chapter: "They left." It is commonly accepted by scholars that when Luke was a part of Paul's company, he used the pronoun "we," but when he was not, he used "they." From that inference, we can deduce that Luke joined them at Troas on the second mission trip (Acts 16:10), but stayed in Philippi after they had left. He rejoined Paul's company when Paul came back through Philippi in Acts 20:6, and then was with or around him until Paul was ultimately sent to Rome (Acts 27:1).

The early part of the second missionary journey was, from heaven's standpoint, quite glorious and successful, but from man's vantage point, it was also quite painful. The continuation of this journey follows in the same vein. The enemies of the cross are always plentiful when the message of the cross is preached boldly and consistently. Paul's path of destiny was strewn with the persecution which accompanies a true spiritual revolution. The closer we follow God's ideal plan for our personal destiny, the rockier will be our road. If we are not facing increased resistance from the forces of Satan, we are not fulfilling our destiny as God intends. This is a sobering thought, to be sure, but it is an unavoidable conclusion of the book of Acts (not to mention the teachings of Jesus). If we ever change our thinking and begin to see persecution as an odd thing or a thing to be avoided at all costs, we will have strayed far from God's mission. How closely are you walking in your pathway of divine destiny? Being a serious follower of Jesus is no place for the fainthearted!

Questions for Further Study

1. How did Paul handle "closed doors" to what his plans and wishes were?

2. How do you usually handle God's failures to answer your prayers as you had asked them? Explain.

3. What did you learn about "personal fruitfulness" in this section of the book?

4. In Acts 16:14, it says of Lydia that God "opened her heart." What do you think that means and doesn't mean? Explain.

5. Describe the conversion process of the Philippian jailor, and explain why the "faith only" protestant doctrine will not fit this situation.

Chapter Thirteen

CAMPAIGN TWO
(Part Two)
ACTS 17:1-18:22

A life that is given to the mission of Jesus is never boring. Sometimes it is wildly exhilarating, and sometimes it is painfully heartrending. When the difficult times come, we cannot give up and give in. When the victorious times come, we cannot rest on our laurels. With Paul we must say:

> "But one thing I do: Forgetting what is behind and straining toward what is ahead, I press on toward the goal to win the prize for which God has called me heavenward in Christ Jesus." (Philippians 3:13b–14)

This great warrior of the cross was never thrown off track by victories or defeats.

As Paul began the second missionary journey, he quickly encountered both highs and lows. Life in the kingdom will always be thus. Christians are not without challenges and heartaches, but neither are we without God in the enduring of them. Mountaintop experiences are to be embraced and enjoyed, but so are the valleys. All experiences of those devoted to Christ are under his control and will ultimately figure into his victory plan (Romans 8:28). Paul and his company departed Philippi in a rejoicing mode, but they would continue to face the flaming arrows of the archenemy, Satan. Their response would remain ever the same: the preaching of Jesus Christ and his cross.

Bad Characters, Noble Characters (Acts 17:1-15)

[1]When they had passed through Amphipolis and Apollonia, they came to Thessalonica, where there was a Jewish synagogue. [2]As his

custom was, Paul went into the synagogue, and on three Sabbath days he reasoned with them from the Scriptures, [3]explaining and proving that the Christ had to suffer and rise from the dead. "This Jesus I am proclaiming to you is the Christ," he said. [4]Some of the Jews were persuaded and joined Paul and Silas, as did a large number of God-fearing Greeks and not a few prominent women.

[5]But the Jews were jealous; so they rounded up some bad characters from the marketplace, formed a mob and started a riot in the city.

Having planted the church in Philippi under the most unusual circumstances, Paul and his companions continued on in Macedonia to Thessalonica—an important city then and now. Many different types of people were receptive to Paul's message: some Jews, many God-fearers[1] and prominent women. This was a fairly standard mixture, seen also at Berea, according to Acts 17:12. However, the ones who did not accept his message were much more vindictive in Thessalonica than in Berea, for they started a riot in their home city and then followed Paul and the brothers to Berea to incite the same kind of mob scene there. Those who did accept in Berea will forever be famous for demonstrating what constitutes a noble heart:

> Now the Bereans were of more noble character than the Thessalonians, for they received the message with great eagerness and examined the Scriptures every day to see if what Paul said was true. (Acts 17:11)

They were neither suspicious nor naïve. The purpose of preaching and teaching is not to keep people from doing their own thinking, but to point them to appropriate Scriptures from which they can reach their own heartfelt conclusions. The Bereans understood as well as anybody the process of coming to personal faith with the help of others, and thus they provide a great example for us moderns to follow.

Idols and Wise Fools (Acts 17:16-34)

[16]While Paul was waiting for them in Athens, he was greatly distressed to see that the city was full of idols. [17]So he reasoned in the synagogue with the Jews and the God-fearing Greeks, as well as in the marketplace day by day with those who happened to be there.

[18]A group of Epicurean and Stoic philosophers began to dispute with him. Some of them asked, "What is this babbler trying to say?" Others remarked, "He seems to be advocating foreign gods." They said this because Paul was preaching the good news about Jesus and the resurrection. [19]Then they took him and brought him to a meeting of the Areopagus, where they said to him, "May we know what this new teaching is that you are presenting? [20]You are bringing some strange ideas to our ears, and we want to know what they mean." [21](All the Athenians and the foreigners who lived there spent their time doing nothing but talking about and listening to the latest ideas.)

Seizing the Moment

This text teaches us a lot about the heart of Paul. Try to imagine how he must have felt when he entered the famous city of Athens. He had planted a church in Philippi that would be one very close to his heart, but in the process was beaten severely, jailed and asked to leave town upon his release. Then, in Thessalonica another church was planted, but a riot had erupted in the city, instigated by those who claimed that the Christians had "turned the world upside down" (Acts 17:6, KJV). (As much as we may have developed a fondness for that phrase, the brothers were actually attempting to turn the world "right side up"!)

Under the cover of darkness, Paul's group fled toward Berea, about fifty miles west of Thessalonica. In spite of the gracious initial acceptance they enjoyed there, Paul was soon run out of that town also. Under the direction of some local brothers, he proceeded to Athens without Silas and Timothy. He was likely tired, possibly discouraged and most certainly lonely without his coworkers. But what did he do in such circumstances? What disciples on a mission should always do—he stayed in the battle!

As he looked out on a lost city full of idols, he was distressed![2] What do distressed disciples do? They reason with anyone who will listen, whether the religious people in the synagogue, the pagans in the marketplace or the philosophers in the halls of academia. What distresses you most—personal discomfort and challenges, or the lostness of people? How do we respond to the challenging times in our lives, and how do we respond to the call of the mission when those times strike? This is a continual challenge in the life of a disciple. As I look at the life of Paul, and the life of Jesus whom he imitated, I am amazed and convicted by their single-mindedness and focus. In Paul's situation many of us would be thinking about taking a break for some rest and relaxation (especially we who are in North America or similar cultural settings).

For example, we think that we somehow owe it to ourselves to enjoy regularly scheduled breaks for recreation. I have heard some brothers say, "I play golf or basketball every week because I won't be worth much to anyone unless I do." Now, that is a wonderful bit of psychobabble! Those who embrace false religious doctrine refuse to imitate the example of Jesus in evangelism, discipling or prayer—and we are appalled. But we feel that we can turn right around and refuse to imitate his lifestyle, work ethic and focus—and feel fine about it. Something is wrong. Certainly we all need some "down times" for true "re-creation," but some of us are more like our cultures than Christ when it comes to pouring our lives out and allowing our schedules to reflect it. You are not owed regularly scheduled fun times, for slaves of the cross have no rights. When you do take the opportunity to enjoy some special entertainment, view it as a privilege and not as your right!

Paul's example in Acts helps us answer a basic question about evangelism: Should we focus on building relationships or publicly sharing our faith? The answer is *yes*—on both counts. Some people will be open enough to respond favorably to an invitation to a Bible study or church meeting from an absolute stranger. Others will not be converted until after a relationship has been built, allowing them to see, in an up close and personal way, what being a child of God entails. In both situations the relationship must be built, but with some it will be built while studying the Bible together, and with others it must be built before they begin studying. Any of us who become too sophisticated to share our faith with strangers are wimpy rationalizers, and any of us who become too impatient to build close relationships are uncommitted and unloving. Imitate Jesus and Paul in their approach to evangelism, and no further discussions will be needed.

A Lesson for Pagans

Paul began delivering his more formal lesson to the Areopagus, the famous council of leading philosophers, by trying to establish some common ground. First, he noted their religiosity. The city had idols erected to every known god of that pluralistic society and to at least one unknown god. This last altar had been so designated lest they offend some overlooked deity, but Paul found this presented him with the ideal opportunity to declare the true God, the Creator of heaven and earth. Since the Athenians were enamored with man-made gods of idolatry, Paul stressed that God was in no way dependent on man for anything. He created man and even determined the boundaries within which man settled.

Second, he declared that all mankind has much in common via our ancestry. In the intellectual and perhaps snobbish setting of the Areopagus, the statement that all men came from one prototype, Adam, may have convicted their prejudicial hearts. It is almost startling to realize that all races came out of Noah's ark together. Our differences are not nearly as notable as our similarities, but this commonality will never be accepted and appreciated outside as it is within God's kingdom. Nationality, skin color and cultural variations are a source of mistrust and disunity in the world, but in the kingdom they are a source of rich diversity within one unified family.

Third, as Paul proceeded with his speech, he quoted two heathen poets, Aratus and Cleanthes, to help his listeners accept his point about God as Creator. Paul was a well-educated man in the secular and sacred realms, and he did not hesitate to use any of his knowledge to help persuade people of the truth. In 1 Corinthians 15:32, he quoted another heathen poet, Menander, and in Titus 1:12, yet another—Epimenides. One of the oldest discussions in the history of Christendom has been over the validity of utilizing non-biblical sources or philosophies which appear to be truthful and beneficial. Those who approve of such usage believe that all truth is from God, including areas outside the scope of the Bible. For example, who could argue with the fact that the established truths of science have been helpful to man in many ways?

But what about psychology and psychiatry—how do they fit in with discipleship and the spiritual life? Some of us seem tentative about using principles from these areas, and while these fields can be esteemed too highly and are prone to misuse, I think there are benefits to be gained by those who are well-grounded in the word of God. All philosophies outside the Bible must be weighed by the Bible, but behavioral and educational principles discovered by man can have valid applications. It is, as always, a question of balance and perspective. Paul used outside sources to build trust in Scripture, not to exalt the sources themselves.

After Paul had established common ground with the Athenians through careful reasoning, he proceeded to preach the same basics that he preached to those who were more biblically informed: He condemned their sins of idolatry and warned them that failure to repent would not be countenanced by God. Further, they would have to face God on the Judgment Day, a fact guaranteed by the resurrection of Jesus from the dead. Paul was quite aware of how this message would fall on the ears of those steeped in philosophical thinking, but he was simply unashamed of the gospel. The truth is the truth is the truth, no matter the inclination of the audience. And this audience was inclined to sneer at the thought of a bodily resurrection, for to them death forever freed the spirit from its captivity in a material body and world. To modern ears, the old truths of the Bible may seem outmoded and archaic, but these same truths will arise to judge those who yet sneer in their educated foolishness. Never be ashamed of the basics of the message!

Paul's audience had mixed reactions to his sermon about sin, righteousness and judgment. Some sneered, some said "maybe later," and a few accepted the truths he presented. One of the latter was Dionysius, a member of this esteemed body of philosophers, and another was Damaris, no doubt a woman who would have been among those called elsewhere "prominent" or "of high standing." Again Luke reminds us of the absolute necessity of reaching opinion leaders in establishing and building churches. Like Paul, we must avoid remaining within our comfort zones in evangelizing. It is more threatening to share with the high-powered, but it is essential, especially for leaders, who must always be laboring to reproduce themselves. All of us will naturally tend to reach out to people less talented than ourselves, but we must plan to reach people with more talents than we have.

Keep On Preaching (Acts 18:1-22)

[1]After this, Paul left Athens and went to Corinth. [2]There he met a Jew named Aquila, a native of Pontus, who had recently come from Italy with his wife Priscilla, because Claudius had ordered all the Jews to leave Rome. Paul went to see them, [3]and because he was a tentmaker as they were, he stayed and worked with them. [4]Every Sabbath he reasoned in the synagogue, trying to persuade Jews and Greeks.

[5]When Silas and Timothy came from Macedonia, Paul devoted himself exclusively to preaching, testifying to the Jews that Jesus was the Christ. [6]But when the Jews opposed Paul and became abusive, he shook out his clothes in protest and said to them, "Your blood be on your own heads! I am clear of my responsibility. From now on I will go to the Gentiles."

[7]Then Paul left the synagogue and went next door to the house of Titius Justus, a worshiper of God. [8]Crispus, the synagogue ruler, and his entire household believed in the Lord; and many of the Corinthians who heard him believed and were baptized.

[9]One night the Lord spoke to Paul in a vision: "Do not be afraid; keep on speaking, do not be silent. [10]For I am with you, and no one is going to attack and harm you, because I have many people in this city."

Movers and Shakers!

Aquila and Priscilla are introduced in Acts 18 for the first time and are mentioned in six other passages.[3] Five of the seven times their names appear, Priscilla is mentioned first. It is likely that she was the more dominant personality of the two—perhaps a "prominent" woman in a somewhat different sense. This powerful couple evidently was converted in Rome but came to Corinth when Jews were banished by the Roman emperor. Suetonius, a Roman historian, spoke of tumults among Jews instigated by one "Chrestus" (a reference to Christ, evidently). Hence, the Christian Jews (and perhaps some who were just Christians) along with those who were involved in the uprisings were apparently among those expelled by Claudius. (The Romans had little ability to distinguish Christians from Jews in the earlier days of the movement.)

Next we see Aquila and his wife in Ephesus, where they were brought and left to minister by Paul (Acts 18:19). It was at this time that they met and influenced the eloquent preacher, Apollos. Still later we find them in Rome (Romans 16:3) and yet again in Ephesus (2 Timothy 4:19). Although they were tentmakers by trade, they were stellar examples of those who were first of all disciples of Jesus—willing to go anywhere, do anything and give up everything. Leaders in the early church were indeed movement leaders—they moved often and led a movement! Priscilla and Aquila are examples of leaders who were not supported by the church. From them we must learn a valuable lesson about the absence of a clergy/laity system in the early church. One of the biggest threats to the success of God's Cause is the development of such a system—a system we must oppose most deliberately.

Clergy and Laity?

The clergy/laity concept has been created in religion generally, and its development can be traced to a number of sources. One point that could help us avoid the concept better is tied to the terminology we use in distinguishing those on the church ministry staff from those who are not. Specifically, the phraseology "full-time ministry" is likely the worst offender along these lines. Everyone who is a true disciple is (or should be) in the full-time ministry. That is how people are going to be converted from disciples' spheres of influence: in classrooms, workplaces, grocery stores, neighborhoods or wherever. Certainly the Bible does speak of different types of ministry, such as that of the apostles (Galatians 2:8), but it also speaks of all of us having the "ministry of reconciliation" (2 Corinthians 5:18). And we often preach that we must be disciples seven days a week and twenty-four hours a day. Is that not full-time?

Perhaps you are asking, "Does it really matter?" Does it matter how we use the term "Christian" or "disciple" or "church" or "kingdom"? The problem with some of our terminology is that it can contribute to an unhealthy "us and them" mind-set rather than a team mind-set, and it can discourage those not on staff from feeling the importance that all disciples who share the same mission should feel. No one in the kingdom should see themselves as second-class citizens, for each has their ministry from Christ. The specifics of those ministries differ, but all are from God whether a disciple is on staff or not. Actually, some of my greatest heroes in the church are among those not on staff: the single moms, those with nonmember spouses, the leaders of small groups (who often have many other responsibilities to fulfill along with this leadership) and those with severe physical challenges.

I do not want any disciples to feel inferior to me before God because of not being on staff. (Actually, I am not on staff either, choosing to support myself at this stage of life through a teaching ministry.) I have a specific role, which happens to be fairly high profile and often up-front. In my teacher's role, for example, I am fulfilling my specific ministry, but when I step down from the teacher's platform, I then am simply one of the brothers on level ground at the foot of the cross with all other brothers and sisters. I am no more special to God than they are, even though my role may allow me to have more visible impact than many others. Only on the Day of Judgment will we totally understand the impact of anyone's life, whether it was quite visible or relatively invisible during their earthly sojourn. None of this means that the ministry staff is not highly important and absolutely essential to the accomplishment of the mission. But it does mean that we must work to eradicate all vestiges of a clergy/laity system and the feelings and attitudes which ultimately create it. I appreciate very much the appreciation expressed to me for trying to fulfill my ministry, but I want all disciples to feel appreciated similarly. And that will not take place without the forethought and planning of all leaders, whether on staff or not.

Fear and Faith

Back to Acts 18, we come to something some of us would not have expected in the life of Paul: fear. In verses 7–8, we are impressed with the conversion of two more opinion leaders, Titius Justus and Crispus, followed by the conversion of many of the Corinthians. Paul was one of the most remarkable leaders in the early church, constantly driven by his convictions and love for the lost. It is almost difficult to imagine him being afraid of anything. But in God's honest description of his heroes, Paul is described as someone who became low in both faith and courage. And Paul vulnerably described this Corinthian situation in these words: "I came to you in weakness and fear, and with much trembling" (1 Corinthians 2:3). He was a super human, but not superhuman. He had his doubts and down times with which to contend, a fact that should encourage us. God told him to be unafraid and to keep on speaking (not to start speaking) because Corinth had people in it with open hearts.

God always has people with open hearts who will listen to those who persevere in sharing his message. When my faith weakens, I remember the principle of Acts 18 and start envisioning open people in my area. In a town of thousands there must be someone who has a heart for God and is awaiting my sharing. I like to think that every "no" moves me closer to a "yes." It is never a question of whether there are open people; it is only an issue of which ones are open and when God will lead my path to intersect theirs. Can you not imagine one person who is open in your town or city this year? Paul's example teaches us that success at one point does not preclude fear and failure at another, but if we follow him by not giving in to those fears, God will stand by us and lead us to fruitful labor. Courage is not the lack of fear, but rather the refusal to be controlled by it. The spiritual mission of which we are a part will only be advanced by humans of the ordinary kind, who in Christ accomplish extraordinary things. He will sustain us through all challenges, real or imagined, and will bless us with the victory for which he longs more than we do.

Questions for Further Study

1. What can we do in studying with others to encourage the attitudes expressed in Acts 17:11 by the Bereans?

2. What were the emotional and intellectual obstacles that Paul had to overcome in evangelizing in Athens—and how did he overcome them?

3. What are the positives and negatives offered the Bible believer by various philosophies of men?

4. What are the insights you gained about the "clergy/laity" challenges from the section "Keep on Preaching" (covering Acts 18:1–22)? What are your own insights about this issue?

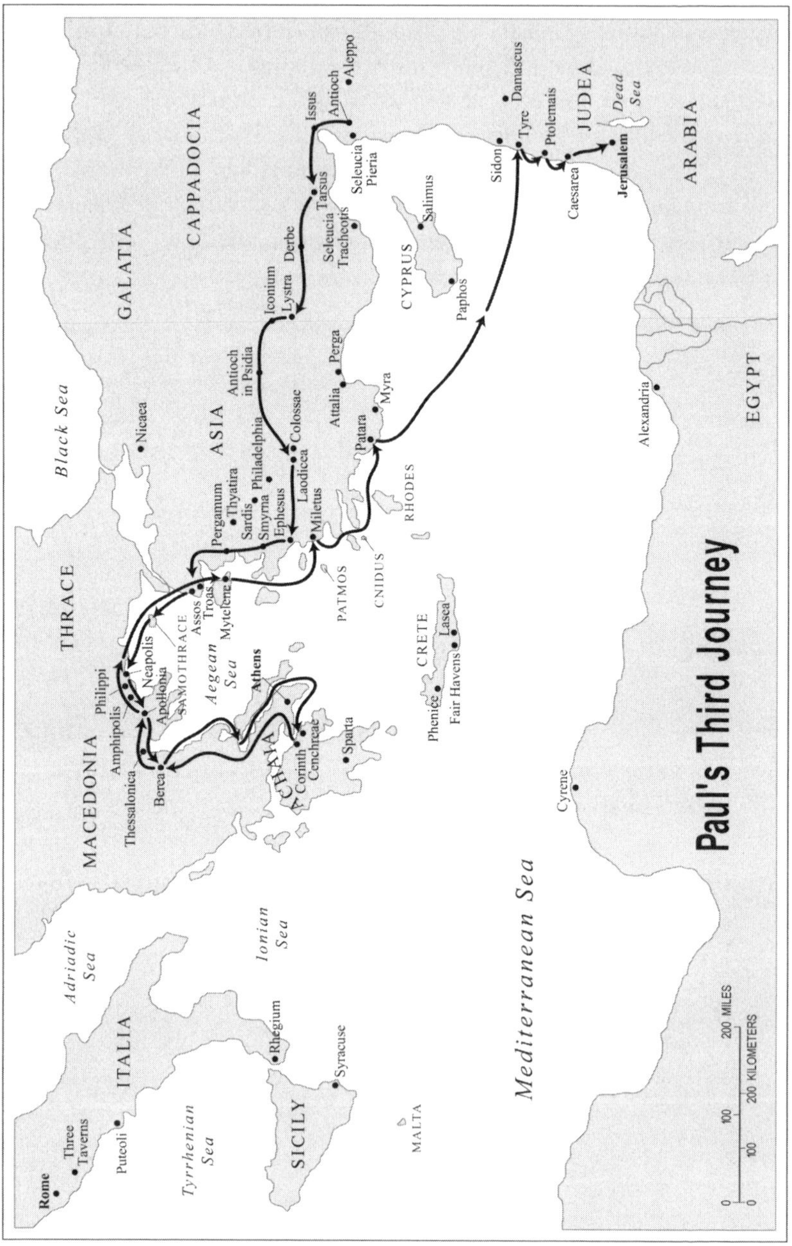
Paul's Third Journey
Black Sea
THRACE
MACEDONIA
GALATIA
CAPPADOCIA
ASIA
ACHAIA
ITALIA
SICILY
CYPRUS
CRETE
RHODES
PATMOS
CNIDUS
SAMOTHRACE
MALTA
JUDEA
ARABIA
EGYPT
Adriadic Sea
Ionian Sea
Tyrrhenian Sea
Aegean Sea
Mediterranean Sea
Dead Sea
Rome
Three Taverns
Puteoli
Rhegium
Syracuse
Thessalonica
Berea
Amphipolis
Philippi
Apollonia
Neapolis
Athens
Corinth
Cenchreae
Sparta
Assos
Troas
Mytelene
Pergamum
Thyatira
Sardis
Smyrna
Philadelphia
Ephesus
Laodicea
Colossae
Miletus
Nicaea
Antioch in Psidia
Iconium
Lystra
Derbe
Tarsus
Issus
Antioch
Aleppo
Seleucia Pieria
Seleucia Tracheotis
Attalia
Perga
Patara
Myra
Salimus
Paphos
Sidon
Tyre
Damascus
Ptolemais
Caesarea
Jerusalem
Alexandria
Cyrene
Pheniće
Fair Havens
Lasea
0 100 200 MILES
0 100 200 KILOMETERS

Chapter Fourteen

Campaign Three

Acts 18:23-21:16

Paul, like Jesus, kept the balance between the two main aspects of disciple making: converting and maturing. He was always on a quest to convert as many as possible, but he was equally concerned about those new converts being well-grounded in the faith. In this third mission campaign these two concerns shine through clearly. He began the campaign by going back to areas with established churches, but quickly went on to the province of Asia where he was previously forbidden by the Spirit to go. Arriving in Ephesus, he planted the church by teaching and baptizing a dozen "disciples." There he labored for two years, establishing a pillar church from which all Asia would ultimately hear the message. His shepherding instinct was again shown upon his return, as he preached to the church in Troas and to the Ephesian elders at Miletus.

The true shepherd must be concerned for the sheep already in the fold, as well as for those not yet in the fold (John 10:14–16). No disciple, regardless of specific role, can allow himself to specialize either in gaining initial conversions or in maturing those converted. Jesus did not, Paul did not, and neither can we, for our task is never simply to help people get saved. Unless and until new disciples make other disciples, multiplication has not occurred and the Great Commission is not being fulfilled. The multiplication process in discipling is well-described in 2 Timothy 2:2:

> And the things you have heard me say in the presence of many witnesses entrust to reliable men who will also be qualified to teach others.

Note the four spiritual generations involved here, beginning with Paul, then Timothy, then reliable men and finally, others. Converting someone is never the ultimate goal of a disciple. The goal is to convert and train them to convert and train others so that the chain will continue. When discipling is passed down through several generations, we can be assured that the discipleship concept is understood and will continue in the pattern Jesus established.

A Humble Leader (Acts 18:23-28)

23After spending some time in Antioch, Paul set out from there and traveled from place to place throughout the region of Galatia and Phrygia, strengthening all the disciples.

24Meanwhile a Jew named Apollos, a native of Alexandria, came to Ephesus. He was a learned man, with a thorough knowledge of the Scriptures. 25He had been instructed in the way of the Lord, and he spoke with great fervor and taught about Jesus accurately, though he knew only the baptism of John. 26He began to speak boldly in the synagogue. When Priscilla and Aquila heard him, they invited him to their home and explained to him the way of God more adequately.

If the conversion of opinion leaders was—and is—important, the conversion of religious opinion leaders was even more pivotal in the spread of the gospel. In Acts 4 Luke informs us that Barnabas was a Levite. In Acts 6:7 we read about a large number of priests being obedient to the gospel. Acts 9 describes the conversion of a most influential rabbi, Saul of Tarsus. In Acts 18:8 we find mention of Crispus, a synagogue ruler, being converted. Acts 18:23–28 gives us more in-depth insight about how such conversions came about.

Religious leaders were not, and are not, easy to convert. Their biblical knowledge has been gained with a traditional point of reference, and because they do know a lot, they do not easily capitulate to another view. Additionally, they have a reputation to protect and probably a paying job as well. Yet when converted, they are able to provide influence through their leadership experience that often proves invaluable. Certainly this was true in the case of Apollos. While Apollos may not have been in need of conversion, he was in need of correction.[1] What can we learn from Priscilla and Aquila about how to approach educated and talented leaders who still have some things to learn?

One, they were not confrontational in their approach. They realized, while hearing Apollos speak, that he was ignorant in some key areas, yet they took him into the privacy of their home to discuss these areas. Two, they apparently focused on his strengths and not on his limitations. Certainly, this is what Luke did as he penned the passage. His general education was noted, along with his biblical training and the considerable knowledge produced by it. He was characterized by fervor and boldness, and taught many things about Jesus accurately. The inclusion of his many positive points could hardly have been coincidental, and we must not miss the reason for this inclusion.

In studying with religious people who have a good deal of knowledge, we will nearly always uncover an equal amount of spiritual pride. This can cause us to focus on this unsavory attitude to the point that we fail to grant them due credit for the many things they may understand and practice correctly. Then they will be left with this commonly expressed feeling: "Do you mean to say that I am still lost and that all of my knowledge and experience means nothing?" To answer that entire query affirmatively is not only insensitive, it is just plain stupid. Even if they are not right with God, the things they know and have done can be a part of the process of conversion that God is now blessing. Cornelius was religious, but unsaved, and God commended him for his prayer life and his financial contributions. In fact, he gave those as reasons for the direct divine intervention in his life. Paul (as Saul) was not only unsaved—he was the worst persecutor in the early days of the church. Yet, God chose him and used his background training in rabbinic Judaism to lead the new movement through the theological minefield of Jew/Gentile relationships. What he knew coming into the kingdom may have been off base in some very important ways, but once sanctified and "fumigated" by the Spirit, it was unequaled in value except by the inspired message itself.

While it is true that religious leaders may have much pride to overcome, patiently leading them out of it will usually prove much more effective than trying to rebuke them out of it. Having been converted from this category and then helping convert several others in this category, I know that our patience will be tested beyond our human ability to remain calm and loving. But with the Spirit's help, we can put the words of the following key passage into practice, thus greatly enhancing our chances of being a vessel used by God to reach religious leaders:

> Don't have anything to do with foolish and stupid arguments, because you know they produce quarrels. And the Lord's servant must not quarrel; instead, he must be kind to everyone, able to teach, not resentful. Those who oppose him he must gently instruct, in the hope that God will grant them repentance leading them to a knowledge of the truth, and that they will come to their senses and escape from the trap of the devil, who has taken them captive to do his will. (2 Timothy 2:23–26)

Those of us who were spiritual leaders in other churches before finding greater truth were most likely led carefully and patiently out of the labyrinth of denominational doctrines through which we viewed the world. I know I was. Therefore, we are going to have to allow others with whom we are working the same opportunity and the time it requires. One way our pride manifests itself is in expecting others to accept our present conclusions very quickly, even though it may have taken us a long time to accept them. If we are to win those like Apollos in our day, we are going to have to avoid this pitfall and imitate Aquila and Priscilla closely. They had been well-trained by Paul, whose own patience was predicated on his realization of how sinful he had been before conversion. Remember whence you have come, and help those like you once were.

Ephesus: Pillar Church Three (Acts 19:1-41)

[8]Paul entered the synagogue and spoke boldly there for three months, arguing persuasively about the kingdom of God. [9]But some of them became obstinate; they refused to believe and publicly maligned the Way. So Paul left them. He took the disciples with him and had discussions daily in the lecture hall of Tyrannus. [10]This went on for two years, so that all the Jews and Greeks who lived in the province of Asia heard the word of the Lord.

Baptizing "Disciples"

The dozen disciples Paul met soon after his arrival in Ephesus may well have been taught earlier by Apollos. Since his own understanding of baptism into Christ was deficient, his discipling of them was likewise deficient. Even though they had made the decision to be disciples, they had not received the Holy Spirit. This caused Paul to realize their baptism was not valid. However, they showed their disciples' hearts by readily being baptized in the name of the Lord Jesus. Technically speaking, one can learn about what it is to be a disciple and put what one has learned into practice before being baptized into Christ.

Many leaders, including myself, have done exactly that, which means that we were disciples before being saved. John 4:1–2 in speaking of baptizing disciples reflects that very situation. Other people learn what it is to be a disciple and make a decision to be one shortly before getting baptized. Many conversions in Acts reflect this sequence. In the former case, baptism does not coincide with becoming a disciple (although it does with becoming a saved disciple), whereas in the latter case it does.

With this distinction in mind, we are in a better position to avoid being confused and creating confusion. In one sense it is quite accurate to say that we should baptize only disciples, meaning those that make the decision to live as disciples. In another sense, it can be said that the process of becoming a disciple is parallel with becoming a Christian and being saved. Baptized disciples are the only ones who are saved. That is why Paul was so urgent about teaching and baptizing these good-hearted people that he found in Ephesus.

Leadership, Authority and Unity

From Acts 19 and Paul's work in Ephesus, several lessons about church plantings are obvious. The first is that churches in large cities of influence must become pillar churches from which the gospel radiates to other regional cities. Initially, it was Jerusalem, then Antioch of Syria, then Ephesus and later, Rome. We can also safely assume that churches were planted out of cities like Corinth as well.

A second lesson is that one church per city was the singular example. The New Testament knows nothing of a multiplicity of churches in any one city. Of course, the one church in a city may have met in smaller groups like house churches (Romans 16:5, 1 Corinthians 16:19, Colossians 4:15), but they were under one united leadership in each city, as evidenced in Acts 15:1-4, 22 (Jerusalem); Acts 13:1-3 (Antioch); 20:17 (Ephesus) and Titus 1:5. Unity of heart and mission is impossible unless we adhere to this pattern we see in the early church.

Another lesson is that the key leader in a church planting raised up other leaders who were sent out to plant congregations in other towns and cities. They subsequently followed that leader's example and became trainers and senders themselves to yet smaller cities in the area. The progression was a very natural one. Strong leaders raise up other strong leaders, and such are destined to exert a great influence over large numbers of people. God has always called strong leaders to lead his people in this manner. It should be noted that Paul gave his key leaders responsibility (with its necessary accompanying authority) over fairly large segments of the world—Timothy in Asia and Titus in Crete, and others, presumably, in other areas. Titus was to appoint elders in every town, and having done this, he did not then disappear from their sight. He must have maintained an ongoing relationship with these churches. Paul also maintained relationships with churches he planted, and his key men surely followed the same basic plan.

Leadership and authority issues cannot be settled without both the Bible and common sense, but if we use both, key developments in the church today can be seen to be entirely appropriate. Actually, the issue is primarily a matter of influence. A key leader, in the first or twenty-first century, always influences leaders who themselves become key leaders. The early leaders will find that their leadership influences a number of spiritual generations and levels of leadership as time passes and the church spreads. It would be both unnatural and unspiritual for later leaders not to seek input and direction from those earlier ones who had discipled and trained them as leaders.

It should not be assumed that leaders with continuing influence over other leaders somehow have desires to be popes or dictators. But great leaders always surround themselves with other strong leaders, men of strong personality and strong opinions, not "yes men." They develop close personal relationships with these men and lead out of those relationships. Two-way communication is inherent. They always allow these men to lead the churches which are now under their care and oversight. But they still give input, which is obviously limited by the size of the ministry territory and the distances involved.

We cannot evangelize the world without a plan, and we cannot carry out the plan without organization. (That organization must always be within a biblical framework and follow biblical principles even though time and circumstances may affect the exact form that organization takes.) If churches have no plan (and this describes the majority in the religious world), they thus need no organization to carry out a "nonplan"! If the task of evangelizing the world was left up to them, the world would die without having heard the Good News. We must stick to the plan that is working, both because it is working and because it is an imitation of the approach of the early church.

Pretending or Repenting?

The account of the sons of Sceva in Acts 19:13–16 is one of the most humorous in the Bible. (Read it carefully.) But why is it included? Perhaps for several reasons. One may be to show that religious people doing religious things are not necessarily right with God. The seven used spiritual phraseology and acted the part of exorcists—but they were charlatans. Paul described similar men with these blunt terms:

> For such men are false apostles, deceitful workmen, masquerading as apostles of Christ. And no wonder, for Satan himself masquerades as an angel of light. It is not surprising, then, if his servants masquerade as servants of righteousness. Their end will be what their actions deserve. (2 Corinthians 11:13–15)

Another lesson in the broader context shows the close connection between religion and finances. These seven men were not likely doing what they were doing for free. Given their deceitful motives, they had financial intent attached to their activities. Then in Acts 19:17–20, the repentant new disciples burned up sorcery scrolls worth 50,000 days' wages. Finally, in Acts 19:23–41, Demetrius the silversmith instigated a riot over the temple of Artemis and its attendant commercial ventures. Religion was, and is, big business. Those seeking a profit from it are numerous, deceitful and influential. If their mission cannot be shown to be the same as that of Christ—and its effects the same as that of the early church—beware!

A third lesson involves the inducement to, and the power of, repentance. The wording of Acts 19:18–19 indicates that some disciples (we would assume newer disciples) were very convicted by what happened to Sceva's sons and repented more deeply than they had previously. Repentance is tied to knowledge, for we can only repent of what we know to be wrong. In order to come to the point of baptism we must repent (Acts 2:38), which means that we change our minds about sinning, leading to a change of behavior. However, it is impossible to know everything that is wrong before baptism, and equally impossible to know everything that is right to be practiced. The basics we must know, but the rest we learn as we are trained (Matthew 28:19–20). Repentance before baptism is a decision to follow all that we know and to immediately follow all that we learn as our training unfolds. It is, in that sense, a onetime decision that affects all future decisions to be righteous and follow Jesus.

The power of repentance in this passage was remarkable, prompting much financial sacrifice on the part of disciples and much subsequent evangelistic fruit (Acts 19:20). Changed lives attract the attention of all who see them. For this reason, Jesus told the healed demoniac, "Go home to your family and tell them how much the Lord has done for you, and how he has had mercy on you" (Mark 5:19). Fruitfulness is inseparably connected to life change. As those who know us observe the changes, they are utterly amazed by the power of the message we preach because they see it working. Conversely, if they are not seeing change, they are not favorably impressed. Therefore, for disciples to be consistently effective in making disciples, they must be growing spiritually in an observable way. (Consider carefully the wording of 2 Peter 1:5–9 in this vein.)

Some of us who have been around longer appear to be too easily satisfied with our level of spirituality. It is hopefully true that we have overcome many wrong behaviors, but it is also true that our attitudes have a distance to go, since Jesus is our model. And it is likewise true that our zeal and effectiveness levels are a far cry from his. Thus, we must be much more diligent about personal growth and the repentance which prompts it, for unless those who know us best see these changes clearly, they will not be inspired to make the changes they need to be making. Repentance on the part of Christians is a magnet to draw others in, while a lack of repentance is a repellent. Let's "burn our scrolls" and show that living as a vessel for Jesus is the most consuming quest in our hearts and lives!

Preaching to Eutychus and to Elders (Acts 20:1-38)

[7]On the first day of the week we came together to break bread. Paul spoke to the people and, because he intended to leave the next day, kept on talking until midnight. [8]There were many lamps in the upstairs room where we were meeting. [9]Seated in a window was a young man named Eutychus, who was sinking into a deep sleep as Paul talked on and on. When he was sound asleep, he fell to the ground

> from the third story and was picked up dead. [10]Paul went down, threw himself on the young man and put his arms around him. "Don't be alarmed," he said. "He's alive!" [11]Then he went upstairs again and broke bread and ate. After talking until daylight, he left. [12]The people took the young man home alive and were greatly comforted....
>
> [17]From Miletus, Paul sent to Ephesus for the elders of the church. [18]When they arrived, he said to them: "You know how I lived the whole time I was with you, from the first day I came into the province of Asia. [19]I served the Lord with great humility and with tears, although I was severely tested by the plots of the Jews. [20]You know that I have not hesitated to preach anything that would be helpful to you but have taught you publicly and from house to house."

Preaching and Communion in Troas?

After arriving in Troas, Paul and his company remained there for seven days, assumedly in order to meet with the church during its regular Sunday service. From this passage, we learn that they met on the first day of the week and that a major reason for meeting was to observe the Lord's Supper. The special day of meeting under the Mosaic period was on the seventh day, our Saturday, but the first day of the week superseded it in the new covenant.[2]

Both early church history and 1 Corinthians 11 indicate that communion was originally observed in the context of the Agape Meal (the Love Feast). This combination is not surprising, since Jesus instituted this special memorial meal at the Passover meal with his disciples. Just as the Passover commemorated deliverance from the bondage of slavery in Egypt, the Lord's Supper commemorates our deliverance from the bondage of slavery to sin.

In the New Testament the communion is normally believed to be in view when "breaking bread" is mentioned without accompanying details. Acts 20:11 evidently refers to ordinary eating, for details are included. Additionally, the emphasis in this verse is on what Paul did, not the church (although they likely joined him). Acts 2:42 and 2:46 contain a parallel statement, in which the communion is first mentioned, followed by a later reference to eating an ordinary meal.

The connection of communion to a fellowship meal teaches us a very valuable lesson. Fellowship with God and with other Christians is inseparable. We cannot be united with him without being united with our brothers and sisters. As Paul was correcting abuses of the

Lord's Supper in the Corinthian church, he had this to say:

> For anyone who eats and drinks without recognizing the body of the Lord eats and drinks judgment on himself. (1 Corinthians 11:29)

In this context, the "body" is the church. The brothers in Corinth were not viewing and treating each other with mutual love and respect, which made their communion a travesty. (See 1 Corinthians 11:17–34 to get the flavor of the broader context of the abuses.) The same principle was addressed by Jesus in Matthew 5:23–24:

> "Therefore, if you are offering your gift at the altar and there remember that your brother has something against you, leave your gift there in front of the altar. First go and be reconciled to your brother; then come and offer your gift."

John addressed the same basic issue in 1 John 4:20 with succinct bluntness:

> If anyone says, "I love God," yet hates his brother, he is a liar. For anyone who does not love his brother, whom he has seen, cannot love God, whom he has not seen.

Thus, the message to us must be that we cannot countenance the least amount of disunity among ourselves, even if it is hidden deep in one's heart and kept secret from all but God and oneself. A spiritual principle is at work here: God cannot bless us if we are like the world in harboring bitter roots. No amount of rationalization will cover up bad attitudes before God. As Hebrews 12:15 puts it: "See to it that no one misses the grace of God and that no bitter root grows up to cause trouble and defile many."

From the passage in 1 Corinthians 11, we learn that the Lord's Supper points backward to the time of Christ's sacrifice; forward to his coming again; inward to the self-examination of our heart; and outward to others as we proclaim his death. It is a beautiful connection with his death and all the purposes of that death. And as with all highly important doctrines, which tie us spiritually to that death, Satan works hard to misdirect and pollute our understanding and practice. Communion, from the beginning of the early church, was a weekly observance on the first day of the week. In that sense, it was "common," but it cannot be common in the sense of becoming virtually a meaningless ritual. Like baptism, it provides us with a spiritual connection to the death of Christ, as it ties us together with him and with one another. With that "otherworldly" type of unity, let us proclaim his death and the almost unbelievable impact it has made on his church—complete unity of heart and soul.

Preaching and Remembering in Miletus

Paul's sermon to the Ephesian elders is one of the more memorable in the book of Acts. His great convictions for truth and his great heart for people are combined here in rare form, even for Paul. If the book of 2 Corinthians is the letter in which Paul pulls back the curtain most clearly on his inner life, this portion of Acts 20, recorded by Luke, is the sermon in which he does the same. His urgent appeal to them reveals much about his work ethic, his attitudes and his teaching.

First, let's look at his astounding work ethic. His claim to have worked harder than others (1 Corinthians 15:10, 2 Corinthians 11:23) was no idle claim. His sermon in Acts 20 opened with the comment in verse 18 that his labor of love with them began on the day of his arrival and extended through the entire time he was in Ephesus (three years, v31). He continued to serve in spite of being severely tested by the plots of the Jews (v19). What he almost summarily stated here must have been far more intense than we realize. If he became a target of Jewish opposition in a matter of days in locations that he visited only briefly, we can only imagine what the opposition must have been like when they had three years to take aim.

Further, his work ethic moved him to teach publicly and from house to house (v20). As he looked to the future, he had been assured by the Holy Spirit that prison and hardships faced him in every city through which he passed (v23). His consuming concern was simply that he finish the race and complete the God-given task assigned him (v24). For three years, he never stopped warning the leaders individually day and night (v31). Finally, in a "secular" job, he earned money for himself, his companions and the weak (vv34–35). Dare any of us complain about how difficult our role is in the kingdom of God as we compare ourselves with Paul?

Second, consider Paul's attitudes underlying his hard work. He demonstrated great humility, laced with tears (v19). He felt compelled to do anything the Lord wanted him to in order to fulfill his ministry (v22). He was self-denied to the extent that he could honestly claim that his life meant nothing to him (v24). His great concern for the spiritual welfare of his converts moved him to tears again and again (vv19, 31, 37). His total absorption in the mission of Christ left him with no interest in material possessions (v33).

David Bercot's book, *Will the Real Heretics Please Stand Up?*, contains a disturbing element to North American disciples in his treatment of second-century Christianity: the radical renunciation of materialism, especially on the part of leaders.[3] I will hazard one strong prediction in this arena: If Christianity is to flourish in the coming years and continue being blessed by God with rapid, multiplying growth, all disciples (especially leaders) must imitate Jesus and the apostles far more closely in our lifestyles, materialistically speaking. I will not comment further, except to say that this observation may prove to be one of the most important made in the book. I would, however, urge you to read carefully Douglas Jacoby's comments on this subject in "The Spirit of the West: The Curse of Consumerism" in his book *The Spirit*.[4]

Third, look at the teaching approach of Paul. He had no hesitation in laying out the most challenging truths needed by the disciples (vv20, 27). Whatever the tendencies of his sinful nature, people-pleasing and conflict avoidance were not allowed into his life. Truth removes Satan's shackles, while sentimentality cinches them up even tighter. Friends don't let friends live unspiritual lives! Verse 20 informs us that Paul preached publicly and from house to house ("in season and out of season," 2 Timothy 4:2). The School of Tyrannus may have been his lecture hall (Acts 19:9), but the world was his classroom.

As he taught, he omitted no subject that might be helpful. He preached the whole will of God, including repentance and faith in his Son (vv20–21, 27). By such preaching, he declared himself free from the blood of all men (v26). The laws in some US states recognize the principle that having the opportunity and the ability to help others in a life-threatening situation makes us responsible for trying to bring them to safety. Paul recognized the validity of a spiritual application of the same principle. The prophet Ezekiel expressed it in these sobering words:

> "Son of man, I have made you a watchman for the house of Israel; so hear the word I speak and give them warning from me. When I say to the wicked, 'O wicked man, you will surely die,' and you do not speak out to dissuade him from his ways, that wicked man will die for his sin, and I will hold you accountable for his blood. But if you do warn the wicked man to turn from his ways and he does not do so, he will die for his sin, but you will have saved yourself." (Ezekiel 33:7–9)

We are not only our brother's keeper (in Christ) via discipleship; we are our brother's keeper (in Adam) via evangelism. Make no mistake about it: This teaching is not relegated to an OT setting in a "harsh" age. It is part and parcel of our mission for Jesus. When we have opportunity to share him with others, it is a matter of obligation. In Romans 1:14–15, Paul clearly said that he was "obligated both to Greeks and non-Greeks, both to the wise and the foolish," which made him eager to preach the gospel to them. In simple terms, before we share with those in our sphere of contact and influence, the issue is between God and us. After we share, it is between God and them.

Continuing to look at Paul's teaching, we find that he showed no favoritism toward his kinsmen Jews or the Gentiles of his mission assignment (v21). All had sin-stained, but highly precious, souls to be salvaged. As he pursued the salvation of those souls, his emphasis was on the task of testifying to the gospel of God's grace (v24). The gospel was based on what God has done for us in Christ (1 Corinthians 15:1–4), and properly preached, it will motivate us to do more than any other type of motivation will (1 Corinthians 15:10). To state the principle once more, our emphasis must be more on who God is and what he has done than on our response—as important as our response is. It is a matter of lasting motivation. Paul's letters are full of teachings about the greatness of God, Christ and the Spirit for a reason. If we "get" God, he gets us. Read Ephesians and Colossians with this principle in mind, and examine your emphases in teaching in light of his.

Paul's teaching was solidly biblically based, for his trust was in God and his Word (v32). It had to remain the standard, for the ungodly leaders who would attempt to lead the flock astray would do so by distorting the Word (vv29–30).

Finally, Paul closed out his sermon with an admonition to help the weak in response to the words of Jesus himself (v35). This great apostle so embodied the spirit of Jesus in loving both the saved and the lost that our feeble efforts pale in comparison. But by God's grace, we can grow to be much more than we are and leave behind a far greater legacy than we dream possible. As Paul aged, his contribution to the spiritual revolution intensified because he understood God better. Let's imitate him and the Lord he served so completely, and the Cause for which he lived and died will once again cover the earth with the message of salvation, as the waters cover the sea (Habukkuk 2:14).

Questions for Further Study

1. What did you learn from Aquila and Priscilla about dealing with very spiritually mature leaders with whom you have theological differences?

2. Explain 2 Timothy 2:23–26, and list some evidences of what a person looks like when they are "out of their senses."

3. What does it mean to "baptize only disciples," and how can that be misunderstood?

4. What are ways in which leadership and structure work together effectively and what are ways in which they can be misused?

5. What did you learn about repentance from the section entitled "Pretending or Repenting?"

6. What do you learn about doing the ministry from Paul's statements to the Ephesian elders when they met at Miletus, and what lessons do you most need to put into practice right now?

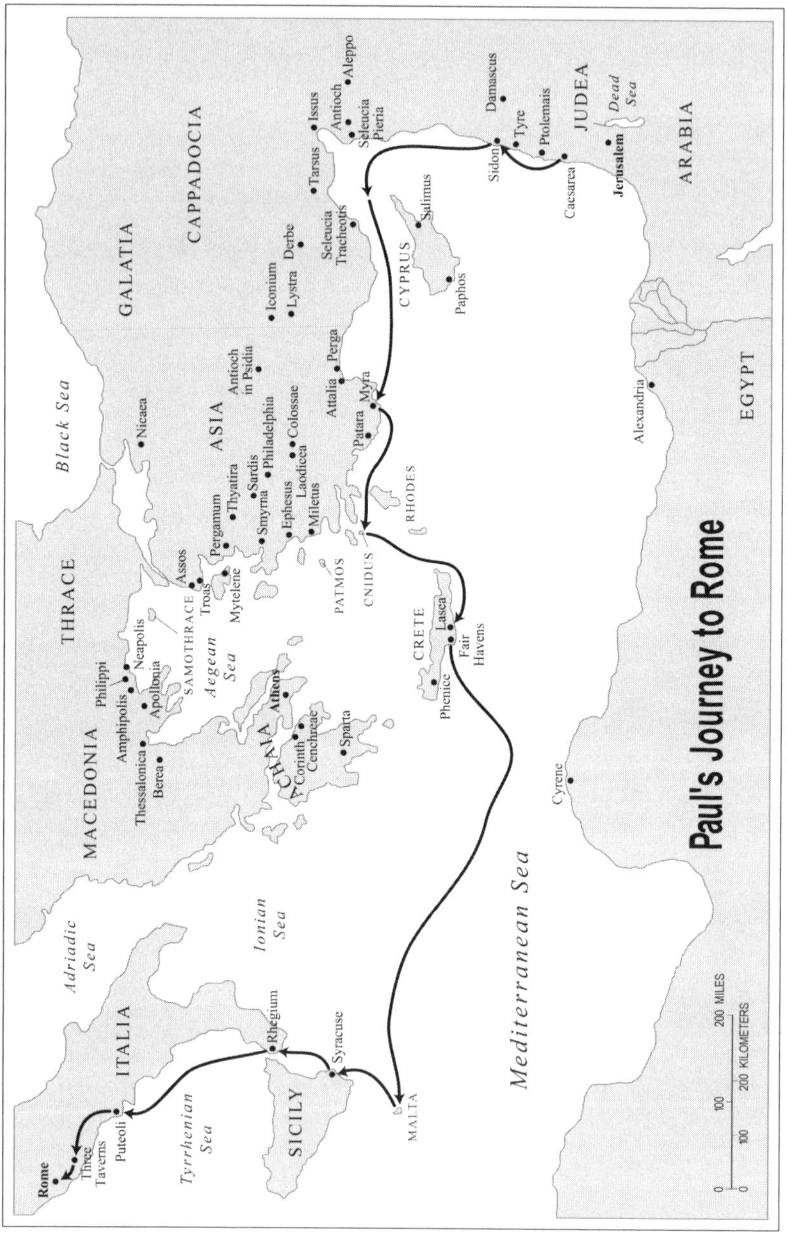
Paul's Journey to Rome
Black Sea
THRACE
MACEDONIA
GALATIA
CAPPADOCIA
ASIA
ACHAIA
CYPRUS
CRETE
JUDEA
ARABIA
EGYPT
ITALIA
SICILY
MALTA
RHODES
PATMOS
CNIDUS
SAMOTHRACE
Aegean Sea
Ionian Sea
Adriadic Sea
Tyrrhenian Sea
Mediterranean Sea
Dead Sea
Rome
Three Taverns
Puteoli
Rhegium
Syracuse
Nicaea
Philippi
Neapolis
Amphipolis
Apollonia
Thessalonica
Berea
Athens
Corinth
Cenchreae
Sparta
Assos
Troas
Mytelene
Pergamum
Thyatira
Smyrna
Sardis
Philadelphia
Ephesus
Laodicea
Colossae
Miletus
Antioch in Psidia
Iconium
Lystra
Derbe
Attalia
Perga
Patara
Myra
Seleucia Tracheotis
Tarsus
Issus
Antioch
Aleppo
Seleucia Pieria
Salimus
Paphos
Damascus
Sidon
Tyre
Ptolemais
Caesarea
Jerusalem
Lasea
Fair Havens
Phenice
Cyrene
Alexandria
200 MILES
200 KILOMETERS

Chapter Fifteen

THE FINAL STEP: FROM JERUSALEM TO ROME

ACTS 21:17-28:31

The remainder of Acts is focused on Paul's final frontier,[1] the capital city of the mighty Roman Empire. By the direction and power of the Holy Spirit, he had planted churches in many of the key cities of the empire. He had set in motion the evangelization and discipling process which had already been responsible for spreading the flame of the Spirit's message to the known world of that day. Within a few years of Paul's arrest in Jerusalem, he would write these words:

> This is the gospel that you heard and that has been proclaimed to every creature under heaven, and of which I, Paul, have become a servant. (Colossians 1:23b)

Looking back at the events of these final chapters in Acts, we see the work of God quite clearly. Paul, however, had to wait patiently to see these events unfold from the mighty providential hand of his God. At times, he easily saw God in these circumstances, and at other times, he was probably perplexed and perhaps frustrated or frightened. He was human. But he was a remarkably faith filled human, who was supernaturally chosen and destined to accomplish what even now seems impossible. As we enter into the final chapters of the life of God's unique apostle, let us do so with humble appreciation for a life well spent and with a dogged determination to imitate his unique faith.

Jerusalem's Jews Cannot Be Appeased (Acts 21:17-23:22)

[21:17]When we arrived at Jerusalem, the brothers received us warmly. [18]The next day Paul and the rest of us went to see James, and all the elders were present. [19]Paul greeted them and reported in detail what God had done among the Gentiles through his ministry.

[20]When they heard this, they praised God. Then they said to Paul: "You see, brother, how many thousands of Jews have believed, and all of them are zealous for the law. [21]They have been informed that you teach all the Jews who live among the Gentiles to turn away from Moses, telling them not to circumcise their children or live according to our customs. [22]What shall we do? They will certainly hear that you have come, [23]so do what we tell you. There are four men with us who have made a vow. [24]Take these men, join in their purification rites and pay their expenses, so that they can have their heads shaved. Then everybody will know there is no truth in these reports about you, but that you yourself are living in obedience to the law.

What Was Paul Thinking?

Reading this section of Scripture without understanding the underlying issues—the Jew/Gentile controversy—discussed in Chapters 8 and 11 of this book would leave us perplexed and confused. The natural question that arises is: How could James and Paul, two of the top leaders in the movement, be parties to such a blatant observance of Mosaic Judaism? Many years have passed since Jesus' death on the cross and its subsequent termination of the old covenant and inauguration of the new. Articles and books have been written by Bible scholars accusing or excusing Paul's decision here in Acts 21. Did he give in to the influence of James (who perhaps was still too close to the forest to see the trees) and just make a serious mistake in judgment, with even more serious consequences? Many have alleged this very thing. And another question looms large: If what he did was permissible, even advisable, what does that say about people continuing to observe many aspects of their former denominational religions today? Good questions, don't you think?

Let's examine the denominational issue first, for it is much simpler. Biblical Judaism (not tradition-bound Judaism) had been established by God. Denominationalism was neither introduced nor approved by him. His plan was for one body (see Ephesians 4:4–6), not many different splinter groups calling themselves "Christians." Thus, the two really do not compare—one is biblical and the other is not. Much in the Old Testament is still quite applicable in principle today, excepting the ceremonial laws. Therefore, knowing which biblical principles were to remain in effect required, both then and now, good judgment and discrimination. Even the ceremonial practices could be seen as nationalistic and cultural rather than as requirements for serving God (as in Timothy's circumcision). Therefore, with God's tacit approval, much of the Law continued to be followed in one way or another. Ultimately, the destruction of the city and the temple in 70 AD ended the transition period described in Hebrews 8:13 and settled most issues once for all. But until that time, the God given Law could be honored by those with Jewish backgrounds, as long as they met two requirements: They could not bind their Judaism on Gentiles, and they could not trust Judaistic practices for salvation. On the other hand, denominationalism is a perversion of Christianity, and as such, does not compare to the first-century transitional period of Judaism.[2]

Now to the other key question: Did Paul go too far in trying to please his Jewish brothers in Christ and make a serious error in judgment? The text says nothing to indicate that God was displeased with what he did, unless the ultimate result of going into the temple—false accusation and arrest—is taken to mean that. Certainly his concession did not accomplish its desired end, but this cannot be viewed as proof that he made a mistake. The principle of 1 Corinthians 9:19–22, becoming all things to all men, was to achieve only the saving of "some." My opinion is that Paul did not sin in what he did but went as far as possible to satisfy his critics. The failure was with them, not him.

We face the same challenge today. We try to do all that we can to answer logically and sensitively those who criticize us. We refuse to compromise biblical issues, but we are willing to make concessions if we think such will yield favorable results in the overall mission. How well does it work? Usually not very well, but we still try to obey the principle of Romans 12:17–18, which states:

> Do not repay anyone evil for evil. Be careful to do what is right in the eyes of everybody. If it is possible, as far as it depends on you, live at peace with everyone.

The real issue is not whether what we do will be approved by men, but whether it will be approved by God. However, we still want to do all we can to be viewed by non-Christians as those deeply desiring to do the right thing. 2 Corinthians 8:21 states the principle that is apropos: "For we are taking pains to do what is right, not only in the eyes of the Lord but also in the eyes of men." The early church was soundly criticized and condemned for their determination to follow Jesus. Did they make mistakes which could be rightly criticized? Probably so, since they were human. But their condemnation by the large majority of the society in which they lived was not due to these well-intentioned mistakes. It was because of their convictions and lifestyles which condemned the sins of their fellow men. When young disciples today hear the charges of persecutors, with the familiar cry of "Where there is smoke, there must be fire," they are tempted to doubt our movement and its leaders. "Maybe we really are doing something wrong," they may think. Just remember that the founder of your religion was God in the flesh, without sin, yet charged as a blasphemer of God and murdered as a criminal. We can make all of the concessions possible without compromising principles, and the result will be the same as Paul experienced: emotion filled outrage and shameless slander. When God's church is falsely charged, stand tall for Christ. You are in good company with the saints of old.

Calling on His Name

While his opponents swirl around him and as he is taken into custody by the Roman guard, Paul asks for an opportunity to speak to the crowd. As he makes his defense, we hear his conversion story for the second time in Acts. We have already discussed this when we looked at Acts 9 back in Chapter 7 of this book, but a few more comments might be helpful. In Acts 22:16 Ananias asked Paul for a response to the cross with this question: "And now what are you waiting for? Get up, be baptized and wash your sins away, calling on his name." Once again, baptism for forgiveness recalls for us Peter's earlier words in Acts 2:38 and Acts 3:19. The additional phrase, "calling on his name," is very interesting. Back in Acts 2:21, quoting from Joel 2:32, Peter said that "everyone who calls on the name of the Lord will be saved." Later in his Pentecost sermon those in his audience with convicted hearts asked what they should do about their sins. In essence they were asking for specific instruction about how to call on the name of the Lord and be saved. His reply?

> "Repent and be baptized, every one of you, in the name of Jesus Christ for the forgiveness of your sins. And you will receive the gift of the Holy Spirit." (Acts 2:38)

Putting together Acts 2 and Acts 22:16, it should be quite clear that "calling on his name" is no more and no less than repenting and being baptized into Christ. If Luke be allowed to interpret Luke, no other answer is possible.

Well, what about Paul's statement in Romans 10:9–13? Isn't "calling on the name of the Lord" (also quoting Joel 2:32) defined as just confessing and thereby being saved? Admittedly, at first glance, Romans 10 would appear to be teaching that. But first glances are often misleading and may prove to be downright dangerous. We need to look more carefully at the context of Romans 10 before coming to a conclusion, especially one which would definitely contradict what we read in Acts. Romans 10:9–10 cannot be used to exclude baptism from the salvation process—for several reasons: First, chapter 10 follows chapter 6, in which baptism is clearly taught to be a part of dying to sin and being raised to begin a new life; and second, "trust" in verse 11 and "call on him" in verse 12 go further than simply believing and confessing. The progression in verses 14–15 is preaching, hearing, believing and calling. Calling on the name of the Lord includes baptism, as may be readily seen in the Acts accounts mentioned above.

In Romans 10:9–10 Paul is talking about the Jews who had failed to accept Christ and addressing the reasons for that rejection. He was making the point, beginning in verse 5, that the righteousness which comes by faith is neither a complex issue nor an unreachable goal. God has already done the difficult work by sending his Son to the cross. Now in response to what he has done, we need to accept him as Lord and Messiah. That was the challenge to the Jew. Being baptized was not a hard concept for them. It had been a part of John's ministry, and large numbers of Jews had received it from his hands. This was not their stumbling block.

The problem that the Jews did have was accepting Jesus as the Messiah and then making this crucified Jew from despised Nazareth their Lord and King. Now that was a challenge! This background focus explains why the passage was worded as it was. Similarly, the problem with Gentile acceptance of the gospel was repentance. Therefore,

Luke focused on that need all through the book of Luke. In fact, his account of the Great Commission only mentions repentance (Luke 24:46–47). Luke's failure to specifically name faith or baptism in this account does not mean that he was excluding them from the conversion process. He was simply focusing on his primary audience's greatest challenge. And Luke's approach follows exactly the same principle used by Paul in Romans 10. Neither was limiting the steps of accepting Christ; both were emphasizing the real faith hurdle for their audiences. Paul was not senile when he wrote Romans 10, forgetting his own experience and his earlier writing in Romans 6. He and Luke were in perfect accord in their understanding and teaching of what was necessary to be forgiven of sins, as were Peter, Philip and the others in their evangelistic work. Let's call on Jesus' name biblically, and teach others to do the same.

Take Your Hands off Me!

After Paul's arrest, the Roman soldiers were preparing to flog him as a part of their standard questioning process. However, he appealed to his Roman citizenship in order to halt the process (Acts 22:23–25). Why did he make this appeal before his beating here, but only afterward in Philippi (Acts 16:37)? It is possible that Paul made the appeal earlier in Philippi, but it went unheeded. In either case, he did not make the appeal simply to avoid pain, but to advance the Cause. In Philippi, he had to leave a fledgling church behind, and he wanted the officials to understand that they were dealing with respectable citizens, not illegal troublemakers. In this way, his appeal provided the possibility of protection from immediate persecution for the Philippian church and its apparent leader, Luke.[3]

In Acts 22, the appeal sprang from Paul's understanding that he was to reach the capital city of Rome. Had he allowed the Romans to treat him as a non-Roman Jew, he likely would have been killed in Jerusalem by the Jews. Hence, the appeal was necessary to allow him to fulfill his divine destiny. In this approach, he imitated Jesus, who never tried to circumvent the personal pain of persecution. When his reputation was at stake, he endured faithfully. When God's reputation was attacked, Jesus spoke out forcefully. The more self is denied, the more God is defended. To which do you respond most forcefully: attacks against you, or against God and his Cause?

Trials in Caesarea (Acts 23:23-26:32)

[23:31]So the soldiers, carrying out their orders, took Paul with them during the night and brought him as far as Antipatris. [32]The next day they let the cavalry go on with him, while they returned to the barracks. [33]When the cavalry arrived in Caesarea, they delivered the letter to the governor and handed Paul over to him. [34]The governor read the letter and asked what province he was from. Learning that he was from Cilicia, [35]he said, "I will hear your case when your accusers get here." Then he ordered that Paul be kept under guard in Herod's palace.

Once Paul arrived in Caesarea, he ended up in the courtroom making defenses a number of times. First, he faced his accusers from Jerusalem before Felix, the governor (Acts 24:1–22). Next, he appeared before Felix and his wife Drusilla (Acts 24:24–25). This passage also indicates that Felix had a number of personal conversations with Paul in the interest of obtaining bribe money from him. Two years later, Felix was succeeded by Porcius Festus (Acts 24:27), before whom Paul was questioned in the presence of Jerusalem Jews once again (Acts 25:1–12). At the end of this session, Paul appealed to Caesar to avoid being taken back to Jerusalem for trial. Finally, he gave his defense before King Agrippa and Bernice (Acts 25:23–26:32).

In all of these sessions, Paul calmly and painstakingly argued his case as Christ's ambassador. His keen mind and extensive education were quite apparent, causing Festus (who understood very little of Judaism) at one point to interrupt Paul thusly: "'You are out of your mind, Paul!' he shouted. 'Your great learning is driving you insane'" (Acts 26:24). By any unbiased estimation, Paul's argumentation abilities and accuracy of content far exceeded that of his most learned opponents. At the end of it all, Agrippa, whose knowledge both of Judaism and Roman law was quite thorough, told Festus: "This man could have been set free if he had not appealed to Caesar" (Acts 26:32). From man's perspective, the preacher was on trial, but from heaven's, his accusers were.

Agrippa and Bernice, with their "great pomp" (Acts 25:23) would have been shocked to look into the future at history's verdict of them and the prisoner with whom they toyed. About the only historical record read today with their names in it is the Bible, and in it they look like pompous, empty shells. The prisoner, on the other hand, has been written about in thousands of books and is far better known in our world than even the emperors of the Roman Empire.

Paul's life shows us the importance of holding deep convictions about our mission and its truths in all circumstances. Even before kings, Paul was unflappable. He was neither bashful nor apologetic about his faith. When King Agrippa was taken aback by Paul's unabashed attempt to convert him, he in derision asked Paul if he really thought he could persuade him to be a Christian in such a short time. Paul's reply was classic:

> "Short time or long—I pray God that not only you but all who are listening to me today may become what I am, except for these chains." (Acts 26:29)

We must not only have truth, but we must hold to that truth with deep convictions. Some have the truth but are insecure in the way they hold it, being easily unsettled before those who do not share their views.

The good news is that our faith is built on evidence that has stood the test of time and inquiry for centuries. Truth has nothing to fear. All of the godless atheists in the world cannot explain away the supernatural nature of the Bible or the empty tomb of Jesus Christ. Do not allow yourself to be apologetic about what you believe. Study it out. Ask your questions. Examine the questions of other people and dig for answers in the Scripture. Ask for help from those whose hearts are filled with deep convictions. Read the writings of those who have penned the reasons for the hope they hold dear. The answers are there. Never be afraid to examine the truths affirmed by the Bible. "Heaven and earth will pass away, but my words will never pass away" (Matthew 24:35). Modern man may think he is sitting in judgment of Scripture, but in truth, it is sitting in judgment of him and one day will judge him and his eternal destiny (John 12:48). Stand up and shout it from the housetops, for it cannot be wrong!

Through the High Seas to Rome (Acts 27:1-28:31)

28:16 When we got to Rome, Paul was allowed to live by himself,
with a soldier to guard him.
17 Three days later he called together the leaders of the Jews.
When they had assembled, Paul said to them: "My brothers, although
I have done nothing against our people or against the customs of our
ancestors, I was arrested in Jerusalem and handed over to the Ro-
mans. 18 They examined me and wanted to release me, because I was
not guilty of any crime deserving death. 19 But when the Jews object-
ed, I was compelled to appeal to Caesar—not that I had any charge to
bring against my own people. 20 For this reason I have asked to see you
and talk with you. It is because of the hope of Israel that I am bound
with this chain."
21 They replied, "We have not received any letters from Judea
concerning you, and none of the brothers who have come from there
has reported or said anything bad about you. 22 But we want to hear
what your views are, for we know that people everywhere are talking
against this sect."
23 They arranged to meet Paul on a certain day, and came in even
larger numbers to the place where he was staying. From morning till
evening he explained and declared to them the kingdom of God and
tried to convince them about Jesus from the Law of Moses and from
the Prophets. 24 Some were convinced by what he said, but others
would not believe.

Destiny, Confidence and Encouragement

Paul was a man of destiny, and he knew it. The Jews in spontaneous anger may have longed to kill him (Acts 22:22), and then with calculated hatred hatched up a plot, bound by their own extreme vows, to murder him (Acts 23:12–15), but God was in control. When we know that we are walking in the purpose for which God called us, we have a confidence that belies the facts. Perfect love casts out fear of God's judgment (1 John 4:17–18), and a committed spirit casts out fear of man's, for we know we are caught up in our destiny and will be preserved until we have fulfilled it. If we are plagued by fears, we had better examine just how well we feel we are living out God's plan for our lives. Confidence is based not simply on whether we think we have met the biblical terms of initial salvation, but in how we view our walk in his mission. How bold are you feeling right now?

One of the most touching passages in the book of Acts is found in Acts 28:15. Paul had survived a long voyage and a near fatal shipwreck. At long last, he and his traveling companions landed near Rome at Puteoli. He no doubt was filled with relief, but he likely was also feeling some apprehension. He had not met the church in Rome personally and wasn't sure just how he would be viewed and received by them. When he wrote his letter to the Romans, he had spent most of the last chapter trying to establish rapport by mentioning many disciples with whom he was acquainted who were in Rome or known by the church there. As a prisoner, Paul's presence would no doubt intensify any persecution the Roman brothers and sisters were already receiving. Just how would they view him?

While he was still about thirty miles south of Rome, some brothers traveled down to meet him. In that age, thirty miles was a long way, and in order to be there when he arrived, they no doubt came early and waited patiently. And now that endearing little verse:

> The brothers there had heard that we were coming, and they traveled as far as the Forum of Appius and the Three Taverns to meet us. At the sight of these men Paul thanked God and was encouraged. (Acts 28:15)

If ever a verse was pregnant with meaning, it is this one. The sisters would have baked some fresh breads and pastries and sent their labors of love in a nice basket. Perhaps little tokens of affection and brief notes were included as well. Paul must have been feeling the burden of the unity of the movement as he walked along the Appian Way, but in one moment in time, the clouds of uncertainty lifted and revealed the sunshine of God's love through his messengers. Encouragement is a wonderful thing.

All of us need more encouragement than we realize. Wise parents learn early to encourage far more than they correct. How much encouragement it takes to offset the corrections, I don't know, but it takes myriad encouragements to offset the emotional beating that the devil and his hordes manage to dish out to us. Encouragement is a gift of the Holy Spirit (Romans 12:8). God himself gives us encouragement (Romans 15:5), but as in Paul's case on the road to Rome, he most often gives it through his servants. "Therefore encourage one another and build each other up, just as in fact you are doing" (1 Thessalonians 5:11).

Paul received much encouragement. Why? One, he gave much encouragement, and those who give, receive. We reap what we sow. But beyond that, God made sure that encouragement came because Paul's life was so completely dedicated to the mission for which Jesus died. He had God's heart for the lost people of the entire world, and his life showed it. When that happens, God will send whatever his messenger needs, whenever he needs it, through whomever can best deliver it. How much encouragement are you receiving? The answer to that question is found in how much you are giving, first of all, and ultimately, in how wrapped up in the mission your heart and life really are.

From Sect to Cult

Paul arrived in Rome to find that it was home to many of his fellow Jews. F. F. Bruce estimates that between 40,000 and 60,000 Jews were living in Rome at this time. His estimate is based in part on a study of six Jewish catacombs and in part on the names of eleven synagogues that have been discovered.[4] (Christian influence in these likely led to the expulsion of the Jews under Claudius in Acts 18.) The Jewish leaders who visited Paul initially had little firsthand knowledge of his work (amazingly), but they were quite aware of the controversial nature of the movement of which he was a key leader. In their terms, it was a "sect."

A sect to them meant simply a segment of Judaism, such as were the Essenes or Zealots. Up until this time, Christianity was known as the "Nazarene sect" (Acts 24:5) and still a part of Judaism. This was destined to change as increasing numbers of Gentiles were converted, and by the latter part of the first century, that transition had been made. Both Jews and Roman officials recognized the change. Prior to that time, the government was not overly antagonistic toward the new movement. However, once they were viewed as a separate movement, the die was cast. Roman policy allowed any country annexed into Rome to keep their existing religions, but they could not later introduce new ones. Such introductions were called *religio illicita,* illegal religions. Thus, in the eyes of Rome, Christianity moved from legal status to illegal status. At that point, it became a hated group, a cult if you will, falsely charged to be subversive and dangerous. The Jews were no longer the worst enemy of the disciples—the Romans were.

The sword was destined to fall, and fall it did.

The book of Acts closes with Paul still a prisoner, but not in prison. He was in his own rented house, guarded by Roman soldiers at all times (Acts 28:30). From this setting he wrote the four letters that are commonly called the "prison letters" (Ephesians, Philippians, Colossians and Philemon). In these, he frequently mentioned his chains.[5] Although Acts closes at this point, from Paul's later writings we can safely assume that he was released from this confinement after having been acquitted. He then made the travels written about in 1 and 2 Timothy and Titus, after which he was rearrested and executed.[6] All three of these letters were evidently written between 63 and 67 AD. In the last of them, Paul wrote of his impending death: "For I am already being poured out like a drink offering, and the time has come for my departure" (2 Timothy 4:6). Nero died in 68, and it is thought that Paul died at his hand in 67 or 68, beheaded by the sword, the customary mode of execution for convicted Roman citizens.

When his head was severed from his worn-out old body, his divine destiny had been fulfilled and his battles in the world's greatest mission were over. As long as he lived, he fought the good fight of faith, whether as a free man, a prisoner in his own rented house, or as a prisoner in the Roman Mamertime jail during his final days. It has been observed that the closer one lives to his destiny, the more he will suffer. Paul's life is a testimony to that premise. Our view of suffering obviously needs some serious adjustment, doesn't it? How much are you suffering for your part in the kingdom of God? As a result of Paul's ministry, thousands were ultimately saved, even though an apostasy was looming large after his death (1 Timothy 4:1–3; 2 Timothy 4:1–4). Let's now do our part in the battle, trust God and save our thousands today as the battle goes on.

The final words of Luke are a fitting testimony to Paul's mission for which he lived daily and ultimately died:

> For two whole years Paul stayed there in his own rented house and welcomed all who came to see him. Boldly and without hindrance he preached the kingdom of God and taught about the Lord Jesus Christ. (Acts 28:30–31)

From his own pen came the immortal words most appropriate for his epitaph:

> I have fought the good fight, I have finished the race, I have kept the faith. Now there is in store for me the crown of righteousness, which the Lord, the righteous Judge, will award to me on that day—and not only to me, but also to all who have longed for his appearing. (2 Timothy 4:7–8)

May God help us to fight our good fight in such a way that these words could be inscribed on our tombstones. Then it will be said of us that we fulfilled our destiny in the most important engagement ever fought on this earth—until we all gather before the throne of him who allowed us the solemn privilege of volunteering in his great army, joining with the very hosts of heaven who fight for the souls of men!

Questions for Further Study

1. Paul's actions in Acts 21 regarding the observation of certain Judaistic practices raise some significant questions. What are the main issues raised and how would you answer them? (Note: this is highly significant material with many ramifications.)

2. Explain "calling on his name" in view of Acts 2, Acts 22 and Romans 10—in a way that harmonizes all three passages.

3. "From Sect to Cult"—what does that mean and what effect did this distinction have upon Christianity in the Roman Empire?

Appendix 1

THY KINGDOM COME

Thy kingdom come, Thy will be done in earth, as it is in heaven. (Matthew 6:10, King James Version)

This brief verse has been used as the basis of songs, poems and quotations for centuries. It provides the most basic and ideal definition of the term "kingdom of God" to be found in Scripture—a place where God's will is done. It pictures that desire disciples have to see all inhabitants of earth submit to the King of kings and the Lord of lords, in the same way that all of heaven submits to him. Who could imagine a better portrayal of life on planet earth than that one? However, looking at all sides of what the Bible says about the kingdom and trying to harmonize it leaves one's head spinning. It almost defies a description in which all loose ends are tied up tightly. But is that unexpected? Can any human look at everything said about God and describe him in simple terms without similar loose ends hanging out everywhere? Obviously, no. Then we should not be surprised to find the same challenges when trying to describe his ruling realm.

As was stated in the exposition of Acts 1:3–6, the kingdom is a very broad and complex subject. I sometimes find it easier to explain what it is not than what it is. I appreciate other authors' efforts to deal with the subject, but I never finish reading any article or book on the kingdom without questions and without a sense of unsettledness, a feeling that something still isn't quite clear about the topic. Likely that says much more about the subject itself than about men's efforts to delve into it. I am quite sure that anyone reading my comments about it will finish with similar feelings. But it is a glorious subject, one of great significance in Old Testament prophecy and one that prompted many comments in the New Testament, from Matthew to Revelation. With all of that in mind, please begin reading with the thought in mind that you are going to receive some introductory knowledge that will hopefully prompt in you the desire to dig deeper, and that the subject deserves to have you start (or continue) digging soon.

The Universal Kingdom

If we were to accept the Matthew 6:10 definition of the kingdom as a realm in which God's will is done, we would soon encounter the complexity of which we spoke earlier. For example, consider these broad, sweeping comments regarding the reign of God:

> "Yours, LORD, is the greatness and the power
>   and the glory and the majesty and the splendor,
>   for everything in heaven and earth is yours.
> Yours, LORD, is the kingdom;
>   you are exalted as head over all.
> Wealth and honor come from you;
>   you are the ruler of all things.
> In your hands are strength and power
>   to exalt and give strength to all." (1 Chronicles 29:11–12)

> The LORD sits enthroned over the flood; the LORD is enthroned as King forever. (Psalm 29:10)

> The LORD has established his throne in heaven, and his kingdom rules over all. (Psalm 103:19)

> "O LORD Almighty, God of Israel, enthroned between the cherubim, you alone are God over all the kingdoms of the earth. You have made heaven and earth. (Isaiah 37:16)

> "I form the light and create darkness, I bring prosperity and create disaster; I, the Lord, do all these things." (Isaiah 45:7)

> "Who can speak and have it happen if the Lord has not decreed it? Is it not from the mouth of the Most High that both calamities and good things come?" (Lamentations 3:37–38)

> He changes times and seasons; he sets up kings and deposes them. He gives wisdom to the wise and knowledge to the discerning. (Daniel 2:21)

> "'The decision is announced by messengers, the holy ones declare the verdict, so that the living may know that the Most High is sovereign over the kingdoms of men and gives them to anyone he wishes and sets over them the lowliest of men.' (Daniel 4:17)

So, what are all of these passages saying? That God reigns over all of creation, animate and inanimate, and nothing happens without his knowledge of it, and in one sense, his approval of it. He indeed is King of kings, and not a sparrow falls to the ground without it fitting into the will of God in one way or another. Because of his absolute sovereignty, he can call Nebuchadnezzar his "servant" (Jeremiah 43:10) and use one wicked nation after another to punish his own people or one another. All of these sinful, rebellious kings were instruments of God to accomplish his purposes, for he is King over all and the whole universe is thus his kingdom!

In this broadest sense of the kingdom, are those in it doing his will? Yes and no. The pigs, lizards, and the like are doing pretty well. They are doing what they were created to do, and without any comprehension of it whatsoever, they are doing his will for them—fulfilling their purpose. Similarly, human beings in general, including those in rebellion, are involuntarily doing his will in some ways. But as we begin this consideration, we have to keep Paul's words in mind when he wrote: "Oh, the depth of the riches of the wisdom and knowledge of God! How unsearchable his judgments, and his paths beyond tracing out!" (Romans 11:33). God has always had spiritual goals in mind as he led history toward Golgotha, and while choices have always been left up to man, especially spiritual choices, he still had his way in working all things together for his purposes. When the time was fully ripe for his coming, he sent his Son into the world (Galatians 4:4). As McGuiggan described it, "Within the scope of God's rule are two classes of men, those in his favor (and in subjection to him) and those who don't have his favor (and who are in subjection to him)" (*The Reign of God,* page 20).

A Kingdom Within a Kingdom

This statement brings us to a consideration of men who are in the favor of God. Everyone from Adam onward who were (or became) people of faith, were a part of a kingdom within a kingdom. They voluntary submitted to their God as their King, which made them a part of two kingdoms at once. The spiritual part of the kingdom has gone through various phases and can easily be overlooked or misunderstood. Before the Law of Moses was given at the inauguration of the Judaistic kingdom, those who were faithful to God were in his spiritual kingdom—whether it was officially called a kingdom or not. If he was the king, they were his subjects. If his will was being done by them, they were in his kingdom of the redeemed. This kingdom before the cross was nonetheless based on the sacrifice made on the cross, for Jesus was the Lamb slain from the creation of the world—Revelation 13:8. The citizens of that early kingdom understood none of this, but they didn't have to. God did. They just had to be faithful to the light God had given them.

Then historically, the kingdom of the Jews was established at Sinai. God's will was for all of those descendants of Abraham to be a spiritual kingdom under his kingship. He made this clear through Moses in Exodus 19:5–6: "Now if you obey me fully and keep my covenant, then out of all nations you will be my treasured possession. Although the whole earth is mine, you will be for me a kingdom of priests and a holy nation." However, although this lofty goal for Israel represented God's ideal will, it didn't play out in an ideal fashion. In fact, by the end of the Wilderness Wandering period, Deuteronomy was written to correct legalistic views of observing the Law that had developed in just a forty year period, which explains why so much in this amazing book was addressing the heart. But Deuteronomy did not halt the slide into legalism (and worse). From its inception, the nation of Israel became a nation within a nation, a kingdom within a kingdom. The whole nation was used as God's instrument to prepare for the coming of the Messiah and to produce him. Sadly, only a remnant (the spiritual kingdom within the physical kingdom) was faithful to him.

Paul certainly made this principle clear with his comments in Romans 9–11. For example, in Romans 9:6 he wrote, "For not all who are descended from Israel are Israel." In those same chapters, he made it abundantly clear that it had always been the case that only a remnant was faithful and a part of the true Israel. The reason the majority were not right with God during the first century can be traced back to their mistaken view of what being an Israelite meant, and did not mean, spiritually.

> "What then shall we say? That the Gentiles, who did not pursue righteousness, have obtained it, a righteousness that is by faith; but Israel, who pursued a law of righteousness, has not attained it. Why not? Because they pursued it not by faith but as if it were by works. They stumbled over the 'stumbling stone'" (Romans 9:30–32).

Thus, the Jews (particularly the religious ones) believed that they were right with God by virtue of being the physical descendants of Abraham. John the Baptist addressed this mistaken view by saying in Matthew 3:9, "And do not think you can say to yourselves, 'We have Abraham as our father.' I tell you that out of these stones God can raise up children for Abraham."

This explains why there had to be a kingdom within a kingdom, a spiritual kingdom and a physical kingdom existing concurrently. The nation may have become a nation at Sinai, and although God used them for his ultimate purposes, they were often a nation in rebellion. Praise God for the encouragement we get from knowing that there was a remnant even in the worst of times, Ruth being a shining example of that—even though a foreign proselyte. Even in the largely apostate Northern Kingdom during the time of the divided kingdom, Elijah was told by God that the remnant numbered 7,000 (1 Kings 19:18).

The most important phase of the Israelite kingdom began when David was made king, for God promised him that someone from his lineage would remain on the throne forever. Saul's family lost the throne due to his sin, but David's family would never abdicate the throne to another family. Of course, the ultimate Davidic king who would reign forever and ever was none other than Jesus the Messiah.

> For to us a child is born,
>   to us a son is given,
>   and the government will be on his shoulders.
> And he will be called
>   Wonderful Counselor, Mighty God,
>   Everlasting Father, Prince of Peace.
> Of the greatness of his government and peace
>   there will be no end.
> He will reign on David's throne
>   and over his kingdom,

> establishing and upholding it
> with justice and righteousness
> from that time on and forever.
> The zeal of the LORD Almighty
> will accomplish this. (Isaiah 9:6–7).

As mentioned in the comments about Acts 1:6, the apostles' question about restoring the kingdom to Israel was not a dumb or naive question. The kingdom of the Messiah was a restored kingdom, especially relevant historically because from the time of the Babylonian captivity until Jesus was crowned, there was not a king on David's throne (meaning from his lineage). Read back over the comments in the Acts 1 exposition if this is unclear to you. The kingdom of Christ was given first to the Jews as a fulfillment of many OT prophecies, and it was a number of years before Gentiles began flooding into his kingdom. Of course, the Old Testament foretold the inclusion of the Gentiles, but the Jews evidently understood this to mean that they would come in through the funnel of Judaism. That misinterpretation led to the Jew/Gentile controversy in the early church that nearly split it.

The Ultimate Kingdom of David

This phase of the kingdom became a reality in conjunction with the Messiah. In this phase of the kingdom, the "kingdom within a kingdom" scenario was destined to become a thing of the past. Although God used the physical kingdom of Judaism for his ultimate purposes to bless mankind, this kingdom essentially failed as a spiritual kingdom, for several reasons. This failure is described by Jesus in Matthew 21:43 thusly: "Therefore I tell you that the kingdom of God will be taken away from you and given to a people who will produce its fruit." In this case, he is saying that the special purpose of the physical kingdom was ending and being given to those who would comprise the Messianic spiritual kingdom. The whole approach to God was undergoing a radical change—a change that few of the Jews understood. The author of Hebrews gives us insight into that change in Hebrews 8:11, as he describes the difference between the old covenant of Moses and the new covenant of Christ. "No longer will a man teach his neighbor, or a man his brother, saying, 'Know the Lord,' because they will all know me, from the least of them to the greatest." In the old covenant, a person was born into the covenant and had to be taught about God (which was a part of the failure mentioned previously). In the new covenant, every person has to be first taught and then born (reborn spiritually). That marked a monumental change and insured that none could enter the covenant of Christ without knowing what they were doing and choosing to do it. Hence, the introduction of the new covenant of the risen Christ marked the end of having a kingdom within a kingdom, in the same sense as during the Mosaic covenant.

The term *kingdom* is used over 100 times in the four Gospel accounts, and about a third that often in the remainder of the New Testament. Jesus' uses of this term were quite varied. Many times, especially in parables, he spoke of kingdom growth (mustard seed, leaven) or the judgment of his kingdom (tares among the good seed, fish in the net) or kingdom value (pearl of great price, treasure in the field). Passages like Matthew 13:38 seem to use the term in the universal sense that we spoke of near the beginning of this article, for the field was referring to the whole world in this passage.

The Inauguration of the Messianic Kingdom

Perhaps the most perplexing aspect of the Messianic kingdom comes in trying to ascertain when it actually was instituted. Keep in mind as we move to this consideration that I believe that the church and the kingdom are not exact equivalents. I said that in the Acts 1 exposition, but I will need to say it again here to avoid any possible confusion.

Traditionally, leaders in our movement have equated the church and the kingdom, and have thus taught that the kingdom (church) was established in Acts 2—as Isaiah 2, Daniel 2 and Joel 2 converged on the Day of Pentecost. I can see what seems to be fairly compelling reasoning for teaching it in this manner. On the other hand, I see passages in the Gospels that seem to clearly say that the kingdom was in existence during the ministry of King Jesus. This complexity is not easily solved, at least in my mind.

The main passages that are used for pointing to the kingdom being in existence during Jesus' ministry are easy to find and list. (All are from the New International Version unless noted.)

From that time on Jesus began to preach, "Repent, for the kingdom of heaven is near." (Matthew 4:17)

"Blessed are the poor in spirit, for theirs is the kingdom of heaven." (Matthew 5:3)

"Blessed are those who are persecuted because of righteousness, for theirs is the kingdom of heaven." (Matthew 5:10)

"But seek first his kingdom and his righteousness, and all these things will be given to you as well." (Matthew 6:33)

"But if I drive out demons by the Spirit of God, then the kingdom of God has come upon you." (Matthew 12:28)

"Jesus said, 'Let the little children come to me, and do not hinder them, for the kingdom of heaven belongs to such as these.'" (Matthew 19:14)

"Which of the two did what his father wanted?" "The first," they answered. Jesus said to them, "I tell you the truth, the tax collectors and the prostitutes are entering the kingdom of God ahead of you." (Matthew 21:31)

"Woe to you, teachers of the law and Pharisees, you hypocrites! You shut the kingdom of heaven in men's faces. You yourselves do not enter, nor will you let those enter who are trying to." (Matthew 23:13)

"Heal the sick who are there and tell them, 'The kingdom of God is near you.'" (Luke 10:9)

"Do not be afraid, little flock, for your Father has been pleased to give you the kingdom." (Luke 12:32)

"Now having been questioned by the Pharisees as to when the kingdom of God was coming, He answered them and said, 'The kingdom of God is not coming with signs to be observed; nor will they say, 'Look, here it is!' or, 'There it is!' For behold, the kingdom of God is in your midst." (Luke 17:20–21, NASB)

In looking at these passages, it cannot be doubted that the kingdom of Jesus was present in his ministry. After all, in Matthew 9:6 Jesus said that he had authority on earth to forgive sins, and if one's sins were forgiven, they were a part of his kingdom. However, the greater question to me is in what *sense* his kingdom was present. Other passages seem to point to a sense in which the kingdom was not yet present, and I don't refer to the kingdom in heaven after the resurrection. Look at these passages also from the Gospel accounts.

> In those days John the Baptist came, preaching in the Desert of Judea and saying, "Repent, for the kingdom of heaven is near." (Matthew 3:1–2)
>
> "I tell you the truth: Among those born of women there has not risen anyone greater than John the Baptist; yet he who is least in the kingdom of heaven is greater than he. (Matthew 11:11)
>
> And I tell you that you are Peter, and on this rock I will build my church, and the gates of Hades will not overcome it. I will give you the keys of the kingdom of heaven; whatever you bind on earth will be bound in heaven, and whatever you loose on earth will be loosed in heaven." (Matthew 16:18–19)
>
> "What is it you want?" he asked. She said, "Grant that one of these two sons of mine may sit at your right and the other at your left in your kingdom." (Matthew 20:21)
>
> "I tell you the truth, I will not drink again of the fruit of the vine until that day when I drink it anew in the kingdom of God." (Mark 14:25)
>
> Joseph of Arimathea, a prominent member of the Council, who was himself waiting for the kingdom of God, went boldly to Pilate and asked for Jesus' body. (Mark 15:43)
>
> While they were listening to this, he went on to tell them a parable, because he was near Jerusalem and the people thought that the kingdom of God was going to appear at once. (Luke 19:11)

Both John and Jesus said that the kingdom of God was near. Given what is said about John in Matthew 11, it doesn't seem possible that he was saying that the kingdom of God was then present when he said that it was near. The apparent interchangeable use of church and kingdom in the same context of Matthew 16, combined with the fact that the apostles didn't begin to use their binding and loosing authority mentioned there until after Pentecost, gives pause as well. In Matthew 20, the request of James' and John's mother seemed to indicate that she saw the kingdom as yet future. Correctly or incorrectly, I've long thought that Jesus joining us in communion (Mark 14:25) happens in the church in a spiritual sense. Joseph of Arimathea evidently wasn't aware of the kingdom being present. Luke 19:11 seems to have been spoken to clarify that the kingdom of God was not going to appear immediately. Of course, it could be argued that this passage was referring to the heavenly stage of the kingdom.

But then we come back to Acts 1. Jesus had opened the minds of the apostles in order to teach and prepare them for all that was soon to occur. The teaching took place over a forty day period. They still were asking about when the kingdom was coming, regardless of what you choose to do about the word "restore." These men who were closest to Jesus all during his ministry and personally were instructed by him in this forty day crash course about the kingdom topic didn't see it as being in existence yet—even after his resurrection from the dead. Something much bigger was to come regarding the kingdom.

Therefore, while it seems apparent that the kingdom of God was present in the person of Jesus during his earthly ministry, those who saw and heard him did not seem to grasp much of what that meant, including the apostles. To assume that it was as much in evidence before Pentecost as afterwards strains my sense of knowledge and my sense of logic. As another writer stated it, could there really have been a crown without a cross? I know that the fairly popular "now, not yet" formula sees two phases of the kingdom as being an earthly phase instituted during the ministry of Jesus and a heavenly phase when time is no more. At this point of my own study, I would propose a "now, not yet, not yet" formula from the vantage point of Acts 1. The *now* was largely the preparatory phase of Jesus' ministry, in which much groundwork was laid for the future and much teaching was addressed toward the Jewish mindset. The first not yet phase was ushered in at Pentecost when the crucifixion and resurrection of Jesus was first publicly proclaimed after it became a reality. It was still a *not yet* phase during the ministry of Christ. And of course the final *not yet* phase would refer to the kingdom after it is delivered up to the Father (1 Corinthians 15:24).

One final consideration leads me to the conclusions stated above—namely, the connection between the Messiah's kingdom and his covenant. Ezekiel 37:15–28 is without doubt a Messianic passage, predicting the new David (Jesus) reigning over his kingdom forever, ruling it with an everlasting covenant of peace. The reign of Jesus as King occurs in conjunction with his new covenant. Therefore, the question must be asked, when was the new covenant instituted? That cannot be other than in Acts 2.

> "For this reason Christ is the mediator of a new covenant, that those who are called may receive the promised eternal inheritance—now that he has died as a ransom to set them free from the sins committed under the first covenant.
>
> In the case of a will, it is necessary to prove the death of the one who made it, because a will is in force only when somebody has died; it never takes effect while the one who made it is living." (Hebrews 9:15–17)

The new covenant is compared to a will, which only goes into effect after the maker of the will dies. The period from the death of Christ to the Day of Pentecost, when I believe the new covenant went into effect, was something like a probationary period before a will becomes totally legal. That is at least the case with manmade wills.

To my way of thinking, the preaching of the gospel of the kingdom that took place during the earthly ministry of Jesus had to be primarily preparatory preaching. The very foundation of the kingdom gospel message is the death, burial and resurrection of Christ (1 Corinthians 15:1–4). If the fulfillment of Isaiah 53 was the heart and soul of the message, it was yet an incomplete gospel. Of course, Jesus taught about his death and resurrection during his earthly ministry, but who really understood it? The apostles certainly didn't, and they were of all people the best candidates to understand it. Instead, even immediately after the resurrection they were fearfully hiding behind closed doors—until the Spirit came on Pentecost. From that time forward, they were boldness personified, preaching and living the gospel of the resurrected, ascended King and spreading his new covenant everywhere. Passages like Isaiah 2, Daniel 2 and Joel 2 come together in Acts 2 in a way that they do not come together elsewhere—including during the earthly ministry of Jesus.

What Are the Real Issues Here?

I don't think the real underlying issue is when the Messianic phase of the kingdom was instituted. 2000 years have passed. In my Appendix about Apollos and whether he was re-baptized or not, I make it clear that it really doesn't matter at all now, one way or the other. You can read that Appendix if you like, but my opinion is that those baptized before the cross and who remained faithful were not re-baptized. That would have included the apostles and others. But what difference does it make to us two millennia later? The same circumstances don't (can't) exist now, so it is a moot question. The same principle could be applied to the institution of the kingdom. Whether that occurred during the ministry of Jesus or on the Day of Pentecost, the kingdom of the Messiah has been around for a long time and the real issue for us is to discover exactly what being a part of that kingdom now should mean to us and how it must show up in our thinking and doing. If we are indeed kingdom people, we must live like it! That's the real issue.

It seems to me that the renewed emphasis on the kingdom in the Gospels comes at least partially from the desire to avoid the malady of equating the kingdom with the church, especially in combination with the strong tendency to have an institutionalized view of the church. I understand that malady, and malady is a good word to describe it. Most who claim to follow Christ have indeed developed a very institutional view of the church, and tend to preach the gospel of the church rather than the gospel of Christ. However, we have two problems to address and hopefully solve—wrong views of both the kingdom and of the church.

If I am correct in my assumption regarding one motivation behind the renewed kingdom emphasis, we have somewhat of a parallel in the motivation behind using the term *disciple* rather than *Christian*. The word Christian is only used three times in the New

Testament, and not defined well at all. Perhaps for that reason, the word has come to be used in so many ways that violate Scripture that those in our movement have opted to use the term disciple. It is used many times and is defined from many angles. In perhaps a similar way, using the term kingdom gets us back into the Scripture with fresh eyes and helps reduce the focus on the term church, which is so misunderstood and misapplied in our day.

However, a real difference exists in these two word choices (kingdom and disciple, in lieu of church and Christian). It is true that Christian is little used and defined in the New Testament. Conversely, it is *not* true that church is little used and defined in the New Testament. From Acts through Revelation, kingdom is used 35 times, whereas church is used 75 times. Most of the times the word church is used, it refers to a local assembly of believers. Perhaps that makes the term easier to institutionalize. However, some of the passages about the church are as lofty as could be imagined, and in these cases, using the word kingdom interchangeably would seem appropriate. Read the following verses and see what you think.

> Keep watch over yourselves and all the flock of which the Holy Spirit has made you overseers. Be shepherds of the church of God, which he bought with his own blood. (Acts 20:28)

> I pray also that the eyes of your heart may be enlightened in order that you may know the hope to which he has called you, the riches of his glorious inheritance in the saints, and his incomparably great power for us who believe. That power is like the working of his mighty strength, which he exerted in Christ when he raised him from the dead and seated him at his right hand in the heavenly realms, far above all rule and authority, power and dominion, and every title that can be given, not only in the present age but also in the one to come. And God placed all things under his feet and appointed him to be head over everything for the church, which is his body, the fullness of him who fills everything in every way. (Ephesians 1:18–23)

> For this reason I kneel before the Father, from whom his whole family in heaven and on earth derives its name. I pray that out of his glorious riches he may strengthen you with power through his Spirit in your inner being, so that Christ may dwell in your hearts through

> faith. And I pray that you, being rooted and established in love, may have power, together with all the saints, to grasp how wide and long and high and deep is the love of Christ, and to know this love that surpasses knowledge—that you may be filled to the measure of all the fullness of God.
>
> Now to him who is able to do immeasurably more than all we ask or imagine, according to his power that is at work within us, to him be glory in the church and in Christ Jesus throughout all generations, for ever and ever! Amen. (Ephesians 3:14–21)

> But you have come to Mount Zion, to the heavenly Jerusalem, the city of the living God. You have come to thousands upon thousands of angels in joyful assembly, to the church of the firstborn, whose names are written in heaven. You have come to God, the judge of all men, to the spirits of righteous men made perfect, to Jesus the mediator of a new covenant, and to the sprinkled blood that speaks a better word than the blood of Abel.
>
> See to it that you do not refuse him who speaks. If they did not escape when they refused him who warned them on earth, how much less will we, if we turn away from him who warns us from heaven? At that time his voice shook the earth, but now he has promised, "Once more I will shake not only the earth but also the heavens." The words "once more" indicate the removing of what can be shaken—that is, created things—so that what cannot be shaken may remain. Therefore, since we are receiving a kingdom that cannot be shaken, let us be thankful, and so worship God acceptably with reverence and awe, for our "God is a consuming fire." (Hebrews 12:22–29)

Again, I think I understand the reluctance some have of in any way equating the kingdom with the church. But both terms need to be clarified, sanctified and perhaps fumigated. I am totally supportive of all efforts to help us see what Jesus envisioned his kingdom to be (regardless of the date of its institution), for we have lost our radical edge as a movement. At one time, using the term disciple called us to that radical edge, but it too has become an institutionalized term for many of us. To those in that category, it means little more than being a part of an ICOC-related church. Therefore, if using the term kingdom can direct us back into studying the kingdom *life*, which is biblically a very radical, cross-cultural life, I say "Amen and Amen!" I just want to make sure I get to that point by employing a correct hermeneutic in the process.

I deeply desire to help us see the kingdom of God in its eternal significance, reaching back into eternity before the world was created and reaching forward into the eternity of which I long to be a part. I also want to help us see the church as the blood-bought Body of Christ, consisting of all the saved on earth, who are at the same time a part of the kingdom—called to be his spiritual representatives to do what Christ did while in his earthly sojourn. While the church is not equal to the kingdom, it is certainly a part of God's kingdom. In the church, we are subjects of the King and we subject our lives to the rule and reign of God. It may not all be simple and easy to understand, hence the need to keep digging, but our study should lead us to a deeper understanding of the kingdom and its ever-increasing glory as we await that day when "Thy kingdom come" is fulfilled in the grandest way possible, for all eternity.

Appendix 2

Judas: Will People Really Be Lost?

Peter, in Acts 1:25, makes the statement that Judas "left to go where he belongs." The story of Judas is a tragic one indeed. He must have been a very talented man when Jesus chose him. It would be difficult to imagine Jesus choosing someone simply on the basis of knowing that a betrayer would be required in the end. Like many leaders who have fallen, he was at one time strong and righteous. Paul proudly mentioned Demas as a fellow worker in Colossians 4:14, but later had to write, sadly, that Demas had deserted him because of a love for the world (2 Timothy 4:10). We are in a spiritual battle, and leaders are going to fall. Along with Judas, they have their opportunities to take a different path but choose not to. Both Peter and Judas betrayed Jesus before he went to the cross, but one had godly sorrow that led to repentance, while the other one had worldly sorrow that led to death (2 Corinthians 7:10). The contrast could not be more clearly demonstrated, leaving Judas without excuse.

Was Peter being judgmental by saying essentially that Judas had gone to hell? No, he was simply allowing God to judge. Jesus said in Matthew 10:32–33 that if we disown him before men, he will disown us before his Father. This is God's judgment, not man's. We live in an existential age, the age of "do your own thing and be your own judge." The thought of saying that people are lost seems shocking and repugnant to many, who quickly make the charge that those who say such are judgmental. But in reality, it is they who are judgmental. They are judging that God's Word is not true or that God will not keep his word on the Judgment Day.

It is true that some sins are obvious, while others may be quite hidden (from men, not from God, 1 Timothy 5:24). In the same way the course of some people's lives is quite apparent, while others' may not be. It is not being at all presumptuous to let God's Word judge the vast majority of the world who make no claim to be disciples of Jesus. The Bible is clear about no one being saved without being a follower of Jesus (John 14:6, Acts 4:12) and equally clear that being a follower is much more than professing to be a Christian (Matthew 7:21, John 8:30–32). Having a judgmental spirit is certainly a bad thing (Matthew 7:1–5), but making biblical judgments is a good and necessary thing (Matthew 7:13–21). May we all have convictions based on the Bible, about which we are in no way apologetic.

In the realm of morals and ethics, we live in a world that eschews absolutes. The downward spiral into moral and spiritual relativity and existentialism can likely trace its roots to religious philosophy. For years religious people have made statements such as: "It doesn't matter what you believe as long as you are sincere"; or "Attend the church of your choice." I remember the early days of the sexual revolution, when young people started living together without being married, and the deep pain it caused in the hearts of their dismayed parents. But the youth were just applying their parents' religious relativism to moral areas: If one's own opinion made religious doctrines right or wrong, why could not opinion determine moral right and wrong? The consequences of accepting such relativity have been devastating to our culture, to put it mildly.

In the realm of science, we would not accept this line of reasoning for a moment. Building a space shuttle is not left up to the "if it feels right, do it" philosophers—we want exactness, according to a well-prescribed standard. We expect the medical community to prescribe just the right medications and to warn us about possible side effects and drug interactions. We want accurate data that consistently follows a standard. Why will we insist on absolutes in many arenas, but glibly accept almost anyone's sincere opinions in morals and ethics—the areas that have everything to do with our lives on earth and after earth? Thank God that the Bible contains absolutes of right and wrong. May we not be led down the primrose path to destruction, strewn with existentialism gone to seed! And may we never be apologetic about the plain teachings of Scripture, including what it takes to be a true Christian and to be saved! As sad as it may be, Peter did not skirt the issue of Judas' lostness. Such sobering truths should move us to be much more urgent about our righteousness and evangelism.

Appendix
3

Harmony of ACTS 9, 22 & 26

ACTS 9

9:1Meanwhile, Saul was still breathing out murderous threats against the Lord's disciples. He went to the high priest 2and asked him for letters to the synagogues in Damascus, so that if he found any there who belonged to the Way, whether men or women, he might take them as prisoners to Jerusalem.

ACTS 22

22:1“Brothers and fathers, listen now to my defense.” 2When they heard him speak to them in Aramaic, they became very quiet.

Then Paul said: 3”I am a Jew, born in Tarsus of Cilicia, but brought up in this city. Under Gamaliel I was thoroughly trained in the law of our fathers and was just as zealous for God as any of you are today.

4I persecuted the followers of this Way to their death, arresting both men and women and throwing them into prison, 5as also the high priest and all the Council can testify. I even obtained letters from them to their brothers in Damascus, and went there to bring these people as prisoners to Jerusalem to be punished.

ACTS 26

26:4“The Jews all know the way I have lived ever since I was a child, from the beginning of my life in my own country, and also in Jerusalem. 5They have known me for a long time and can testify, if they are willing, that according to the strictest sect of our religion, I lived as a Pharisee.

9“I too was convinced that I ought to do all that was possible to oppose the name of Jesus of Nazareth. 10And that is just what I did in Jerusalem. On the authority of the chief priests I put many of the saints in prison, and when they were put to death, I cast my vote against them. 11Many a time I went from one synagogue to another to have them punished, and I tried to force them to blaspheme. In my obsession against them, I even went to foreign cities to persecute them.

12“On one of these journeys I was going to Damascus with the authority and commission of the chief priests.

ACTS 9

3As he neared Damascus on his journey, suddenly a light from heaven flashed around him.

4He fell to the ground and heard a voice say to him, "Saul, Saul, why do you persecute me?"

5"Who are you, Lord?" Saul asked.

"I am Jesus, whom you are persecuting," he replied. 6"Now get up and go into the city, and you will be told what you must do."

7The men traveling with Saul stood there speechless; they heard the sound but did not see anyone.

8Saul got up from the ground, but when he opened his eyes he could see nothing. So they led him by the hand into Damascus. 9For three days he was blind, and did not eat or drink anything.

ACTS 22

6"About noon as I came near Damascus, suddenly a bright light from heaven flashed around me.

7I fell to the ground and heard a voice say to me, 'Saul! Saul! Why do you persecute me?'

8"Who are you, Lord?' I asked.

"'I am Jesus of Nazareth, whom you are persecuting,' he replied.

9My companions saw the light, but they did not understand the voice of him who was speaking to me.

10"'What shall I do, Lord?' I asked.

"'Get up,' the Lord said, 'and go into Damascus. There you will be told all that you have been assigned to do.'

11My companions led me by the hand into Damascus, because the brilliance of the light had blinded me.

ACTS 26

13About noon, O king, as I was on the road, I saw a light from heaven, brighter than the sun, blazing around me and my companions. 14We all fell to the ground, and I heard a voice saying to me in Aramaic, 'Saul, Saul, why do you persecute me? It is hard for you to kick against the goads.'

15"Then I asked, 'Who are you, Lord?'

" 'I am Jesus, whom you are persecuting,' the Lord replied.

16'Now get up and stand on your feet. I have appeared to you to appoint you as a servant and as a witness of what you have seen of me and what I will show you. 17I will rescue you from your own people and from the Gentiles. I am sending you to them 18to open their eyes and turn them from darkness to light, and from the power of Satan to God, so that they may receive forgiveness of sins and a place among those who are sanctified by faith in me.'

ACTS 9

10 In Damascus there was a disciple named Ananias. The Lord called to him in a vision, "Ananias!"

"Yes, Lord," he answered.

11 The Lord told him, "Go to the house of Judas on Straight Street and ask for a man from Tarsus named Saul, for he is praying. 12 In a vision he has seen a man named Ananias come and place his hands on him to restore his sight."

13 "Lord," Ananias answered, "I have heard many reports about this man and all the harm he has done to your saints in Jerusalem. 14 And he has come here with authority from the chief priests to arrest all who call on your name."

15 But the Lord said to Ananias, "Go! This man is my chosen instrument to carry my name before the Gentiles and their kings and before the people of Israel. 16 I will show him how much he must suffer for my name."

17 Then Ananias went to the house and entered it. Placing his hands on Saul, he said, "Brother Saul, the Lord—Jesus, who appeared to you on the road as you were coming here—has sent me so that you may see again and be filled with the Holy Spirit." 18 Immediately, something like scales fell from Saul's eyes, and he could see again.

ACTS 22

12 "A man named Ananias came to see me. He was a devout observer of the law and highly respected by all the Jews living there.

13 He stood beside me and said, 'Brother Saul, receive your sight!'

And at that very moment I was able to see him.

ACTS 26

ACTS 9

He got up and was bap-
tized, 19and after taking
some food, he regained his
strength.

Saul spent several days
with the disciples in Damas-
cus. 20At once he began to
preach in the synagogues
that Jesus is the Son of God.
21All those who heard him
were astonished and asked,
"Isn't he the man who raised
havoc in Jerusalem among
those who call on this name?
And hasn't he come here to
take them as prisoners to
the chief priests?" 22Yet Saul
grew more and more power-
ful and baffled the Jews liv-
ing in Damascus by proving
that Jesus is the Christ.

23After many days had
gone by, the Jews conspired
to kill him, 24but Saul learned
of their plan. Day and night
they kept close watch on the
city gates in order to kill him.
25But his followers took him
by night and lowered him in
a basket through an opening
in the wall.

ACTS 22

14"Then he said: 'The God
of our fathers has chosen
you to know his will and
to see the Righteous One
and to hear words from his
mouth. 15You will be his wit-
ness to all men of what you
have seen and heard. 16And
now what are you waiting
for? Get up, be baptized and
wash your sins away, calling
on his name.'"

ACTS 26

19"So then, King Agrippa,
I was not disobedient to the
vision from heaven. 20First to
those in Damascus, then to
those in Jerusalem and in all
Judea, and to the Gentiles
also, I preached that they
should repent and turn to
God and prove their repen-
tance by their deeds.

ACTS 9

26When he came to Je-
rusalem, he tried to join the
disciples, but they were all
afraid of him, not believing
that he really was a disciple.
27But Barnabas took him and
brought him to the apostles.
He told them how Saul on
his journey had seen the
Lord and that the Lord had
spoken to him, and how in
Damascus he had preached
fearlessly in the name of
Jesus. 28So Saul stayed with
them and moved about
freely in Jerusalem, speak-
ing boldly in the name of
the Lord. 29He talked and
debated with the Grecian
Jews, but they tried to kill
him. 30When the brothers
learned of this, they took
him down to Caesarea and
sent him off to Tarsus.

31Then the church
throughout Judea, Galilee
and Samaria enjoyed a time
of peace. It was strength-
ened; and encouraged by
the Holy Spirit, it grew in
numbers, living in the fear
of the Lord.

ACTS 22

17"When I returned to
Jerusalem

and was praying at the
temple, I fell into a trance
18and saw the Lord speaking.
'Quick!' he said to me. 'Leave
Jerusalem immediately, be-
cause they will not accept
your testimony about me.'

19"'Lord,' I replied, 'these
men know that I went from
one synagogue to another
to imprison and beat those
who believe in you. 20And
when the blood of your
martyr Stephen was shed,
I stood there giving my ap-
proval and guarding the
clothes of those who were
killing him.'

21"Then the Lord said to
me, 'Go; I will send you far
away to the Gentiles.'"

ACTS 26

21That is why the Jews
seized me in the temple
courts and tried to kill me.

22But I have had God's
help to this very day, and so
I stand here and testify to
small and great alike. I am
saying nothing beyond what
the prophets and Moses
said would happen—23that
the Christ would suffer and,
as the first to rise from the
dead, would proclaim light
to his own people and to the
Gentiles."

Appendix 4

Was Apollos Rebaptized?

Most Bible readers assume that Apollos was re-baptized as a part of being taught the way of God more adequately by Priscilla and Aquila. Let's begin by reading the end of Acts 18 and the beginning of Acts 19.

> [24]Meanwhile a Jew named Apollos, a native of Alexandria, came to Ephesus. He was a learned man, with a thorough knowledge of the Scriptures. [25]He had been instructed in the way of the Lord, and he spoke with great fervor and taught about Jesus accurately, though he knew only the baptism of John. [26]He began to speak boldly in the synagogue. When Priscilla and Aquila heard him, they invited him to their home and explained to him the way of God more adequately. [27]When Apollos wanted to go to Achaia, the brothers encouraged him and wrote to the disciples there to welcome him. On arriving, he was a great help to those who by grace had believed. [28]For he vigorously refuted the Jews in public debate, proving from the Scriptures that Jesus was the Christ. (Acts 18:24-28)

> [1]While Apollos was at Corinth, Paul took the road through the interior and arrived at Ephesus. There he found some disciples [2]and asked them, "Did you receive the Holy Spirit when you believed?" They answered, "No, we have not even heard that there is a Holy Spirit." [3]So Paul asked, "Then what baptism did you receive?" "John's baptism," they replied. [4]Paul said, "John's baptism was a baptism of repentance. He told the people to believe in the one coming after him, that is, in Jesus." [5]On hearing this, they were baptized into the name of the Lord Jesus. (Acts 19:1-5)

In spite of the normal assumptions, much discussion has occurred about whether Apollos was in fact baptized at this point. The text does not say so, nor does it say anything more generally that would necessarily imply it. A related question is whether the apostles or even the 120 in Acts 1 and Acts 2 were re-baptized. If they had come into a saved relationship during the ministry of Christ (and they had; see John 15:3), then his dying would not have made them become unsaved. John's baptism was for the forgiveness of sins (Mark 1:4), called in Acts 19:4 a "baptism of repentance" that had to be followed by belief in Jesus. Since the Israelites were born into a covenant relationship with God, the forgiveness through John's baptism was not the forgiveness of initial salvation, but rather the forgiveness of repentance for those in the covenant, much like what prayers on the part of Christians accomplish today (1 John 1:9).

My opinion is that those who had experienced John's baptism before Christ died and maintained faith in him were not re-baptized. I don't think the 3,000 baptized on the Day of Pentecost included the apostles. If the principle is true that those who had received John's baptism before the cross and remained faithful would not need a re-baptism, then Apollos would not have needed another baptism. However, John's baptism would have been invalid if experienced *after* the cross, for it was superseded by Great Commission baptism, and that was likely the case of those described in Acts 19:1–5. The probable scenario is that Apollos was baptized with John's baptism before the cross but then taught and baptized the dozen men in Ephesus with John's baptism after the cross, which was no longer valid. Hence, Paul re-baptized them with the baptism of the Great Commission. The whole issue is mostly a moot point, for it cannot be applied in any way to those living today. Even if John's baptism remained valid for men who were baptized before the cross and who maintained faith in Jesus, no such person is alive today! Therefore, while such discussions may be interesting, they tend to produce more heat than light, and have no direct application today. However, in the interest of honest inquiry, I am glad to provide the answer that seems to me most likely correct.

ENDNOTES

Chapter 1

[1] For a fuller treatment of the futurist view of the kingdom, see Appendix 1 in my book *Mine Eyes Have Seen the Glory*, 177–184.

[2] Matthew uses the term "kingdom of heaven" more than thirty times and "kingdom of God" only four times. In 19:23–24 he clearly uses the two terms interchangeably. Matthew, writing to a Jewish audience with a materialistic, nationalistic view of the kingdom, may have wanted to emphasize the spiritual nature of the kingdom. He also could have been following the Jewish tradition of using "heaven" as a euphemism for "God"—a tradition that arose from the feeling that the name of God was too holy to pronounce.

[3] Judas, according to Luke's parenthetical explanation in Acts 1:18–19, had bought a field in which he met a gory death. But Luke's explanation, when compared to Matthew 27:3–8, seems to contain two contradictions: how Judas died and how his "field of blood" received its name. Matthew says that he hanged himself, whereas Luke says that he fell into the field and burst apart. The apparent contradiction is solved by harmonizing both accounts and assuming that he hung until the rope broke, at which time he burst open (made more likely by decomposition). As to the origin of the field's name, both explanations were evidently held by various inhabitants of Jerusalem, which is not surprising when you think of variations in explanations of how names of current locations are derived.

[4] See Appendix 1: "Judas: Will People Really Be Lost?"

Chapter 2

[1] See Luke 21:5–24, 23:27–31, Acts 2:14–21 and Malachi 4:1–6 for examples.

[2] For a fuller discussion of the "one time only" view of Holy Spirit baptism and of how Cornelius' situation relates, see my book *Prepared to Answer, Second Edition* (Spring, Texas: Illumination Publishers International, 2009), pp. 144–148.

[3] Edward J. Anton, *Repentance* (Waltham, Massachusetts: Discipleship Publications International, 2005).

[4] See also Matthew 28:19, Romans 6:3–4, Galatians 3:27, 1 Peter 3:20–21 for passages that tie baptism and salvation together.

[5] G. R. Beasley-Murray, *Baptism in the New Testament* (Grand Rapids: William B. Eerdmans, 1973), 393.

[6] Douglas Jacoby, *The Spirit* (Spring, Texas: Illumination Publishers International, 1998), 65. This statement comes in Chapter 9, which contains some great common sense admonitions regarding being led by the Spirit.

Chapter 3

[1] While we do not have the same miraculous gifts of the Spirit today, we certainly have many available gifts from him. See Romans 12:5–8 for one listing of such non-miraculous, but highly important, spiritual gifts that enable us to do great works for God.

Chapter 4

[1] See Leviticus 11:44, 19:2, 20:7, Ephesians 1:4, Hebrews 12:14, 1 Peter 1:15–16.

[2] The word translated "kept back" in verse 2 is found in the New Testament only here and in Titus 2:10, where it is translated "to steal." It is the same word used in Joshua 7:1 in the LXX (Septuagint Greek version dating back to 250 B.C.) to describe breaking faith with God.

[3] It is interesting to note that the word "church" occurs in Acts for the first time here (5:11).

[4] In this "High Court" of Judaism, the Pharisees were in the minority but had a powerful influence due to being more favorably viewed by the public than were the majority Sadducees. Bruce estimates that the Pharisees numbered only about 6,000 at this time (F. F. Bruce, *The Book of Acts, revised edition* (Grand Rapids: William B. Eerdmans Publishing Co., 1988), 114–115, footnote 51).

Chapter 5

[1] For more detail regarding miraculous gifts in the early church, see my *Prepared to Answer,* Chapter 10.

[2] For a thorough treatment of these predictions, see my *Mine Eyes Have Seen the Glory,* Appendix 2.

[3] Of nineteen speeches recorded in Acts, this one by Stephen is the longest. Like Stephen, James had one speech recorded, Peter eight and Paul nine (of which five were sermons and four were defense speeches). Thus, about twenty percent of Acts is comprised of speeches by Paul and Peter, and including this one by Stephen, the percentage increases to twenty-five.

[4] Saul was convinced at the time that he ought to oppose Jesus (Acts 26:9), but in the words of this same Jesus, it was "hard to kick against the goads" (Acts 26:14). This proverb referred to a stubborn person rebelling against a powerful authority. A goad is a sharp stick used to prod oxen or mules, and a stubborn animal will kick back against the goads even though it hurts. Paul said in Acts 23:1 that he had acted in all good conscience, and in this there is an important lesson for us: As Paul would later say in 1 Corinthians 4:4: "My conscience is clear, but that does not make me innocent. It is the Lord who judges me."

Chapter 6

[1] The scattering of the believers might have involved more the Hellenists than the Hebrews, which, if true, would explain at least a part of the reason the apostles did not leave. Certainly the church in some form remained in Jerusalem and was no doubt more Hebrew in makeup. According to Eusebius, just prior to the destruction of Jerusalem in 70 AD, the Christians fled the city. Then in 135 AD, the emperor Hadrian reestablished Jerusalem as a Roman colony, after which time the church was reported to be almost entirely Gentile.

[2] See my exposition on Romans: Gordon Ferguson, *Romans: the Heart Set Free* (Billerica, Massachusetts: Discipleship Publications International, 2001) and Sam Laing's book, *The Guilty Soul's Guide to Grace* (Spring Hill, Tennessee: Discipleship Publications International, 2005).

Chapter 7

[1] The school of Hillel is generally considered to be somewhat more liberal in its interpretation of Scripture. For example, in Deuteronomy

24:1 the "indecency" found in a wife was said to be adultery by school of Shammai, whereas, those in the school of Hillel interpreted it more broadly so that it could mean nearly anything that displeased a husband. Today almost all Jewish student centers on college campuses are named for Hillel.

[2] Appendix 3 contains a parallel harmony of these three accounts.

[3] At least two alleged discrepancies regarding Paul's vision are raised by the texts. One, his companions stood speechless, but in Acts 26:14 Paul said that they had all fallen to the ground. Two, they heard the voice, but 22:9 in some Bible versions said that they did *not* hear the voice of him who spoke. The first is solved by them getting up quickly while Paul remained on the ground longer, and the second is answered by them hearing an audible sound, yet not "hearing" in the sense of "understanding." We use the word "hear" in the same two ways today. See John 12:29 for a good example of the latter situation.

[4] For more detail regarding Christ's deity and the Trinity, see my book *Prepared to Answer, Second Edition* Chapter 12, which examines these teachings in light of the false claims of the Jehovah's Witnesses.

[5] See *Prepared to Answer, Second Edition* Chapter 8, for a more thorough treatment of denominational baptism and the biblical answers to it.

Chapter 8

[1] A centurion led one hundred soldiers, with responsibilities corresponding to a modern army Company Commander Captain. Interestingly, the biblical record indicates that Jesus' dealings with Gentiles also began with a centurion (Matthew 8:5–13).

[2] The frequent mention of God-fearers in Acts may lend itself to the idea that Luke himself came from this group.

[3] For Peter to have been staying with Simon the tanner shows that he was already losing some of his "Jewishness," because those who worked with animal skins of necessity worked with dead animals, which would have made a Jew ceremonially unclean.

Chapter 9

[1] Not being an apostle, he would not have been able to pass on spiritual gifts. However, he soon brought Saul to Antioch, who was able. He was not an apostle in the technical sense of being one of the Twelve (plus Paul), although he is called an apostle right along with

Paul in Acts 14:14. Just as the term "disciple" was used in both a technical sense in reference to the Twelve and in a broader sense to the followers of Christ generally, "apostle" (basic meaning: "one sent") could be used in a restrictive or more general sense. See also Galatians 1:19 in which James, the Lord's brother, is so designated.

[2] This Herod is the elder Herod Agrippa, grandson of Herod the Great, more popular with the Jews than others in the Herodian family due to his Hasmonaean (Maccabean) roots. Also mentioned in Acts were his children Agrippa the younger, Bernice and Drusilla (Acts 24:24; 25:13).

[3] For an in-depth discussion of pride and humility see Michael Fontenot and Thomas Jones, *The Prideful Soul's Guide to Humility* (Woburn, Mass: DPI, 1998).

Chapter 10

[1] For more detail regarding the denominational teaching about salvation often called "faith only," see my book *Prepared to Answer, Second Edition,* Chapter 8: "Protestant Doctrines of Salvation."

[2] Some have surmised that 2 Corinthians 12:2–4 refers to this time and that Paul was actually dead when he was "caught up to the third heaven." However, at least two problems call that supposition into question. One, Paul himself did not know if he was in or out of the body on the occasion described in 2 Corinthians 12. If it had been clear that he was dead, those comments would seem unusual. Two, most scholars do not feel that the chronology of Acts 12 and 2 Corinthians can be arranged to coincide. If the writing of 2 Corinthians was in about 55 AD, as most conservative writers think, then fourteen years earlier (2 Corinthians 12:2) would have been 41 AD—too early for the events of Acts 14.

Chapter 12

[1] Citizenship could be obtained in several ways: (1) A soldier received it after 24 years of service. (2) It could sometimes be purchased, although there was great selectivity (Acts 22:26–28). (3) The emperor might grant it to someone who had done him a favor. (4) It was sometimes granted to certain people in a favored area of the empire when that area had contributed significantly to the Romans' cause. (5) A child born to Roman citizens was automatically granted citizenship. Our best assumption is that Paul's parents or grandparents had been

given citizenship in accordance with number 4 and he had become a citizen at birth. Those who were citizens did have a certificate which they could produce as proof of their status.

Chapter 13

[1] See the following for mentions of God-fearers, not all of whom were receptive to the gospel: Acts 2:5, 10:2, 10:22, 13:26, 13:50, 17:4, and 17:17.

[2] The Greek term translated "distressed" is found only once more in the New Testament, where it carries a negative connotation, being translated "angered" (1 Corinthians 13:5). In both cases the presence of strong emotional reaction is clear. Paul's distress in Acts was that of a strong righteous indignation.

[3] Acts 18:18, 18:19, 18:26, Romans 16:3, 1 Corinthians 16:19, and 2 Timothy 4:19.

Chapter 14

[1] Much discussion has occurred about whether Apollos was in fact baptized at this point. See Appendix 4 for a fuller treatment of the subject.

[2] For more detail about the difference between the Jewish Sabbath and the Christian Sunday, see *Prepared to Answer, Second Edition,* Chapter 13, which deals with modern Sabbath keepers.

[3] David W. Bercot, *Will the Real Heretics Please Stand Up?* (Tyler, Texas: Scroll Publishing Company, 1989). See especially Chapters 5 and 9.

[4] Douglas Jacoby, *The Spirit* (Spring, Texas.: IPI, 1998), 110–120.

Chapter 15

[1] Paul wanted to go to Rome, but then after this, all of the way to Spain (Romans 15:23–24). Whether he actually carried out that desire we cannot know. From Luke's perspective, the final frontier for Paul's ministry was definitely Rome.

[2] Some see the possibility of a broader application of the "disputable matters" in Romans 14, extending to non-Judaistic religious practices which would correspond to denominational practices. However, the thrust of Romans makes such applications questionable, for Paul is therein consistently correcting the understanding of the basis of salvation held by those with Jewish backgrounds.

[3] See comments in Chapter 12 about the rationale for Luke remaining behind to lead the church in Philippi for at least a period of time.

[4] F. F. Bruce, *The Book of Acts,* 57–58.

[5] Ephesians 6:20; Philippians 1:7, 13, 14, 17; Colossians 4:3, 18; Philemon 1:10, 13.

[6] See Merrill C. Tenney's excellent explanation of the sequence of these events in *New Testament Survey, Revised edition,* Grand Rapids: Eerdmans Publishing Company, 1985, 334.

Illumination Publishers International

Toney Mulhollan has worked in Christian publishing for 35 years. He has served as the Production Manager for Crossroads Publications, Discipleship Magazine/Upside Down Magazine, Discipleship Publications International (DPI) and on the production teams of Campus Journal, Biblical Discipleship Quarterly, Bible Illustrator and others.

Toney serves as Executive Editor of Illumination Publishers International. He is happily married to the love of his life, Denise L. Mulhollan, M.D. They make their home in Houston, Texas along with their daughters, Audra Joan and Cali Owen.

For the best in Christian writing and audio instruction, go to the Illumination Publishers website. We're committed to producing in depth teaching that will inform, inspire and encourage Christians to a deeper and more committed walk with God. You can e-mail us at our website below.

www.ipibooks.com

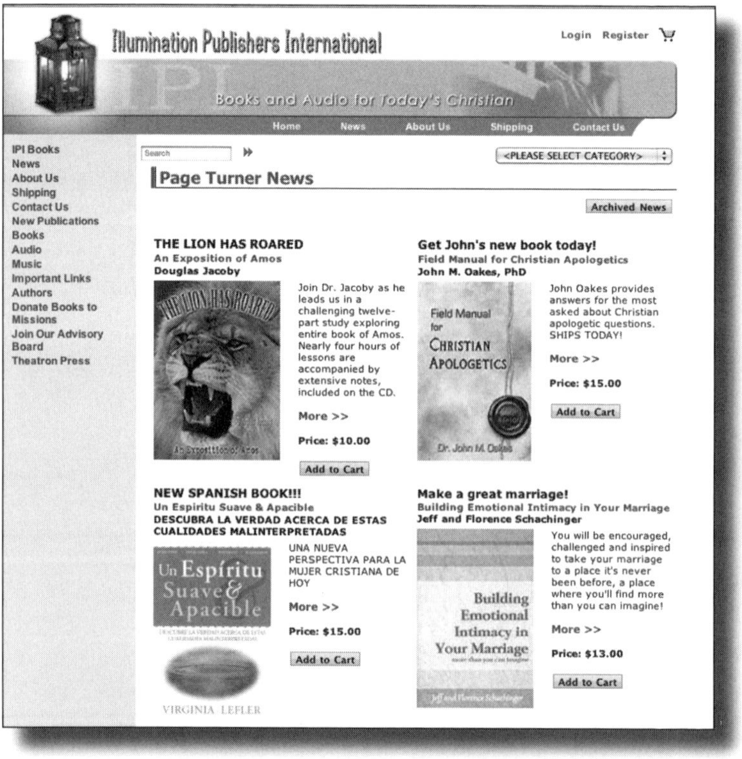